ADDITIONAL PRAISE FOR *TEAM GENIUS*

"As technology moves ever faster, teamwork in business becomes ever more critical. *Team Genius* offers great advice on how to do it right."
—Tom Staggs, chief operating officer, Walt Disney Company

"*Team Genius* reveals a science-based breakthrough to building teams of people as small as a pair and as large as thousands. Leaders are only as good as the teams they build. If you want to be a standout leader, you must read *Team Genius*."
—Cameron Herold, executive coach, former chief operating officer of 1-800-GOT-JUNK and author of
Double Double: How to Double Your Revenue and Profits in Three Years

"*Team Genius* is a rewarding look at one of the most fundamental of human forms—the team. Building on relevant and readable theories, the authors draw from an abundance of real-world (and fun) examples to show what it means to understand, develop, improve, and retire successful teams. Highly recommended!"
—John Schlifske, chairman and chief executive,
Northwestern Mutual

RICH KARLGAARD
and
MICHAEL S. MALONE

HARPER
BUSINESS

TEAM
GENIUS

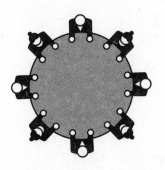

The New Science
of High-Performing
Organizations

HarperCollins books may be purchased for educational, business, or sales promotional use. For information, please e-mail the Special Markets Department at SPsales@harpercollins.com.

FIRST EDITION

Designed by Fritz Metsch

Library of Congress Cataloging-in-Publication Data
has been applied for.

ISBN 978-0-06-230254-0

15 16 17 18 19   OV/RRD   10 9 8 7 6 5 4 3 2 1

To all of our teammates through the years—
and all that they taught us about creating
something bigger than ourselves

Contents

Introduction:
The Power of Teams

Successful teams are at the core of powerful organizations. But what explains game-changing teams—start-up teams, creative teams, R&D teams, project teams, and sales teams? What makes them stand out? Can we decode their winning algorithms? Can we apply this knowledge at different companies and industries—even across different cultures and generations?

The authors of this book have spent their lives in the petri dish of successful team formation—in both our home base of Silicon Valley and around the world. We have started companies, sat on boards, and observed winning and losing teams up close. But in *Team Genius*, we've gone further than anecdotal observation. We've tested our observations and theories against cutting-edge research in anthropology, sociology, neuroscience, and cognition science. We will explain our research and methodology later and in copious footnotes. Readers of this book will be the beneficiaries of this work.

We believe that the pace of technological innovation plus rapid changes in the global economy, combined with huge demographic shifts now under way, will raise the stakes for team performance. Average will die. High mediocrity won't be enough to win and sustain success.

Let us be clear. When we talk about teams, we are not talking about formal teams as depicted in company org charts and those

"About the Company" Web pages. *Team Genius* is about how work *really* gets done. The sum of our experience says that the world's most creative and impactful work—at start-ups, inside large organizations, in sports, and within creative operations in arts and entertainment—gets done by informal teams.

Business literature is remarkably clear about this. After Nazi Germany put the world's first fighter jet—the Messerschmitt 262—into action in 1943, before World War II's outcome was known, the Allies faced a problem. Lockheed's chief aircraft designer, Kelly Johnson, promised an American fighter jet in six months. Today, as then, it would normally take six months just to write a proposal for funding the jet. But Johnson picked a team of Lockheed rebels like himself, installed them in a tent next to a smelly plastics factory, and delivered the P–80 Shooting Star right on schedule. Steve Jobs famously put his informal Macintosh development team away from Apple headquarters in a low-rise building next to a Good Earth organic restaurant. IBM built its first personal computer not in Armonk, New York, but in a few ratty buildings in Boca Raton, Florida. Twitter was designed largely on a bus heading from San Francisco to Austin, Texas, for the 2007 South by Southwest conference.

In the years ahead, will virtual teams and crowdsourcing change the way we think about teams? Well, it so happens that Mike co-wrote a best-selling book called *The Virtual Corporation* . . . in 1992. His answer is yes—but it doesn't change everything, as some futurists like to assert. The deeper answer is what neuroscience and anthropology have to say about teams . . . and you will be surprised by their findings.

As we began putting the final touches on *Team Genius*, both of us were struck by conversations we'd recently had on a pair of themes. One was speed of change in the global economy and how even the most dynamic companies are challenged to build teams that can cope. Rich had dinner with a top executive of Lenovo, the

US $40 billion-annual-revenue Beijing-headquartered maker of personal computers, laptops, tablets, and phones. (Lenovo, if you recall, bought IBM's PC division in 2005.)

Lenovo is known for its nimble management—much of it based in the United States, in the Research Triangle Park area of North Carolina—as well as for its rapid response to opportunities and threats. Lenovo is a rare elephant that can dance. And yet the Lenovo executive explained at dinner how a Chinese phone upstart, Xiaomi, had outmaneuvered Lenovo in Asian markets. How so? Was this a case of the "innovator's dilemma," as defined by Harvard Business School's Clayton Christensen? In the innovator's dilemma, a profitable incumbent company (Lenovo, in this case) can see a disruptive threat. It just can't figure out what to do about it. Matching the prices of the Xiaomi's products would surely hurt the profit margins of Lenovo's. Was it that?

No, Lenovo had seen Xiaomi coming. It had seen Xiaomi's products gaining fast acceptance in Asian markets. And Lenovo was perfectly willing to get in a price war with Xiaomi. The problem was more practical. Lenovo just couldn't build local market teams fast enough to stop Xiaomi's momentum.

The second conversation we heard again and again was that of senior managers worried about the demographic shift to the millennial generation. And their concern wasn't about market shifts, product tastes, social media, and the other usual sources of concern. Rather, it was about whether millennials could actually lead companies and manage other people. For all that generation's known skills in science, technology, social media, and risk taking, senior managers in large organizations everywhere complain about a general lack of managerial talent coming up in their ranks.

Let's stop here. Is this the perennial phenomenon of a grouchy older generation complaining about the shortcomings of up-and-comers? A bit, perhaps. But in the main we don't think so. Absent in these complaints was any of the usual carping about work ethic, education, creativity, and abilities. Rather, the complaints were specific to management experience and team-building skills.

What we do know is that millennials will soon be populating the management ranks of corporations around the globe. They will preside over a world that is so fast-changing and competitive that they will have to do markedly better job at building, managing, and motivating teams than has been demanded of any previous generation. The stakes will be that high.

That's why one of our chief purposes in writing this book was to bring together both the best practices of today and the past, with the latest in scientific research, to show the next generation of leaders in every field how to build the dynamic, robust, and *great* teams they will need in order to compete in this new world. Their learning curve will be shockingly steep—and we want to help them survive the climb. If they can succeed, it will benefit us all.

TWENTY QUESTIONS

Teams compose a large part of our private and public lives. We depend on them for both our success and our happiness. Isn't it odd how little scrutiny we give them? The teams that make up our lives are created mostly by luck, happenstance, or circumstance—but rarely by design.

Success by serendipity is risky enough in the small matters of our life—a bowling team, the leadership of a neighborhood group, a holiday party committee. But it can be downright dangerous when it comes to actions by major corporations, nonprofit institutions, and governments. No one would launch a billion-dollar product into the global marketplace without months of product testing, customer polling, and analysis; or without establishing distribution and retail channels, marketing campaigns, sales kits, and so forth. Yet we are likely to place this entire project in the hands of a leadership team that, right from the start and by its very nature, is doomed to failure.

As we'll show in the chapters that follow, the planning for and designing of great teams no longer have to be a black art. To help you get started thinking differently, perhaps even more scientifically, here are twenty questions you ought to be asking about the teams you manage and those to which you belong:

1. Is your organization, and the teams that compose it, up to the challenges they face in a hypercompetitive global economy?
2. If not, is there some way to accelerate your understanding of teams?
3. Can you apply that new knowledge in a way that lets you build teams both fast and appropriately for the ever-changing challenges that face you?
4. Can you find the right team at the right moment?
5. Can you identify the right moment when one team needs to be dissolved to create another, perhaps in a very different form?

These first five are not idle questions. They are very real and their implications are imminent. Every organization you are a part of is composed of teams, and every one of those teams is currently at some point in its life cycle. Some of those teams are clearly dysfunctional; others are suboptimal in their performance; and still others are approaching the end of their usefulness. Even great teams aren't always being challenged to do all that they are capable of doing.

6. If the fate of your organization depended on it, could you identify those great teams?
7. Do you know how to staff a team for a specific task?

8. If you were assigned the task of reorganizing the subpar teams to ensure their top performance, would you know how to do it?

9. Would you even know where to start?

10. By the same token, if you were to look at the top-performing teams in your company—in management, manufacturing, R&D, sales—would you be able to identify which ones were reaching the end of their life span?

11. Would you have the courage to shut them down?

12. Would you know how to handle that retirement without creating acrimony and killing morale among some of your most talented employees?

13. Would you know how to recompose a replacement team to be just as effective and without losing any time?

Thirteen, and we've only just begun! Those were questions about your own skills in creating and managing teams. Here are some questions about your organization's capabilities that you have likely never considered:

14. Can your company's teams stay ahead of the changes affecting your industry and customers?

15. Are your teams able to anticipate and respond to sudden disruptions in technology, economics, and customer behavior?

16. Are your teams leveraging globalism and multicultural values as strengths?

17. Is mobile technology helping or hurting your team's performance? How are you performing in this area relative to your competition?

18. Are your teams' missions and values being supported or undercut by social media?

19. Do you have the right people in the right positions in the right teams?

Last but not least, here's a question that almost no one asks and even fewer organizations get right:

20. Are your teams the right size for the job?

The goal of this book is to help you answer all of these questions—and more. And to help you do so, we've brought together acquired wisdom that is as old as humankind, along with some of the latest and most stunning research just now emerging from the brand-new field of social neuroscience. Many of these findings will surprise you and challenge your prejudices. We guarantee they will make you a better manager of teams.

SOME SURPRISING NEW TRUTHS

As a preview of what is to come, here are some of the ideas we will explore that contain surprising truths about teams:

- What science says about racial and gender diversity. Warning: it's provocative.
- Why cognitive diversity yields the highest performance gains—but only if you understand what it is.
- How to find the "bliss point" in team intimacy—and become three times more productive.
- Why too much conformity will kill you—as will too little.
- How to create "whole-brain teams" with the right amount of "creative abrasion."
- How to identify destructive team members before they harm you.
- Why small teams are 40 percent more likely to create a successful breakthrough than a solo genius.

- Why groups of 7 (plus or minus 2), 150, and 1,500 are magic sizes for teams.
- Why everything you know about performance compensation is probably wrong.
- How to keep a successful team fresh and when to break up teams.
- How to identify the one person you should never lay off when downsizing.

All that we ask is that you keep an open mind as you read the pages to come. Some of these theories and discoveries may seem counterintuitive, at least, and perhaps even impossible, the first time you encounter them. We felt the same way. But if you look back into your life you will find successful team experiences that, at first encounter, seemed equally unlikely.

For example, if you took part in sports, you probably played at least once for a team that looked great on paper, but on the field just never meshed—and fell far short of its potential. On the other hand, you may have been assigned a partner in college or on the job with whom you had nothing in common, whose personality was incompatible with yours, and with whom you shared no skills or experience. Yet the two of you proved to be surprisingly productive. How did that happen?

And how many times were you part of a team that did well—until the wrong members were rewarded—or that continued to operate long after you and your teammates stopped respecting one another? And, of course, how many times have you been part of a team that would have been perfect if you had just kicked out that one person who was a destructive force?

TEAMS: TOMORROW'S NEW PERFORMANCE LEVER

We begin by offering four imperatives that every leader must recognize:

First, your teams must be capable of surviving whatever today's brutal economy throws in their path. Indeed, today's teams will have to be able to survive on their own, often with little support from headquarters. They will have to take serious risks and make decisions, sometimes fateful ones, very quickly.

Second, your teams must be designed to work with, not against, your members' brain structures. Why? It's the oldest reason of all, one we've long suspected but only recently proved scientifically: *Humans are genetically wired for teams.* This is the message emerging from the latest brain research. What's more, as many of us learned as children, being on a team can rewire our brains and make us *better* as people. In other words, we are meant to be part of teams. This imperative is not some external social construct, but an innate part of who we are.

Third, your teams must be given the support they need to reach their full potential—rather than putting too much faith in any one individual in your organization. Businesspeople around the world share a common misbelief. It is one promoted by the media for its own reasons. It is this: the faith in the power of solitary entrepreneurs, leaders, and trendsetters. Confession: Both authors of this book are members of the media, but we have also started companies and served on boards of directors. We can state with authority: Boards and investors almost always overrate individual genius and underrate genius *team* contribution.

Fourth, the size and composition of your teams matter greatly when setting strategic goals. We will show you that when teams fail, they are almost always too big. We will show you that a large size ironically works against diversity, which itself is a very poorly understood concept. We will also argue that many of the most successful endeavors have depended on the smallest team size of all: the pair—a coupling that occurs in more forms than you may have ever imagined.

If this book teaches you nothing but (1) how to think about team size, and (2) how to staff and manage for diversity, you will be pleased and so will we.

Are you up to improving your team management skills? You'd better be! How you build, manage, and reconfigure teams in a fast, disruptive, and turbulent economy will play an ever larger role in your success or failure. To prepare ourselves for the world to come in the rest of this century, we need to find the genius that resides in great teams.

It is time to revisit the idea of the teams—and not just in story and lore (and perhaps a few rules of thumb). It's time to take a look at teams systematically, *scientifically*, using the latest discoveries in anthropology, sociology, cognition, and neuroscience. To prepare ourselves for the world to come in the rest of this century, we need to find the genius that resides in great teams. And to do that, we need to develop a *new science of teams*.

TEAM
GENIUS

Change Kills—If You Don't Have the Right Teams

Talking about the rapid pace of technology-driven change has become commonplace. These days, even schoolchildren are taught about the power of *Moore's law,* that measure of semiconductor memory chip development that has now become the metronome of the modern world. But our acceptance of the reality of this change doesn't necessarily mean that we understand it, or that we have developed effective strategies to cope with it. In fact, the reality of this ever-accelerating change is stranger and more challenging that we can imagine.

Gordon Moore, a cofounder of Fairchild Semiconductor (and later of Intel Corporation), first devised his law in 1965 in an article for *Electronics* magazine. The point Moore wanted to make was that memory chips, invented just a few years before, were improving at a dizzying speed. He tried to plot their price and performance points on regular graph paper, but they took off too fast, so he switched to logarithmic graph paper (that is, to show exponential growth), and he got a nice straight and shallow line. It showed that the performance of these chips was doubling every couple of years (eighteen months at the time, twenty-four months now).

It was an impressive graph, but no one then, not even Moore, realized that this graph would continue to hold for *fifty years* and set the blistering pace of change for the modern world. We all now live in the world of Moore's law, and we likely will for at least another quarter century. It's interesting to note how shallow that curve is for the first forty years, until about 2005. Yet along that comparatively flat curve can be found the births of the minicomputer, the microprocessor, the digital calculator, computer gaming, the personal computer, the Internet, robotics, wireless telephony, the smartphone, and electronic commerce. After 2005, as we race toward twenty-five billion transistors per chip, the curve goes almost straight up, heading toward infinity. Are we really prepared for this? If the entire digital age occurred in the foothills, what happens now that we are entering the Himalayas?

We have grown so accustomed to living in the world of Moore's law that we forget we're dealing with one of the most explosive forces in history. We've become so adept at predicting, incorporating, and assimilating each new upward click of the curve that we assume we have this monster under control. We don't.

There is a second great exponential law that has emerged out of the digital world to redefine modern life: *Metcalfe's law.* It says that the value of a network is proportional to the square (or a similar multiple) of the number of users. In other words, each new addition adds value to the Web out of the usual proportion to its presence. And with the emerging Internet of Things, those "users" may soon include 100 billion new smart devices as well—sensors, cameras, robots, drones, and the like. As far back as 2005, Google's CEO, Eric Schmidt, estimated the Internet's data size to be 5 million terabytes (that's *eighteen* zeros).[1] Today, the Internet is 60,000 times larger, at 300 exabytes.

John Chambers, CEO of Cisco, says the "Internet of Everything" is worth $14.4 trillion, growing more than 20 percent per year.

But, as with Moore's law, the exponential implications of Metcalfe's law are less noticed. Fifteen years ago, about a billion people regularly jumped onto the Web. Even then, that number already made the Internet the largest market in human history. But that was just the beginning. As of 2010, another billion people had joined the global marketplace. By 2012, *2.5 billion* people around the world had joined the global, Internet-based marketplace.[2] Today that number likely exceeds 3 billion. And that number has yet to include those scores of billions of sensors and smart devices that will also soon be joining the Internet. Thus, according to Metcalfe's law, the number of possible digital connections among people and sensors will grow into the trillions times trillions—a practical infinity.

But just sticking to humans, we find that the third billion is very different from the first two. Most of this cohort lives in the developing world and probably in a teeming metropolis that barely existed twenty years ago. These users may never see an annual income of more than a few hundred dollars per year, and may have never driven in an automobile, much less flown on an airplane. Nonetheless, even if they are just selling items on eBay from a cellphone rented by the minute in a corner of some Third World city, they are adding value to the global economy. Just as important, they are helping create yet one more new submarket in addition to the millions springing up throughout the world. Even in developed countries, the Internet's contribution to global GNP is now 21 percent, double what it was just five years ago.[3] It is growing at an even faster pace in the developing world.

Let's keep going—because waiting out there is a fourth billion, about which we know almost nothing. They live in some of the poorest and most isolated places in the world, with little contact with even the products of the developed world—many have never used money or been in a car, and have seen an airplane only from afar. But they will join the global economy when the planet is completely covered with wireless connectivity. They will do so through minutes rented on a smartphone offered from a cardboard hut on a corner in some teeming Third World supermetropolis, or from one of the free phones handed out by the millions by the big telecom companies looking for new customers.

Soon these third and fourth billions will be part of the Internet-based global economy. Companies, desperate for their business and the benefits of Metcalfe's law, will use creative new means to seek them out and bring them onto the Web—even as the nature of that Web will be continuously transforming, thanks to Moore's law.

TWO LAWS BUT NO GUARANTEES

So where does that leave us? Mass scale and, with it, global reach, will be incredibly valuable in the twenty-first century. But will they be enough to capture the huge opportunities offered by the third and fourth billions? Our conclusion: no. That's because scale and reach are rapidly being commoditized. You can be a small company, and your opportunities to make products and services with large-scale efficiency are better than ever—and will become better yet in the future. A crucial understanding of Moore's law is that it creates excess capacity—and not just in the world of electronics. For instance, extremely precise horizontal drilling far beneath the earth's surface makes it possible to tap new oil sources trapped in shale rock. This level of precision is made possible by advanced electronics, itself made possible by Moore's law. As the oil billionaire T. Boone Pickens told *Forbes*, "You can drill two miles down, take a right turn, drill another two miles, and pick the lock to someone's front door. That's how precise it is."[4] Moore's law, then, describes a tendency to create excess capacity not just of electronic chips but of oil, factories, shipping—everything.

As for global reach, you might wish you had a billion-dollar advertising budget to reach the global marketplace. But no budgets will be large enough in the future, because of our other friend, Metcalfe's law, which describes the exponential creation of a near infinite number of connections and ways to reach customers. Fast-moving small companies can find more niches and customers than ever. The same is true of technology power. The cloud is rapidly commoditizing the availability of top-class technology. You don't have to buy equipment from IBM; you can rent it by the second from Amazon, Alibaba, Google, Microsoft, and others.

Our point is to show you that although access to scale, global reach, and powerful technology is a requirement for success, it is not sufficient to create *sustained* success. It is being commoditized. It is losing its former status as a barrier to entry. It is becoming, as poker players like to say, mere table stakes in the game of economic competition. Instead, it is *maneuverability* that will be the new barrier to entry, the new essential for sustained rising value. Such maneuverability will come from the combination of global reach, great technology, *and* highly optimized teams—*team genius*, as we call it.

Here is the uncomfortable truth: Humans run to a much slower evolutionary clock than our inventions. To use an engineering term, we are the "gating factor" that keeps a process from running faster. It is people, not scale or technology, who determine how well an organization adapts to change.

So, whether we know it or not, the difference in our rapidly accelerating world between a perpetually successful enterprise and a struggling, dysfunctional also-ran comes down to the people in those enterprises—and even more, to how those people relate to each other as they form and re-form into teams.

Thus, even as the companies that expand their reach around the world grow bigger and more ambitious in their vision, they will, paradoxically, also have to become smaller and more focused in their execution. And, contrary to what many business prognosticators have assumed for the last half century, the more gigantic the enterprise and the more virtual and wired it becomes, the more likely that it will be dependent on dozens, hundreds, even thousands, of small, closely knit internal teams.

That's why, at the nexus of two almost unprecedented forces in human history—the unrelenting, exponential advance of technological performance (speed), and the explosion of new connections in the global marketplace (reach)—one of the oldest human cultural phenomena, *the team*, finds itself as vital as ever before.

MASTERING MANEUVERABILITY

Both of the authors of this book knew Bill Walsh, the great San Francisco 49ers football coach of the 1980s. Walsh won three Super Bowls and left his successor with a team that won two more. Walsh died in 2007, but his playbook and team innovations redefined professional football for two generations.

We once asked Coach Walsh why he drafted Jerry Rice, a little-known wide receiver out of tiny Mississippi Valley State University. Rice went on to become the National Football League's all-time scorer. But in 1985, Walsh was alone among scouts and coaches in perceiving Rice's true potential as a future Hall of Famer.

"Rice was considered to be too slow for NFL greatness," explained Walsh. "His time in the forty-yard dash was only 4.7. Most great NFL receivers run 4.4 or faster. But when you studied the film from Rice's college games, you saw two things different about Rice. One, he could turn on a dime. He could run sideways faster than anyone I'd seen. His *maneuverability* left defenders wondering what happened. Two, Rice always finished his pass route within one foot of where he needed to be. Like he had a GPS in his head. [Quarterbacks] Joe Montana and Steve Young could count on him."

Rice's abilities give us an insight into success in the modern economy beyond scale, reach, and speed. In today's economy, it is essential to be *maneuverable*.

Maneuverability is more than rapid evolution. Sometimes even that is too slow. Rather, maneuverability is the capacity to turn, even reverse direction, quickly, to deal competently with whatever new change—technology, market opportunity, or competition—has just burst onto the scene, and to do so without losing internal cohesion and breaking up. This is a challenge facing almost all institutions, from small retailers to the governments of great nations around the world.

The exponential forces at work in today's culture and economy reward winners quickly and punish losers mercilessly. Over here you'll find a resurgent Apple, but over there is sad, old Eastman Kodak. Germany on the one hand, Greece on the other. South Korea and North Korea, Silicon Valley and Detroit. As this book goes to press, prosperity and futility are being sorted out more swiftly, and dispersed more unevenly, than at any other period in our lifetimes. Whether the global economy improves or worsens, this new unevenness is here to stay.

History, of course, is filled with stories of maneuverable teams somehow surviving in incredibly dangerous situations—and even triumphing—against almost impossible odds. Xenophon's march, Magellan's and Cook's voyages, Marco Polo's journey to the East, Cortés and Pizarro, Stanley's search for Livingstone, the Bolsheviks, Shackleton's expedition, *Apollo 13*. There are a multitude of such stories, and no doubt thousands more that were never recorded, such as the inhabitation of the South Pacific islands, the first exploration of North America across the Bering land bridge, and, most important of all, the survival of those few families of early humans who managed to avoid near extinction on the northern coast of Africa and gave birth to modern humankind.

What does this mean for those of us who lead businesses and organizations? Where will we find maneuverability? One answer, and one that seems counterintuitive at first glance, is *structure*. The size and composition of the most successful teams match archetypes that are as old as humankind, which suggests (as we'll see in later chapters) that there is a kind of organic strength and stability to these structures that cannot be matched by other, synthetic groupings—much less by very large organizations.

Stability enables these teams to move with a common purpose, sometimes even when a situation demands that a team move in a different direction than the one for which it was created. The Silicon Valley legends Bill Hewlett and David Packard pursued bowling pin resetters, automatic flush urinals, and other failed ideas before they lit upon Hewlett's old grad school project, the audio oscillator. Jim Clark, Marc Andreessen, and the other founders of Netscape were originally planning to go into the computer game business. Google was founded with no clue whatsoever about advertising. Amazon launched by selling books to consumers, not cloud services to businesses. Who knew Apple would become a giant in music? Organizations lacking maneuverability find such moves—almost second nature to proper teams—almost impossible to execute.

That's not to say that older and larger organizations cannot maneuver effectively and even make stunning reversals in direction. But it is exceedingly rare. And it almost never happens unless a small, cohesive team is found at the center or top of that organization and is endowed with two other crucial factors: the *power to execute* its decisions across the entire organization, and the *trust* of its players in the periphery around that team. Indeed, even the largest organizations can maneuver widely and with stunning speed in the face of rapid change if they are built out of genius teams in support of an empowered leadership.

APPLE'S COMEBACK

One of the greatest examples in business history of a large organization's maneuverability took place right before our eyes: Apple Inc. In September 2002, Apple's future was thought to be so bleak, you could buy shares in Apple Computer at a price that valued its operating enterprise at less than zero. What you were buying, if you had been so bold, was Apple's cash reserves of $5 billion. Beyond that, you were buying a prayer that Apple could do something with that cash.

Remember, this was five years *after* the return of Steve Jobs. Contrary to myth, Jobs did not immediately turn around Apple's dismal fortunes. Yet just one decade later, Apple would drop the "Computer" from its name but win the world. It would become the richest company on earth in September 2012, valued at $656 billion.

Meanwhile, during that decade of Apple's extraordinary ascent, other great American companies, stalwarts of reliable business success, fared poorly. Among them were Pacific Gas & Electric, Enron, WorldCom, Tyco, Adelphia Communications, US Airways, Trump Entertainment Resorts, Northwest Airlines, Lehman Brothers, Washington Mutual, Chrysler, and General Motors. Thus, even while Apple prospered, a greater number of American companies went bankrupt or out of business altogether than in any decade in the country's history, including during the Great Depression.

How did Apple do it? Why did it succeed while its bigger and (initially) more successful neighbors faltered?

The simple answer is that during this period Apple managed to introduce a series of four monumental products and services—the iPod, iTunes, the Apple Store, and the iPhone and iPad—that created not only new industries but also entirely new multibillion-dollar market *categories*.

To understand how Apple did this, we need to appreciate the real contributions of Apple's cofounder Steve Jobs, who had been out of the company for twelve years, and who returned at the beginning of this historic era in the company's history. It was, in fact, a wiser and more confident Steve Jobs who took command of Apple for the second time in 1997. And though he remained the same mercurial, rash, dangerously unpredictable, and impetuous Steve Jobs who had been driven out of Apple in 1985, he had learned two important pieces of wisdom in the interim: (1) Build a company that rewards risk rather than punishes it; and (2) Never forget that all successful enterprises, no matter how big and wealthy, are an aggregation of teams—large and small, loyal and renegade, stabilizing and anarchistic, from the lowliest engineers to executive row—all of them working, sometimes in harmony and sometimes at cross-purposes, toward the success of the company.

Throughout Apple's story, in good times and bad, freakishly great teams from the unlikeliest corners of the company have arisen to play a crucial role in its future—and have often kept the company alive. They have come from design (the friendly competition between the Lisa and Macintosh teams), education (which gave the company a second chance when IBM captured the corporate market), the Apple operating system (which kept users loyal as company hardware declined in quality), and marketing and advertising (which maintained the Jobs style after he was fired) . . . and ultimately to the team organized by engineering chief Jon Rubinstein that designed and built the iPod and set Apple off on its third era. Many of these teams operated independently from the larger corporation—and a few were outright renegades. Almost every one showed a kind of genius.

Ultimately, it was these teams that built the early Apple, held it together under second-rate management through the hard times, and exploded with innovation in Apple's resurrection and triumph. So the question is, why were Apple's teams, often with many of the same members, so effective during some parts of the Apple story and utterly ineffectual in others? Three reasons:

Technology—Where did the flexibility and adaptability of Apple's teams come from? From the technology itself. As we've already noted, the pace of technological change is so fast that if you can latch on to it and hang on, it will accelerate you past all traditional competition. Unfortunately, as many companies have learned to their dismay, doing so is a lot harder than it looks. But Apple did keep up with Moore's law. Because it incorporated the law (via microprocessors and the latest memory media) into its products, it built rapid change into its culture, and it unleashed its teams to pursue the quickest possible paths to their goals.

People—Like Google, Facebook, and Twitter today, Apple in its first two decades (and in its most recent decade) enjoyed an almost unmatched star quality—and it shrewdly used that charisma to attract the best and brightest young talent to join its ranks. But that's the easiest half of the story. Hot companies can always draw talent; the real challenge is keeping it when the excitement ends, the stock options have been exercised, and the cultural cachet fades. Apple managed to create such a powerful culture in its early years—the "kool-aid"—that it still managed to retain a surprising number of those top employees when the excitement faded and Apple slogged through the dreary early nineties. They were still there to lead the company when Jobs returned.

Risk—Steve Jobs's greatest contribution to the resurrection of Apple was that he reinstilled a culture of risk within the company that had been missing for fifteen years under his replacements. At Apple in the twenty-first century, you were punished for taking insufficient risk—employees quickly learned to never approach Jobs with a careful plan or a conservative design. It is hard to convey just how rare such a risk-embracing culture really is in the corporate world. And Apple did it better, through its risk-taking teams guided by Jobs himself, than any company ever.

Speed, people, and a risk-embracing culture were just the ingredients. What made them work was their expression through

Apple's army of established, loyal, and well-composed teams. Those teams, in turn, felt unleashed to pursue their destinies—and to show their commitment to the company—with the knowledge that their efforts, once again and at last, would be supported by the CEO himself. Together they enabled Apple to maneuver like no giant company ever had before. And for that opportunity, they were willing even to labor in near anonymity and let that CEO take most of the credit.

The result was historic. Unfortunately, the reality of how Apple and Steve Jobs achieved such astonishing results has been overshadowed by an irresistible myth that portrays Jobs as a brilliant lone wolf, executing one miracle at Apple after another, a solitary hero fighting against the high-tech status quo. There is a lot of truth to that image—except for the word "solitary."

For one thing, you can't ignore the thousands of Apple employees who brought their ideas to Jobs (he had few original product ideas of his own) and who, once they got his support, made those ideas real. But more than that, a careful look at Jobs's remarkable career shows that he almost never operated solo; there was always at least one partner, some famous and others all but invisible, whom he could use as a resident genius, as a reality check, as a protector, to execute his ideas or to calm the chaos that he often left in his wake. In fact, Steve Jobs can be seen as a serial partner, pairing up with different business partners who best served each phase in his career: Apple's cofounder Steve Wozniak ("Woz"), chairman Mike Markkula, John Sculley, Bud Tribble at NeXT, John Lasseter at Pixar. Some of these pairings worked brilliantly, for a while; others failed, either because Jobs chose someone too much like himself, or because he retained too much power and overwhelmed his counterpart.

But one of Jobs's greatest strengths was his ability to learn, not least about himself and his weaknesses. Thus, his last choice for a business partner was arguably his best: Apple's COO (and now CEO) Tim Cook, a business partner who completed his skills, and whom he grew to trust completely.

Cook, a computer industry veteran from IBM, had been hired by Jobs soon after he returned to Apple. It was a team pairing of opposites. Low-key, disciplined, and organized, Cook was almost everything Jobs was not. Better yet, Cook seemed to understand Jobs, creating an environment at Apple that, on the one hand, kept him away from the daily functioning of the firm, while on the other implemented structures that made Apple instantly responsive to Jobs's latest creative impulse.

Finally, Cook had to accept that he would have to work almost anonymously and behind the scenes. That's because Jobs always insisted throughout his career—both because it gave him greater control over the company and because it reduced employee raiding—that he take almost all the credit for the company's successes. Indeed, many people still believe that Jobs invented the Apple computer, the iPod, and the iPhone—and even many industry veterans can't tell you who actually did. The trade-off was that Jobs was often intensely loyal to, and rewarded well, those people who acquiesced to this arrangement.

Tim Cook was willing to live with that arrangement. Steve Jobs rewarded him more than anyone by entrusting him with his company in the end. Together, they made the most powerful business pair-team of their generation. And the world learned of it only when Jobs became too sick to continue.

RECONSIDERING STEVE JOBS

The more you study the career of Steve Jobs, the more obvious it becomes that Jobs, the most famous solo businessman of modern times, was partnered at every step along the way with another individual or team, most of them all but unknown to the outside world. Further, when he teamed up with the wrong partners, his career went into a tailspin; and when he found the right partner—an individual or a team—he succeeded beyond anyone's dreams but his own.

We've chosen to directly address the story of Steve Jobs because, for billions of people around the world, he is the very embodiment of the maverick entrepreneur who cast off all ties with those around him to take the unconventional, high-risk path to glory. His solitary, heroic image stands as a role model to uncounted young entrepreneurs in the generations that have followed him. He is the ultimate counterpoint to all of those compromising "team players," the workaday drudges who must forever make nice to their coworkers; to all those mediocrities who are tied down by chains of professional courtesy, friendship, and partnership.

And yet in real life, Steve Jobs proved to be as dependent—indeed, even more dependent—as most of us on those chains. And, rather than tie him down or hold him back, the partnerships and teams in Jobs's professional life (and in his personal life as well, but that is another story) were precisely what liberated him to unleash his genius, what empowered him to successfully run Apple, and, not least, what protected him from the excesses in his behavior.

If that is true for Steve Jobs, of all people, why isn't it also the case for almost every other loner we honor in our culture? Might it be that the lone hero is actually the exception, and the two-or-more-person team the secret rule? Bill Gates? Well, he had Paul Allen, then Steve Ballmer. GE's Jack Welch? Numerous field generals. Facebook's Mark Zuckerberg? Sheryl Sandberg. Alibaba's Jack Ma? Jonathan Lu. Invariably, when you look behind the great man or woman of industry, you find one or more other key players who, for one reason or another, stay in the shadows.

Finally, did Steve Jobs see himself as a lone hero? Perhaps, but it's hard to ignore what he told *60 Minutes*: "My model for business is the Beatles: They were four guys that kept each other's negative tendencies in check; they balanced each other. And the total was greater than the sum of the parts. Great things in business are never done by one person; they are done by a team of people."

The Magic Numbers Behind Teams

Now we turn our attention to another force behind the power of teams, whether teams from a hunter-gatherer tribe of prehistory or today's leading-edge technology start-ups. Teams, it turns out, are not strictly practical responses to immediate challenges and situations. Teams are at the heart of what it means to be human.

Put another way, as human beings, we *must* form teams. It is encoded into our DNA. It has proved to be the critical factor in the rise of civilization.

The human drive to form teams is also a survival mechanism for individuals. Psychologists have long noted that solitary individuals, from hermits to unattached adults, typically have shorter life spans than their more social, mated counterparts.

The archaeological evidence suggests that even the earliest hominids always grouped together to live and hunt. In 1975, the

2.3-million-year-old remains of what appears to have been a hunting party of hominids who died together were found in Hadar, Ethiopia—suggesting that teams existed even *before* the members were fully human. In the Omo Kibish dry lake bed a few miles away, the anthropologist Richard Leakey found the nearly 200,000-year-old remains of another group of humans who, based on their tools and other artifacts, lived together as a family group or a small tribe.

Similar team behavior can still be found in the world's surviving hunter-gatherers. For example, the San Bushmen of the Kalahari almost always hunt in teams, not least because their primary weapons (poisoned arrows and spears) necessitate a long time spent tracking and driving their prey, sometimes requiring days of pursuit by multiple trackers looking for signs. The prey is large—an eland can weigh a ton, an elephant ten times that—so can rarely be taken by a solitary hunter. When the animal is butchered, multiple hands are needed to transport the meat (and the necessary calories for the group's survival) for what can be many miles back to the village.

This team hunting technique is at least as old as Neanderthals hunting mammoths, and likely much, much older than that. It is also as recent as last night's military patrol in a war zone somewhere in the world.

The agricultural revolution took teams—and the division of labor—to a new level. Not only is it almost impossible to conduct planting and harvesting as a solitary farmer, but without a surrounding infrastructure to process, store, distribute, and trade the fruits of the harvest, the system just doesn't work. Consider the special skills needed for a successful agricultural society: planting, harvesting, milling, baking, brewing, shipping and trade, animal husbandry, policing and protection, adjudication of disputes, marketplace management, building, taxation, and distribution.

With agriculture, we began to need the differentiated skills of our fellow human beings more than ever. This division of labor, formed out of aggregations of small teams, is older than human history. Babylon, the first true city, exhibited all of these characteristics six thousand years ago. By the time of the Sumerian, Egyptian, and Chinese civilizations, the process of division and aggregation had already become highly sophisticated. The pharaohs ruled a geographically vast empire of millions of citizens through layers of bureaucracy, their rule ultimately reaching down to small teams manning distant and isolated outposts. The Egyptian army fought in a team structure, and it wasn't an undifferentiated mass of workers and slaves who built the pyramids.

What is crucial to note is that this division has never stopped. At no point in the development of civilization, and across six millennia, have small, fundamental teams ever been abandoned as unnecessary or obsolete. Rather, they remain essential building blocks in the structures of ever-larger institutions. Even the largest human groupings ever created—Xerxes's Persian army, the Soviet Red Army in World War II, China's People's Liberation Army today, the Roman Catholic Church, the million employees of Walmart—are aggregations of an uncounted number of small teams managed by an ever-larger superstructure of larger teams.

Thus the modern army has its army groups, corps, divisions, battalions, and companies. Yet armies still come down to teams, elements, and squads. Great corporations may have country or regional organizations, divisions, and offices. But they too ultimately devolve to partnerships, sales teams, departments, work groups, and pairs. The same is true for the great religions (from the office of the pope to the parish priests) and national governments.

Over and over, the size and structure of these teams are repeated through history, be they Caesar's legions or IBM.

WHY DO TEAMS FORM THE WAY THEY DO?

This kind of consistency and durability, not just in type but also in *form*, through the course of human history suggests that something much more than only coincidence—or even practicality—is at work. It suggests something deeply human. With few exceptions, human beings don't do well alone. We thrive while operating in certain organizational schemes.

Why should this be so? We believe there are several explanations.

One is the nature of leadership itself. Researchers into the nature of leadership recognized decades ago that even the best leaders have a limit to their successful *span of control*, usually six to ten people—the number of individuals whom they can personally manage at the highest levels of productivity. Beyond that, even the most talented leaders simply don't have enough intellectual, emotional, or temporal bandwidth to provide the requisite personal attention. Thus, smart leaders begin to divide up their direct reports into multiple teams, each with a subordinate emplaced and empowered to serve as the new team leader.

As a result, multiples of this basic span of control—with any added command superstructure—consistently appear in larger organizations throughout time.

A second force at work in creating team archetypes is *structural stability*. Here one can draw an analogy with atomic theory. Certain molecules, particularly simple ones (atmospheric oxygen, cyanide, carbon monoxide, benzene), are inherently stable due to the nature of their atomic bonds and their structure. Others are much more volatile (isotopes, ions, radioactive elements, and so forth) and unless constantly maintained in their unstable condition, they will quickly revert to more stable structures.

Human teams exhibit the same combination of stability and

volatility. Some teams, most obviously pairs, but also large group-ings such as the 150–160 people in a typical tribal village, are con-siderably stable. They are, in fact, what unstable teams typically collapse into. Pairs, of course, are the most stable of all, not just because of their simplicity, but also because they manifest those most basic of all human relations: friendship and marriage. Living things have been genetically wired for pair-bonding ever since the first species exhibited sexual differentiation and mating.

But add a third team member and things become much more complicated—sometimes even explosive. Trios work, of course, but often it seems they do so only by serial pairing. After all, his-tory doesn't show many triumvirates and troikas, especially among rulers, that have survived for long. Intel of the 1970s and 1980s was a noted exception, with its famous trinity of Robert Noyce, Gordon Moore, and Andy Grove. More recently, Google's triumvirate of Larry Page, Sergey Brin, and Eric Schmidt has worked well. Chi-na's telecom giant Huawei uses an office of three CEOs, rotating each for six-month stints at the top. Stability is provided behind the scenes by its press-shy founder, Ren Zhengfei. When trios work, it's because their individual members' skills are so different yet dovetail perfectly. Google's cofounder Sergey Brin plays the role of futurist. His fellow cofounder, Larry Page, is the CEO. Chairman Eric Schmidt, fifteen years older than the other two, is the diplo-matic ambassador.

OPTIMAL SIZE AND THE MAGIC FORCE

Beyond three members, the next optimal team size has been the subject of considerable debate.

Here's Susan Heathfield, a human resources expert: "So, opti-mum team size is not an easy answer. From experience and re-search, the optimum team size is 5–7 members. The team size that continues to function effectively is 4–9 members. Teams are known to function cohesively with a size up to 12 members."[1]

Remember that two-million-plus-year-old hominid hunting team? Twelve members. The small tribe discovered by Leakey? Two dozen members. This suggests that small teams of a consistent size are not only intrinsic to being human, but historically are among humanity's most enduring characteristics. Even in the age of global wireless coverage and the World Wide Web, it's hardly surprising that small teams aren't going away any time soon. Indeed, they will likely remain intrinsic to human beings as long as there are human beings.

Certainly, small teams are as important as ever in the modern "hunting party." In its smallest units, the British Army operates at the limits of Heathfield's numbers, with a single "fire team" composed of four soldiers, and a "section" of two fire teams—eight soldiers—commanded by a corporal. In the US Army, a squad is two fire teams of four riflemen and a staff sergeant in command, for a total of nine; in the Marine Corps, it is three four-man fire teams with a master sergeant commanding, for a total of thirteen. In real life, however, such as in Vietnam or World War II, attrition, delays in replacements, and shortages of personnel meant that the typical squad was always short two or more members. Comparable unit sizes can be found in armies throughout the world (for example, the Russian army unit is nine members; the Chinese People's Liberation Army, twelve).

Why this particular size? We've mentioned the normal effective span of leadership. But there are more everyday and pragmatic reasons as well. Once again, they are as old as human beings and combat. For example, a squad was the number of soldiers who could effectively hear the orders of their commander in the clash of battle. In the Roman legions, the size of a squad—eight—was defined by the number of soldiers who could share a standard tent.

Two thousand years later, long after the constraints of tent size are gone and soldiers can communicate in combat via radio to an audience of any size, the squad—that basic unit of military organization—remains the same size. This suggests a force far deeper than tradition or immediate practicality at work, but something deeply human. Any organization forming small teams should be wary of ignoring this magic force.

WHY SEVEN PEOPLE BEAT A HUNDRED

What is that force? It may be, as we'll investigate in depth in upcoming chapters, that the very nature of the human brain—in particular, short-term memory—revolves around what the psychologist George Miller famously called "the magical number seven, plus or minus two." That is, human short-term memory is capable of capturing and briefly holding between five and nine items of information—for example, zip codes—and has only a limited repertoire of tricks to enhance that power (notably, "chunking" small clusters of data, such as the way we conceptualize telephone numbers as a three-digit area code, a three-digit local prefix, and a four-digit direct number at the end).

That the optimal size of small teams is the same as the effective range of short-term memory in our brains is unlikely to be a coincidence. Our minds seem to work best in pairs and in that zone of seven plus two other entities. Below that, the team often devolves into pairs or trios; above that, it moves toward splitting down to the stable quintet or sextet.

It's not surprising then that, wherever you encounter small units and teams even in the modern world, they rarely deviate from the basic half dozen or the aggregated-dozen-member archetypes. This strategy is as old as history and as new as the creation of new product teams at the most cutting-edge technology companies. Here's the Canadian team management consultant Mishkin Berteig on the priority of the right team size:

> Imagine that you have just been "given" a software development group consisting of 100 developers. Now imagine that you are given a really important project to work on. Which would be better?
>
> a. Get all 100 people working on the project (with good project management, leadership, etc.), or . . .
>
> b. Find the 7 strongest people in the group who are willing to work on the project (in other words, the seven strongest people that are actually interested in the project) and get them working on the project, fire the rest of them, and spend the savings on giving the 7 people the absolute best tools and environment they need and want, and spending the rest to make them happy/comfortable.
>
> Personally, despite the severity of scenario (b), I would definitely bet on it and not on scenario (a).[2]

The notion of optimal team sizes has gotten considerable support from other quarters, some of them quite unlikely.

For example, consider Parkinson's law, first formulated in 1955 by the British naval historian Cyril Northcote Parkinson in an article in the *Economist*.[3] In it, Parkinson argued for a rule about the behavior of organizations—particularly government bureaucracies—that has now become part of our language:

> Work expands so as to fill the time available for its completion.

Parkinson wrote the article as satire, but it captured a profound truth about human organizational behavior, and it has posed a challenge to sociologists and human resource managers ever since.

Parkinson even proposed two reasons for this phenomenon:[4]

- An official wants to multiply subordinates, not rivals, and
- Officials make work for each other.

That's why, Parkinson noted, even though the British Empire was shrinking rapidly as he wrote his essay, the total number of people employed in the British government to manage the empire was still growing by 5 to 7 percent per year "irrespective of any variation in the amount of work (if any) to be done."[5]

Besides providing a devastating indictment of unconstrained government growth, Parkinson's law had an interesting secondary effect: it forced social scientists, if they were to defeat the negative impact of the law, to determine the right number of bureaucrats for any given task.

Parkinson himself was fairly flexible. He believed that almost any team of fewer than twenty members could be made to work effectively, arguing that adding any more members would, once again, devolve the group into multiple smaller teams. He did, however, make one exception: in his experience, he said, a team of *eight* members would never reach a consensus decision—apparently because (as 4×4 or 2^3) there was no tiebreaker. That would seem to contradict the ubiquitous eight-man military units—until one remembers the staff sergeant or master sergeant in command, whose decision is final.

THE MYSTERY OF DUNBAR'S 150 AND 1,500

Driven by the demands of Parkinson's law, social scientists and anthropologists fanned out to study everything from factories to primitive tribes—and made some stunning discoveries. Studying everything from Hutterite religious communities to the Yanomamo people of the Brazilian jungle, as well as ethnographic literature, the British anthropologist Robin Dunbar discovered that the same human group sizes appear over and over. He called them "clusters of intimacy," and he identified "cliques" of five people, "sympathy groups" of twelve to fifteen people, and "bands" of up to thirty-five members.[6]

But Dunbar's biggest discovery, now named after him, was that there appeared to be an upper limit to team size. Precisely: 147.8, normally rounded up, as the "Dunbar number," to 150. It is a number that appears with stunning regularity. For example, the Yanomamo people have consistently over the centuries divided their tribes whenever they approach 200 members. As for the Hutterites, they long ago learned to split their colonies when their population reaches 150. In the Domesday Book, the average size of Welsh and British villages at the time of the Norman invasion was . . . 150 residents.

Almost everywhere you look, you can find the Dunbar number. For hundreds of years, that basic unit of almost every army in Western civilization, the company, has consisted of roughly 150 members. The likely number of "friends" you will have on Facebook or regular followers on Twitter? 150 to 190. The total population of households to whom Brits sent Christmas cards in 2000 (that is, before email greetings)? 153.5. Dunbar's explanation? The figure of 150 seems to represent the maximum number of individuals with whom we can have a genuinely social relationship, the kind of relationship that goes with knowing who they are and how they relate to us. To put it another way, it's the total number of people you would not feel embarrassed about joining uninvited for a drink if you happened to bump into them individually in a bar.[7]

Robin Dunbar hasn't stopped at 150 as an archetypical team size. There are other Dunbar numbers as well:

- 3 to 5: This is the circle of our very closest friends. Here Dunbar agrees with other social scientists.
- 12 to 15: The group of friends and family whose death we would deeply mourn. Again, Dunbar agrees with other researchers. He also adds an interesting example of a group of this size, born in historical experience: juries. This group is also connected with the notion of *deep trust*—that is, it's the number of people from whom you can accept a small amount of betrayal without severing ties.
- 50: This is a new number. Dunbar derives it, as usual, from historical sources; it is "the typical overnight camp size among traditional hunter-gatherers like the Australian Aboriginals or the San Bushmen of southern Africa."[8]
- 150: The Dunbar number. In the words of Dave Snowden, a Welsh knowledge management expert, the Dunbar number is "the number of identities that you can maintain in your head with some degree of acquaintances that an individual can maintain. It does not necessarily imply that you trust them, but it does mean that you can know something about them and their basic capabilities. In other words you can manage your expectations of their performance and abilities in different contexts and environments."[9]

Note that these natural groups in Dunbar's theory seem to scale by a factor of three. To date, no one seems to have come up with an explanation for this underlying multiplier.

- 1,500: This largest Dunbar number appears to be something of an outlier, one for which Dunbar himself doesn't seem to have an explanation. Are there one or two still-missing Dunbar numbers in between the last two, whose value and purpose are as yet undiscovered? Dunbar has suggested that there might be one at 500, which would correspond to the average person's number of acquaintances. Then comes this number, 1,500, which once again has a number of historic and contemporary examples and an underlying link to basic human behavior.

In terms of examples, 1,500 members is roughly the size of a large military battalion, the smallest unit capable of independent operation. It is also, as Dunbar has noted, the average size of a tribe in hunter-gatherer societies, and the number of people who speak the same language or dialect. But perhaps the most common and compelling example of the use of 1,500 as a limit on group size can be found in the corporate world.

Hewlett-Packard Co. in the 1950s and 1960s is sometimes described as the greatest corporation of all time. It was as technologically innovative as Apple was fifty years later, it offered more progressive employee programs (stock options, profit sharing, flextime, and so forth) than any company before or since, and—not surprisingly—it set records for employee happiness and morale that have never again been matched by a large corporation.

Interestingly, in 1957, as the company approached 1,500 employees, the two founders began to sense that something had changed in their relationship to other HPers—and something radical had to be done. Wrote David Packard in his autobiography, *The HP Way*, "It [was] increasingly difficult for Bill and me to know everything well and to have a personal knowledge of everything that was going on." So they decided that it was time to break up HP from a monolithic company into a divisional one. Bill Hewlett said, "Out of this came the concept that what we should probably do is divisionalize. We had [nearly] 1,500 people at that point and we thought it was too big. By dividing up into two or three small units, we might be able to keep that personal touch."

From that day to the present, HP's divisions have traditionally split up when they reach 1,500 employees. That decision is credited with making Hewlett-Packard in the 1960s and 1970s one of the most nimble large companies of all time. What Bill and Dave sensed intuitively, and executed with their typical decisiveness, has been imitated by countless other companies in the years since. The 1,500-employee division is one of the most common organizations on the global business landscape.

What Hewlett and Packard sensed on the ground has also been described by Dunbar in human terms:

> You have an inner, inner core of intimate friends and relations, of about five, and then there's the next layer out, it's about 15. If you like to think of those as best friends, perhaps, they're the people you might do most of your social Saturday evening barbeques with, and that of course, includes the five inside. And then this next layer out is 50 (you might think of those as good friends), and the 150, your friends. And then we know there are at least two more layers beyond that: one at 500 which you might think of as acquaintances, so again this is including everybody within the 150 as well; finally, one at 1,500 who are basically the number of faces you can put names to.[10]

WHAT DAVID PACKARD AND BILL HEWLETT KNEW

Another way of looking at Dunbar numbers is that five is the number of your most intimate friends and partners ("clique") and is a number that, not coincidentally, corresponds with the limits of our short-term memory. Fifteen is the number of people with whom we can have deep trust in the face of almost any turn of events ("sympathy group"). Fifty is a familial grouping, a small tribe with whom we can securely travel in dangerous country ("band"). One hundred fifty is the optimal size for a group of people living together in a community ("friendship group"); it corresponds to the number of people whose individual characteristics and behaviors the human brain can effectively remember. Five hundred is the number of people with whom we can remain nodding acquaintances ("tribe"). And fifteen hundred is the limit of our long-term memory, the total number of people to whom we can mentally attach a face if we hear his or her name ("community").

Why this last number, 1,500, works is self-evident. If you live in a community of 150 people, you feel pretty comfortable walking down the street, because you know everyone in town. A stranger—that is, a potential threat—is instantly obvious. With 500 members in the community, that comfort is strained a little, because you are likely to run into people whom you know but haven't spoken to in a long time. But still, strangers stand out. But with 1,500 neighbors, that comfort ends. Now you begin encountering people who you are not quite sure if you've ever met before . . . and the world suddenly becomes a much riskier place.

For Bill Hewlett and Dave Packard, the first threshold was passed in the late 1940s, when they had to end their tradition of personally handing out Christmas bonus checks and greeting everyone by name. By the early 1950s, everyone was still in the same building complex on Page Mill Road in Palo Alto, but the two founders now found themselves nodding at employees whose faces they knew but couldn't name. The tipping point came in the late 1950s, when Bill and Dave began encountering employees they had never seen before and whose only proof of employment was their name badge. And that's when they made their move.

By the end of the 1980s, HP had more than forty divisions, all of them consisting of about 1,500 employees—and was regularly creating new ones. The company even developed a standard architectural design for its divisional facilities, accommodating for a maximum capacity of . . . 1,500 employees.

Other corporations—in emulation of one of the world's most successful companies, or via trial and error—soon found themselves replicating this model. The PC division of Sony in Japan, for example, has 1,500 employees. Interestingly, but probably not coincidentally, 1,500 is usually considered the maximum employment of a medium-size company. And a surprising number of companies—such as Facebook, Google, and Twitter—hit the 1,500-employee mark in the ramp-up to their initial public offering . . . suggesting that there may be an even deeper link between going public, with the inevitable transformation in employment that takes place inside a company between employees of a private versus a public firm, and the boundaries of a natural community. Many employees of private firms remark, often with despair, that their "company is no longer the same place" after the IPO, that it is no longer a big "family but now an anonymous organization that is filled not with true believers but with salary men and women intent on their benefits and résumés."

THE HARD MATH OF IMPOSSIBLE CONNECTIVITY

Before we close out this section about the manifold forces at work in making teams of certain sizes both inevitable and desirable, there is one last structural force, beyond genetics, that appears to be driving the creation of teams. It is *the mathematics of networks.*

The reason the Internet is so powerful—and Metcalfe's law, as discussed in chapter 1, so useful—is that each new user arriving on the Web doesn't just add his or her solitary new node, but the billions of new connections that are then created. To understand the magnitude of this effect, let's look at the smallest number of connections in a team and progress forward, showing the total number of connections:

2 members = 1 connection
3 members = 3 connections

4 members = 6 connections
5 members = 10 connections
6 members = 15 connections
16 members = 120 connections
32 members = 496 connections

Notice that after the low-digit numbers, the equation settles down to $N(N-1)/z$, where N is the number of team members. The sheer complexity of the network grows much, much faster than the number of team members does (at the Dunbar number of 1,500, the number of interconnections reaches 1,124,250).

And that creates an obvious problem. Human beings can handle, much less maintain, only comparatively small numbers of connections. That's why relationships degrade so quickly as the number of team members grows. Most of us are pretty good at remaining in contact with five or six other people on a constant basis. But doing so is a whole lot tougher with a dozen or more. At fifty? Not even those rare individuals with a photographic memory for faces and names can still stay in touch with the team in the same way as they did with a half dozen others. Even with the tools of social networks, texting, wide area networking, and global wireless telecom, we *still* don't have the time or the bandwidth to continuously maintain hundreds or thousands of close personal connections.

That's why bigger teams almost never correlate to a greater chance of success. The noted Harvard psychologist J. Richard Hackman once said, "Big teams usually wind up just wasting everybody's time."[11] He explained that

[the] fallacy is that bigger teams are better than small ones because they have more resources to draw upon. A colleague and I once did some research showing that as a team gets bigger, the number of links that need to be managed among members goes up at an accelerating, almost exponential rate.

It's managing the links between members that gets teams into trouble. My rule of thumb is no double digits. In my courses, I never allow teams of more than six students. Big teams usually wind up just wasting everybody's time. That's why having a huge senior leadership team—say, one that includes all the CEO's direct reports—may be worse than having no team at all.[12]

We are driven not only by biology to form teams of certain predetermined sizes but also by mathematics—or more precisely, combinatorics—to choose the smaller of those sizes whenever possible. And, conversely, combinatorics drives the quality of the relationships in teams to degrade so quickly from close acquaintance to mere recognition.

It also explains why, as we have seen over and over again in recent years, companies and other institutions can spend fortunes on the hottest and coolest new information tools and the latest new management techniques only to end up even *less* competitive. Too often, even the most ambitious and enlightened schemes crash on the rocky shore of human nature—that is, whatever other advantages these schemes enjoy, they have failed to build the *appropriate* teams to employ their strengths.

FROM TEAM ART TO TEAM SCIENCE

If the laws of networking constrain the behavior of human teams, the reality of networks—particularly the Internet—may help us construct them more efficiently than ever before.

One of the most compelling new industries created by the intersection of the Internet, sensor technology, and software analytics is *Big Data*.

Though Big Data has lately suffered the overhyping that comes with any powerful new technology, the reality is that it represents a revolutionary new approach to our ways of looking at the natural world. In particular, it signals the end of *sampling*. Historically, because measuring all cases of a particular phenomenon was all but impossible, humans developed the science of statistics: that is, taking samples and then using mathematical tools to measure correlation and chance of error, blowing up the results to cover *all* cases.

Big Data turns this upside down. Using everything from high-resolution satellite imagery to tiny semiconductor sensors to the cloud-based collection of millions of daily transactions, we now find it possible for the first time to measure *everything*—every fish passing a point in the ocean, every tree in the Amazon, every purchase made at every Walmart, every step taken by every shopper in a retail mall . . . and soon, every gust of wind on earth, and every blood cell in our bodies.

Even better, all of these mountains of raw data, including metadata, can be crunched, using the latest computer-based analytical tools to discover truths about the natural world (for example, long-term trends in climate, animal species, human behavior, and epidemiology), and nonintuitive connections (for example, the connection between childhood behavior and cancer sixty years into the future) never before even imagined.

One of the most interesting consequences of the Big Data revolution is its ability to conduct massive searches, using multiple characteristics. Not surprisingly, this ability has earned considerable attention in the commercial world.

In particular, a brand-new industry has sprung up to use Big Data to aid in the hiring process. Corporations and government agencies now contract Big Data firms to look for the best candidate for a position by not just doing a global search but also by gathering and processing huge amounts of available information about individuals—from school grades to personality tests to past performance—to determine the very best fit for the job. Begun just a few years ago, this industry has already grown to a billion-dollar size . . . not surprisingly, as the value of the perfect candidate for a given job is many times that of rolling the dice on a new hire after a couple of interviews.

"Recruiters and hiring managers rely heavily on instincts, hunches and memory to choose the right candidates," said Mark Newman, the CEO of HireVue, to *Forbes* in 2014. "But there isn't a lot of data to help them predict who will become a top performer, or decide who should be interviewing candidates." The *Wall Street Journal* and *Entrepreneur* magazine ran similar stories hailing the bright new dawn of algorithmic hiring.

But as valuable as using Big Data to hire individual employees can be—count us skeptical—its value pales against the value of a well-designed, high-functioning team. That said, until now, teams have by necessity largely been recruited and formed by hunch, intuition, and experience, with little to no empirical support.

That is about to change.

The New Science of Teams

Think of all of the dysfunctional or barely functional teams that you have known—or worse, been a part of—over the course of your life. Painful memories, aren't they?

Let's go in a more pleasant direction. Think of those one or two teams—a childhood sports team, a best friendship, a Scout patrol, a college study group, a department in your company—that just seemed to gel. The team you felt so much a part of that it was like an extension of yourself. A team that accomplished—and helped *you* accomplish—far more than you ever thought possible. The team that remains the ideal against which you have judged all subsequent teams. The team whose members remained friends long after its tenure ended.

Now imagine if *every* team of which you've been a member had been that successful, that productive, and that rewarding. Imagine *you* at your best, surrounded by teammates at their bests, sharing personal experiences that will be remembered fondly decades later.

HARDWIRED TO WORK AND IMPROVE TOGETHER

The most fundamental questions one can ask about teams are, Are human beings designed to work together? And can each person grow and perform at his or her best if properly fit into the right team? Some of the most compelling new research in brain science in the twenty-first century says yes.

In fact, the human brain is evolutionarily designed so that individuals can adjust to one another's perspectives and emotions in order to engage in cooperative activity.[1] Such adaptation does not occur at a "software" level; rather, as the noted psychologist Daniel Goleman has shown, *humans are actually wired to connect.* That is, when we engage with another person, we are, in fact, embarking on an intimate brain-to-brain connection with that person.

Hints of the depth of that connection pop up in our everyday language—for instance, when we "don't laugh at someone, but with them" or when we say we are "of one mind" with another person. The deeper that engagement—love, friendship, a partnership of complete trust—the greater that relationship affects our brains and our well-being to the point of actually activating genes controlling our immune systems. Thus, nourishing relationships really are beneficial for our health, while toxic ones can actually be physically destructive.

We tend to think of our brains as pure thought and our bodies as physical entities (except when we suffer a concussion or endure a hangover). But in fact, our brains make up 2 percent of our total body weight—the high relative number being one of those things that distinguish us from most other animals. And that bundle of nerve cells is especially hungry: our brains are responsible for 25 percent of our body's total glucose use, 20 percent of its oxygen use, and 15 percent of our total cardiac output.[2]

This hunger for fuel—which we typically credit to that thin and wrinkled bedsheet-size layer of cerebral cortex that gives us higher thinking and consciousness—also appears to come from our need to socialize. Thus, the correlation between brain size and group complexity appears to be the strongest for pair-bonding animals.[3]

One popular explanation for why this is so is that teamwork made us this way. This is the "social intelligence hypothesis," which states that advanced cognitive abilities such as those found in humans and other primates are a result of the selection pressures from the varied demands of their social interactions. In other words, we have big brains because environmental forces—hunting on the veldt, near-extinction events, the Ice Ages—in our distant history *forced us to work together* in complicated ways. Our large brain size is the outcome of that teamwork.[4]

Simulation experiments conducted by the evolutionary microbiologist Luke McNally of Trinity College Dublin and his team found that when groups were faced with cooperative problems, organisms invariably selected for greater cognitive abilities.[5] In other words, we're smarter precisely because we had to work together.

This finding is so important that we want to give you a bit more detail on how the experiment was conducted. The simulation, done on computers, began with fifty simple "brains," each with three to six neurons. Each brain challenged the others to a classic human social interaction scenario: either the prisoner's dilemma (each individual, without any information, either has to betray the others or trust them) or the snowdrift game (a.k.a. playing chicken to see who swerves first). In other words, the brains could either cooperate or cheat.

The "brains" that did well in these games were then programmed to be more likely to have offspring—that is, "winner begets all." After each game, the brains reproduced asexually. In these new generations, all the brains had a chance to undergo a random mutation, in a manner similar to real life, that could change the brain's structure or the number or connectivity of its neurons.

The simulation ran for 50,000 generations (about as many as

we've had as something resembling humans). The slow transition to a more cooperative society resulted in the evolution of more complex brains. Thus, teams have literally helped make us who we are.

Such cooperative behavior was induced in this experiment by external forces (the researchers), but where, you may ask, does cooperative behavior come from in nature? Now it gets even more interesting. It turns out that cooperative behavior appears *everywhere* among living things—from genes to multicellular organisms to societies.[6] Some have even speculated that this cooperative behavior may have been necessary for the emergence of *all* complex biological systems, from genomes to the global human community.[7]

But even if cooperative behavior is ubiquitous in the animal kingdom, this still doesn't quite explain why it not only exists among humans, but—consider nation-states with hundreds of millions of citizens—is almost unimaginably complex.

WHY WE COLLABORATE BEYOND KIN

One likely explanation for the depth of cooperation found in human societies is *kin relations*. Humans have lived as foragers for 95 percent of their history—there is evidence of australopithecine kin behavior dating back one million years. The simple answer is that people cooperated in hunter-gatherer groups because they were related to one another.

But it turns out that this isn't exactly correct: analyses of coresidence patterns in the archaeological record have revealed that kin relations were too few in human hunter-gatherer groups to have been the driving force for the evolution of human cooperation. In other words, there weren't enough distant cousins in these groups to drive real genetic change. Rather, it took large interacting networks of *unrelated* adults to evolve capacities for social learning—which in turn created cumulative culture.[8]

The implications of this discovery go in two directions. The first is that, perhaps from the start, human beings teamed up with people beyond their kin. And that in turn underscores the notion that those humans didn't have to *learn* how to bring nonkin members into their team, but that they already, naturally, had that inclination.

In the other direction, just where that inclination came from is not so obvious. For example, in a comparative study of sequential problem-solving groups, researchers assembled teams of capuchin monkeys, chimpanzees, and human children. Each were given an experimental puzzle box that could only be solved in three stages. As an incentive, successful problem solvers were given ever-better rewards the closer they got toward the solution.

So, what happened? Well, each member of the capuchin (the lower level of the intelligence scale) and the chimp (the middle level) teams tried to solve the problem on its own. By comparison, the groups of children worked as teams, teaching each other, exchanging advice, and sharing their rewards. The more they cooperated, the better they did at the task. Indeed, by working together, many of the teams of children actually solved their puzzles.[9]

As it turns out, contrary to a more selfish notion of humankind—that is, people are only in it for themselves—*cooperation* may be the default tendency in humans, and self-interest may be something you *will* yourself toward. This position is underscored by the results of so-called resource allocation experiments in which subjects are forced to make decisions quickly. These snap decisions result in more cooperation among subjects than is found when they are given time to deliberate and reflect on their decisions.[10] Give us time, it seems, and we'll start thinking of only ourselves.

GETTING AHEAD BY GETTING ALONG

Still don't buy it? Consider the incredible contribution of open-source software—computer code that's freely developed through public, collaborative efforts of programmers around the world. Some of our most important Internet infrastructure has been enabled through open-source development, like Apache's HTTP Web server, Red Hat's Linux operating system, Mozilla's Firefox web browser, Sun's Java programming language, and MySQL database systems.

Or consider Wikipedia. Traditional encyclopedia companies such as Collier's and Encyclopedia Britannica weren't buried by cheap foreign labor or rising paper costs; they were usurped by the collaborative effort of volunteer writers and editors.

Maybe it's an Internet thing, right? Don't be too sure. Work probably doesn't get any more isolated and independent than commercial fishing. Located in the top lobster-producing region of the United States, the Maine lobster industry brings in almost $300 million a year and comprises 5,400 separate businesses employing 35,000 individuals. Yet it's one of the best modern examples of collective action. Just a couple of decades ago, the industry was on the verge of collapse. Century-old businesses were being shuttered and boats dry-docked. But now it's a study in the way people with a common interest can work together to protect a resource through promoting sustainability. Authority over the industry lies with both the fishermen and government agencies; this authority includes the establishment of size restrictions, seasonal boundaries, and trap regulations. Because of this voluntary cooperation, the industry is flourishing and the community is thriving. So even in an industry defined by individual effort, humans naturally seem to work better together.

Still, why this should be so is not yet obvious. One explanation for cooperation being our natural default response—what social scientists refer to as *prosociality*—is that cooperation actually engages the reward regions of our brains; that is, we go there first because it *feels* good. But for now, that is still just speculation.[11]

Supporting this notion that prosociality is deeply engrained in humans is a wide range of both anthropological studies and field anecdotes from around the world and across numerous cultures. Wherever they are, people tend to engage in prosocial behavior—even when it is not obviously to their advantage.

For example, in resource distribution studies in which participants are requested to split resources, people—wherever they are—typically choose to share between 40 and 50 percent of what they have, even when the recipient is anonymous and there is no penalty for not sharing those resources.[12] And we're not just talking about adults here, or acculturated young people, but even toddlers: children as young as fourteen months old will actively cooperate in joint tasks (of course, they'll also hit each other over the head with those "shared" toys on occasion).[13]

SOCIAL NORMS AND "ULTIMATE GAMES"

As you might imagine, these innate prosocial traits are made manifest in *social norms*—and those norms in turn are a distinguishing feature of human beings.[14] What makes social norms so important is that they can shape behavior without the force of law—that is, they are people's beliefs about acceptable social behavior in situations in which the law is not present to enforce it.[15] Think of all those times you waited at a stoplight at 3:00 a.m. when there wasn't a cop, or even another car, in sight; or the items you never took from stores even though no one was watching. Or when you gave the right price to an inquiring cashier who couldn't find the tag on your item.

As it turns out, you are not alone. In-depth ethnographic studies of cultures around the world, from hunter-gatherers to the citizens of modern cities, depict groups as sharing a wide range of social norms, running from food sharing to cooperation to honesty.[16] These attitudes are directed not only at members of the group, but also toward those considered outsiders.

Joe Henrich of the University of British Columbia has spent the last decade working with various colleagues to uncover the cognitive sources of human society. In one of his research projects, he and his team studied social behavior in fifteen different small societies, including foragers, nomadic herding groups, and individuals in settled, agricultural societies in Africa, South America, and Indonesia. They found that within-society social norms even affected individuals' behavior toward strangers.[17]

One of his more interesting findings is that the more that individuals from a particular society have to collaborate to survive, the more they will offer to strangers in "ultimatum" games. (These are games in which two players divide a sum of money; the first player chooses the division, and the second can veto that decision—but then all the money is lost). Henrich and his associates found that the Machiguenga people of Peru, who rarely collaborate outside of their own families, still allocated on average 26 percent of their total resources in ultimatum games to strangers. In contrast, the Lamerala of Indonesia, who fish in highly collaborative groups of individuals from different families, on average allocated 58 percent of their total resources to strangers.

But sharing isn't only about resources. It can also be about shared experiences. In his book *Keeping Together in Time*, the historian William McNeill provides powerful evidence for how coordinated rhythmic movement and the shared feelings it evokes is a powerful binding force for human groups. McNeill shows that shared movements, from ancient village dances to modern-day military drills, create muscular bonding and endow groups with a capacity for cooperation, solidarity, and, in turn, survival.[18] Those few who have spent time in an African village know the binding power—and the solidarity bordering on a kind of delirium—of the village dance. And most of us have experienced this in our own lives, from high school marching band to military boot camp.

But even more remarkable is that we all may have been practicing these coordinating dynamics since *even before we were born*—in particular, the kind of self-organized synchronization that takes place between our brains and our bodies. Just watch a baby, or an adult rehabilitating from a stroke or a major injury, and see how the dynamic between what the brain wants and what the body actually does has to be constantly practiced until that self-synchronization is both fast and precise. A toddler learning to walk can execute the perfection of a pole vault or a triple spin on ice skates twenty years later.[19]

It shouldn't be surprising, then, that this mind-body synchronization takes place not only within human beings, but also *among* them. We may not be a flock of birds seemingly turning with one mind, but the analogy still holds. Indeed, some experiments have shown that humans can exchange behavioral coordination information so quickly that the results can appear to be spontaneous—as when people tend to applaud in unison.[20]

This shared information can be quite limited and yet still achieve coordination, an insight that may prove very useful in this age of Skype and virtual meetings. Experiments in social neuroscience of people watching each other on a video screen show that with visual information exchange alone, humans still immediately and spontaneously coordinate their actions. Incredibly, the aftereffects of these visual social encounters persist even when the vision of the others is no longer available. In other words, we are *changed* by our social interactions.[21] Perhaps not for forever—but the miracle is that, based on such little interaction, we are changed at all.[22]

The anthropologist Robin Dunbar, whom we've already met,

has proposed the concept of a "social brain," arguing that a crucial, distinctive part of human intelligence is its intrinsically social quality, which enables effectiveness in complex social networks.[23] In the words of one of his fellow researchers, "The social brain hypothesis in evolutionary anthropology contends that human brains have evolved to be as big as they are so that we can think about and manage our relationships with other people."[24] In other words, our brains are not bigger because we are smarter, but bigger in order to help us work with—to team with—our fellow humans.

OXYTOCIN, THE BONDING (AND ORGASM) HORMONE

Okay, so human beings seem wired to form teams and to work together. But what is that wiring made of? Now we're getting down to the most basic component of human teams: oxytocin, a mammalian hormone that acts as a neuromodulator on the brain. Oxytocin is produced by the hypothalamus and is stored in the pituitary gland. Oxytocin (sometimes referred to by its trade names of Pitocin and Syntocinon) is often administered to induce labor in pregnant women. It is also regularly used in veterinary medicine to induce both labor and lactation.

This hormone has some very interesting characteristics. For one thing, its effects have a half-life of only about three minutes, and it cannot be introduced into the brain via the bloodstream (it's blocked by the blood-brain barrier)—the latter feature making it safer for use in deliveries. Since digestion also destroys it, oxytocin is typically administered by injection or via nasal spray.

The power of oxytocin on the human body is quite stunning. For example, it appears to play a part in everything from maternal bonding to anxiety to orgasms. But its most important role, for our purposes, is as the basic neurobiological element in the human "social brain."[25]

In particular, oxytocin appears to be one of the most important chemicals for mediating pair bonds and social behavior.[26] It seems to increase our ability to process positive social cues (humans identify human facial gestures more quickly and more accurately after being dosed with the hormone), while also simultaneously decreasing social threat–related cues linked to social-avoidance behaviors.[27]

It would seem that the world of oxytocin is a very friendly place, for even as oxytocin creates positive social interaction, those positive social interactions in turn increase levels of oxytocin.[28] And those increased levels can do all sorts of things, including:

- Increase social interaction between adults.[29]
- Improve the processing of positive social information.[30]
- Enhance in-group trust.[31]

So far, oxytocin sounds like the fabled elixir of love. But all is not sunshine and cupcakes, because researchers have discovered one more, darker, feature of the hormone: It promotes greater defensive aggression toward out-group members.[32] It may also be a major cause of human ethnocentrism. That this hormone should have such a Janus-like aspect—making us love our neighbors but also fear strangers—helps explain why group dynamics can be so complicated and multidimensional.

Most of us would agree that individual behaviors that benefit others—for example, cooperation, compassion, and mutual coordination—are critical for successful teamwork.[33]

Our motivation for prosocial behavior, including affiliation and closeness, appears to arise from neurophysiological processes.[34] And those processes in turn are created by the release of oxytocin and another neuropeptide, called vasopressin. Antecedents of these hormones date back in animals at least 700 million years and are seen across the animal kingdom.[35]

Research has found that the amount of oxytocin released during "dyadic" interactions (two individuals in a sociologically significant relationship) is directly related to the reciprocity of that pair.[36] (The initial research in this area was looking at the early stages of romantic attachment—as we've already noted, there are strong correlations between the functioning of teams and the mating process. . . . Now you know why.) The oxytocin released by these interactions promotes further trust and cooperation,[37] especially toward in-group members.[38] In other words, form a happy team with others and you will feel a lot better toward your group as a whole.

Literally better. One of the effects of oxytocin on the human body is to dampen many of its physiological responses to stress.[39] So, being part of a team actually can make us less stressed—and ultimately, happier. And this is not some secondary effect, or a minor feature, but one that goes right to the heart of being a fully actualized human being: psychologists have found that a child suffering early separation from his or her parents can experience altered oxytocin receptor sensitivity as an adult.[40] So we are talking some powerful, life-changing forces in this singular chemical.

Just how powerful remains a matter of speculation. The psychologists Rick O'Gorman and Kennon Sheldon and the evolutionary biologist David Wilson have proposed that natural selection itself may have favored people with prosocial genetic traits. How so? Because individuals with altruistic traits and a willingness to adopt social roles are rewarded with group inclusion—and thus have a greater chance of breeding. Meanwhile, those with traits harmful to a group, including the disposition for free-riding and selfishness, are punished or alienated.[41] The stress-reducers of the world are always more popular than the stress-inducers.

In fact, this talent for joining and reducing overall stress may prove to be far more important than we ever thought. Marilynn Brewer, a psychologist at the University of California, Los Angeles, has argued that sociobiologists neglect the role of selection in small groups—which she believes is the *most* important aspect of human evolution—and focus too much instead on individuals. For Brewer, it is small cooperative groups that have been the primary survival strategy for humans.

Here is her argument: In order to survive, humans needed to cluster into groups—and those groups needed to meet certain structural requirements: coordination of individual effort, communication, and optimal group size. These structural requirements for group survival in turn imposed selective pressures on individuals who wanted to become part of these small cooperative groups in order to survive and breed. And those individuals with the cognitive and motivational capacities agreeable to cooperative group life survived precisely because they were included.

Meanwhile, those individuals whose cognitive and motivational capacities were disruptive to group organization were selectively avoided, rejected, or eliminated, either by the group or by having to go solo in a dangerous world. Run this filtering process through hundreds of generations, and those social motives—such as cooperation and group loyalty—become dominant and thus characteristic of the human species.[42]

THE STRANGE POWER OF MIRROR NEURONS

The discovery of mirror neurons, among the most important findings of the last decade in neuroscience, helps us understand many heretofore paradoxical social phenomena, including the evolution of language, emotional empathy, and personal social identity.[43]

Mirror neurons are nerve cells in the brain whose purpose appears to be creating a copy of an observed action—either by the owner of that brain, or, even more astonishingly, *the action of others*. In particular, when a person observes an action, neurons that represent that action are activated in the observer's premotor cortex—

creating a "motor copy" of the observed action.[44] And thus visual information is transformed into knowledge.[45]

To better understand the power of mirror neurons, consider the way many of us jump out of our seats at the crack of a baseball bat or pump our fists when a long putt drops—even though we're watching other people perform on TV. Why do we experience such visceral reactions? It's because our mirror neurons fire when we see a familiar action, allowing us to understand the action, its goal, and even the emotions associated with it. By extension, this means that our motor systems trigger when watching a sport that we have physically experienced. And if we're watching strenuous action, mirror neurons even cause a small, but measurable, uptick in our heart rate. In this sense, the spectating brain is also the participating brain. And more important, when our favorite team wins, we win.

A 2008 study by Salvatore Aglioti, a professor at the Sapienza University of Rome, suggests that there's a sliding scale of mirror neuron response among spectators based on their real-life sports experience. This is why we usually take the greatest pleasure in watching sports that we've actually played. Additionally, our mirror neurons show a preference for certain players who touch the ball more often than others, such as quarterbacks in football and pitchers in baseball. Why? Even if we've never played football or baseball competitively, most of us have experienced the action of throwing a ball.

Of course, the evolutionary purpose of our mirror neuron system is not to make us more enthusiastic sports spectators—that's just a fun side effect. Instead, this system is important for social cognition, understanding the mental states of others, empathy, and learning by watching others.

The discovery of mirror neurons in the late 1980s is a classic example of a lucky accident. Italian neuroscientists found that when a monkey raised its arm, a particular cell in the creature's brain was fired. That wasn't the big surprise, that came one day when a lab assistant raised his arm and triggered a similar reaction in the monkey's same brain cell. The researchers discovered that neurons that mimic or mirror what others do are part of the brain's circuitry.[46]

The discovery of mirror neurons could be a game changer, with the potential to offer breakthroughs in everything from how teams are created to the nature of leadership.

It is because of mirror neurons that people are able to emulate, within seconds, the emotions and actions of others. Mirror neurons also allow us to navigate our social world and create an instant sense of shared experience. And they are particularly important to leadership, because followers don't just act out the orders of leaders, they actually tend to mirror the feelings and actions of those leaders.[47]

For example, it is now believed that positive behaviors such as empathy actually create a chemical connection—a form of "mood contagion"—between the brains of a leader and his or her followers. In other words, leaders' empathy and attunement to others' moods actually affect their own and their followers' brain chemistry. And what that means is that the leader-follower dynamic that has been the subject of endless speculation over the last few thousand years may, in the end, be even stranger and more mystical than we ever imagined: a biochemical process in which individual minds fuse into a single system.

This model goes a long way toward explaining the superhuman bond ("chain lightning," as the Steely Dan song calls it) that great leaders—for good or evil—create between themselves and their followers.

Just think of corporate leaders like Howard Schultz, Indra Nooyi, Alan Mulally, Richard Branson, and Ursula Burns, or "field leaders" like Duke coach Mike Krzyzewski and Yankee shortstop Derek Jeter—they all seem capable of *willing* their "teams" to victory. Those superior leaders understand either naturally, or by learned experience, how to leverage this system of brain interconnectedness. How they do so is its own kind of magic. Some appear to have learned this skill from extensive experience as leaders on the way up. But others appear to be born with the specific neural circuits that empower them with either a kind of "social intelligence" or a set of interpersonal competencies that inspire others to do great things.[48]

This offers something of an answer to the age-old question of whether leaders are made or born. They are both, but great leaders are almost always born that way. (By the way, research on hundreds of top executives by Margaret Hopkins of the University of Toledo has shown no significant gender differences in social intelligence among top leaders, contrary to the myth that women have superior social intelligence.)

Look at mothers and their newborn babies, and you will see another phenomenon of mirror neurons: some of them are exclusively tasked with detecting and mirroring the smiles and laughter of others. It is a process that begins with moms soon after birth and quickly extends to include all humankind. Not surprisingly, this innate detector also works between leaders and followers.

For example, a leader who smiles and laughs will trigger similar laughter in his or her team—a process that also helps in team bonding. And bonded groups almost always perform better than their less-well-bonded counterparts. Not surprisingly, top-performing leaders have been shown, on average, to elicit laughter from their subordinates at least twice as often as their less successful counterparts.[49] One reason for this is that laughter appears to increase both creativity and trust within teams.[50] Perhaps more surprisingly, humor also makes audiences listen and retain more of a presentation or conversation.[51] Once again, you can credit our mirror neurons, which predispose us to react to humor, laughter, and general happiness.

This discovery is reinforced by field experiments with actual leaders. When leaders display happiness, it improves their followers' *creative* performance—and interestingly, when they are sad, it enhances those same followers' *analytical* performance. In other words, when the team members think the boss is happy, they feel liberated to try out new ideas; and when they think the boss is unhappy, they hunker down into survival mode.[52] This is probably why positive emotions result in more cooperative and conciliatory behavior.[53]

But it isn't all good news: positive and negative emotions differ in longevity, something you can probably validate by thinking of your own career. Employees invariably remember negative (burdensome) events more often, with more intensity, and in more detail than positive, uplifting events.[54] Although memories of good times are brief, memories of bad times seem to stay with us forever.

Happily, thanks again to our mirror neurons, positive and prosocial behavior can be contagious.[55] People who witness prosocial and cooperative behaviors tend to experience a greater sense of morality.[56] And, in findings that can only be considered comforting for the future of humankind, researchers have also found that people observing helping behaviors engaged in more helping behavior in their own subsequent tasks.[57] Perhaps even more compelling is that subjects participating in experimental economic "dictator games" (in which only one player determines the distribution of rewards to all other players) become more generous after observing other players exhibiting prosocial behavior.[58] It seems that the better we behave, the better people around us behave as well.

"WE" VERSUS "ME"

It should come as no surprise that mirror neurons play a crucial role in human teamwork. When a team is working, members must not only engage with each other but also understand and anticipate the actions of their teammates. Although a number of specific

systems in the brain help humans represent and anticipate the behaviors of others during joint action, mirror neurons seem to play
a key role in enabling observational learning and imitation among
team members.[59] But the relationship between members of a team
and their mirror neurons goes both ways. That is, socializing behavior doesn't just arise from the wiring of our brains. Rather, the
nature of our socializing with others affects the activity of our mirror neurons—to the point that it can change the way those neurons
represent the actions of others.[60] In the best scenario, the result is
a virtuous cycle: the more we socialize with others, the better and
happier we are at doing that socializing—an experience most of us
know from our own lives.

If all this seems literally delusional, the real source of seeing the
world through rose-colored glasses, it is a valuable delusion. Why?
Because delusions are *shared* among the group members. It turns
out that in collaborative settings, team members who work well together will come to a common representation of their project—one
that reduces any emphasis on personal authorship and competition.
In other words, it becomes *our* project, not mine. And, as we will
see, anything that can remove ego and claims of ownership among
team members is a very good thing—not just for team productivity
and durability but also in the long aftermath.[61]

This "learned synergy" influences not only our appreciation
of success, but also our understanding of failure. Indeed, the neural representation of others' *errors* is also influenced by being in
a team.[62] We are much more forgiving of mistakes made by our
teammates than those made by "outsiders"—especially when those
outsiders are in competitive interpersonal settings.[63] At their best,
teams, powered by our mirror neurons, can create a sense of "we,"
in which another's actions are perceived as one's own. Self-other
merging seems to light up our mirror neuron systems. It also makes
us both more vigilant and more understanding of errors made by
our teammates.[64]

WHERE DOES INTUITION COME FROM?

Mirror neurons aren't the only cells in the brain that help regulate how we interact with others in team settings.

For example, take intuition, the irrational sense—gut feeling, hunch, sixth sense, based on no real evidence—that you know the answer to a problem. Intuition is often revered by great executives—that moment when they sense a weakness in a competitor and act decisively; or hire or put their faith in a near stranger; or have an intimation that the market is about to shift directions.

Many people consider chess to be the ultimate application of human logic, but as Garry Kasparov—arguably the greatest chess player of all time—professes, "Intuition is the defining quality of a great chess player. . . . Often, your gut will serve you better than your brains. To me the implication is clear: What made players great was not their analytic prowess but their intuition under pressure."[65]

In practice, intuition can seem like ESP, coming from a place deep in the recesses of your mind. But recent research has found that intuition is partly produced by a class of neurons in the brain called *spindle cells*. The role of these spindle cells is to quickly transmit thoughts and feelings to other cells. And by "quickly" we mean jaw-droppingly fast. Within one-twentieth of a second, spindle cells trigger neural networks designed to make judgment calls with only a minimum of evidence—such as deciding whether one person is trustworthy or whether another is right for a job. In our fast-moving digital world, this ability to make accurate "gut calls" can be crucial for team leaders.

Meanwhile, another class of neurons called *oscillators* regulates physical coordination between people. When two cellists play together, they hit their notes in unison because of their respective oscillators. In a sense, human beings find harmony when their oscillators do.

For now at least, we don't know how to strengthen or regulate the firing pattern of mirror neurons, spindle cells, and oscillators. We can't yet manipulate how we work together at the neural level. But what we can understand is that these fundamental factors do exist and not only are happiness and stress contagious, but they can spread within seconds across a team.[66]

WHEN IN DOUBT, HUG IT OUT

For generations, management and leadership experts (as well as our own mothers) have been telling us to always thank people for their help or for a job well done. Well, now research has shown that *expressions of gratitude* can in fact increase closeness among group members.[67] When managers express gratitude, it can increase employees' sense of social worth and self-conception as viable members of the organization. And that, in turn, promotes prosocial behaviors that tie the team together even more.[68]

By the same token, nonverbal expressions of gratitude can be particularly powerful. For example, touch can activate reward regions of the frontal lobes of the brain,[69] stimulate oxytocin release,[70] and excite the vagus nerve, one of the body's longest nerves, which runs from the brain stem to the abdomen, touching most of the organs in between, and is linked to prosociality and attention.[71] Put all of that together and you can see how (appropriate) touch can enhance cooperation in team activities.[72] Now you understand what all that hand-holding, hugging, and trust-catching was about in team training seminars.

Here's another one you probably already know, but for which there is now empirical evidence: *reputation* matters in teamwork. Studies in organizations and social groups have found that reputations form and spread among group members at the speed of lightning.[73] How fast? Within a week of a team's formation, all its members have likely already acquired groupwide reputations as either collaborators or free riders.[74]

And these good reputations can be extremely valuable to the team members who enjoy them. In experimental studies, group members with a prosocial and generous reputation tend to be rewarded more by other group members. In particular, they tend to receive greater resource allocations than those with less generous reputations. Better yet—and the reader will especially want to remember this—those same prosocial and generous team members are also more likely to be appointed to leadership positions.[75]

You really do get ahead by getting along.

HEALTHY FOR YOU TOO

Being part of a successful, well-functioning team is good not only for your organization but also for you.

Recent research comprising more than 300,000 patients across 148 studies has revealed that individuals who report inadequate social relationships have a 50 percent greater probability of mortality as compared with patients who report adequate social relationships.[76] Loneliness, and its deleterious effects, is at the heart of this. Being on a team can make you happy, sad, angry, or frustrated, but it rarely makes you feel lonely. And loneliness is a killer—literally. As Brad Wilcox, a sociologist at the University of Virginia, revealed in a May 2013 article for the *Atlantic*, there's a strong link between suicide and loneliness. Noting a marked rise in suicide rates, Wilcox convincingly argued that these new statistics challenge the "rugged individualist" myth and indicate that men and women seem to be significantly more likely to kill themselves if they lack support systems.

Additionally, the sleep of lonely young adults is less efficacious as assessed by almost every physiological, behavioral, and self-report measure.[77] Lonely people at all ages show weaker immune responses and a greater vulnerability to viral respiratory infections.[78]

For certain tasks—such as financial forecasts and sales estimates—the team can actually make you look better as an individual. Particularly in such quantitative judgment tasks, teams consistently outperform the average of their members' individual judgments.[79] When teams are also given outcome feedback,[80] share task-relevant information, and are asked to identify their most accurate group member,[81] they outperform their members' average estimates by even more.

Ah, but there is a danger in this collaboration—as anyone who has sat in a meeting with one overbearing member who sucks all of the oxygen out of the room (that is, everyone) knows, teams tend to assign *more* weight to the contributions of their extroverted members. The only way to shift the weight back is through highly visible and shared data about the past accuracy of each member of the team. That usually shuts up the loudmouth.[82]

Individuals also seem to learn better if they are learning as part of a group.[83] One reason for this is that the very process of seeking agreement with other teammates drives more concrete conclusions—and dealing with teammates' contrasting opinions also leads to greater self-reflection. It is better to be challenged by others than to learn in an echo chamber.[84] Studies with adult participants show that performance on reasoning tasks is improved when debate is a requirement for team activities.[85]

It works for kids too. Pairs of eight-year-olds were asked to predict whether an empty metal box or solid rubber ring would float in water. Once they agreed on a prediction they had to test it. The children were then queried right after the experiment and then some weeks later for their understanding of the phenomena. The delayed post-test results proved to be significantly better in groups that sought agreement in their predictions before testing and worked in a group in which contrasting opinions were expressed.

It didn't even matter if agreement was actually achieved—all that was important was that agreement-seeking and contrasting opinions were features of the discussion.[86] That's why postmortems and debriefings are so valuable.

MEASURING TEAMS IN REAL TIME

Teams these days are not just being studied statistically, or as part of isolated experiments, but in real life, and while they are in operation. And the results have often been revealing. For example, the old phrase "It is not what you say but how you say it" is now a mathematically proven statement.

Sociometrics

One finding is that *body language* (that fad of three decades ago) and other nonverbal forms of human communication really do matter. In fact, many of the ancient biological signaling patterns that humans used even before the development of language still dominate our lives.

Alex Pentland, the director of MIT's Human Dynamics Laboratory, and his team have used "sociometers" to generate data on communication patterns and the productivity of teams in real organizations. Sociometers are wearable electronic sensors that measure patterns of communication—including the amount of face-to-face interaction, conversation time, physical proximity to other people, and physical activity levels—using social signals derived from vocal features, body motion, and relative location. They capture tone of voice, how one faces others in groups, and how much people listen and talk.

Crucial to the research is that sociometers are designed to capture the *nature* of human interaction, not its *content*; they capture *how* people communicate, not *what* they are talking about. Pentland and his team show that *how* team members communicate is just as important a predictor of team success as several other, highly prized, factors *combined*—including intelligence, personality, skill, and content of discussions.

For Pentland, great teams do the following:[87]

- They communicate frequently: In a typical project team, a dozen or so communication exchanges per working hour seem to be optimal for team performance.
- Team members talk and listen in equal measure: Conversation is distributed equally among members. By comparison, low-performing teams suffer from teams within teams. They have members who talk or listen, but don't do both.
- They communicate informally: The best teams use half their time communicating outside the formal meetings or as a "side" during team meetings. Informal communications tend to increase team performance. In a study on call center teams, the best predictors of productivity were a team's energy and engagement outside its formal meetings. Those two factors explained one-third of the variations in dollar productivity among teams.
- They look for ideas and information outside the group: The best teams consistently (if intermittently) connect with multiple outside sources—especially sources with skills or knowledge lacking among the team's members. Team members then bring back what they've learned and share it with the team (that second part is just as important). Especially high-performing teams often feature what's called a well-intentioned connector: a person who keeps track of these useful outside sources and who on the team knows them. Then when useful information is captured from those sources, this "connector" takes on the task of disseminating that information to integrate it into the expertise of the team.

- They adjust their patterns of communication: Up to this point it may seem that communications within a team are essentially preset based on the natures of its members, a kind of biological determinism. But, in fact, successful teams employ malleable communications patterns—they learn to communicate and they communicate to learn. Patterns of communication that work best are empirically described, perfected, and then taught to the other members of the team.

Team Neurodynamics

There is another way of looking at teams in real time: *team neurodynamics*. This is the science of modeling teamwork through the measurement of members' neurophysiologic indicators. In other words, wire the team up and send them back to work. The field of neurodynamics is based on the discovery that an individual's brain rhythms become synchronized to the frequency of the stimulus presented to him or her.[88]

Neurodynamics was initially applied to individuals—showing, for example, how the brain synchronized to acoustic musical notes, and so forth. It wasn't until 2009 that the science was applied to teams. This "team neurodynamics" began with the concept of *neurophysiologic synchronies*: the second-by-second coexpression of the same neurophysiologic (or cognitive) response to the same stimuli by multiple members of a team. It seems that while we may never be purely of one mind, our minds do sometimes dance to the same beat.

This process was first described for three-person teams engaged in scientific problem solving and then later applied to groups engaged in complex navigational tasks, including submarine piloting.[89] Lately it has been studied with teams of different sizes, from two to six members, and using different types of disruptions and interruptions to detect different entropy levels among the individual members—in other words, how quickly and intensely they react to this interference. The researchers have gone so far as to propose that organizations can do task-specific comparisons of the rhythms across teams—and in doing so, learn about the dynamics of underperforming teams.[90] This opens the possibility of one day being able to assemble teams, test them in action, and then see if their individual and group responses indicate a team that will work well together. But that's still in the future.

For now, let's get out of the busy corridors of the brain and move up into the larger world of complete human beings and how they work in teams together.

The Power of Difference

Cultures, armies, social organizations, and enterprises—all have long grappled with the challenge of team composition. That is, what is the best combination of team members that will achieve the greatest possible result—and not blow up in the process?

The traditional approach is to look at particular teams and assess the overall level of particular traits. Or, conversely, to look at variations in those traits among the team's members. But that approach has taken us only so far. So, lately, social scientists have taken a different, brain-based approach. This new approach examines how team members' task-specific abilities complement each other in accomplishing particular group tasks. This underscores something we already know from real life: "dream teams" don't always perform as well as teams composed of lesser players who exhibit great chemistry do.

Anita W. Woolley and her colleagues at Carnegie Mellon

University pioneered this extension of cognitive neuroscience to groups.[1] In particular, they've taken the recent discoveries about the coordination of systems in a single brain and mapped them into the multiple individual brains of team members.[2] In their model, each team member plays the part of a specific brain system—while team members working together resemble various brain systems functioning together in a single head.

Their conclusion? All effective teams include individuals who can function together as the "brain systems" required to achieve the group's task.

Here's how they reached this conclusion: In 2007, Woolley and her team formed one hundred two-person teams (think of them as pairs of brains) to examine how brain systems in different members' heads functioned together.[3] They examined two independent subsystems—object memory ability and spatial ability—that reflect the operation of distinct neural systems in the brain.[4] The pair-teams were then given an assignment in which one member had to deliver on a spatial task (in this case, navigation through a virtual maze) and the other to accomplish an object-properties task (in this case, remembering repetitions of complex "greebles"— novel shapes used in facial identity research).

The result? Teams whose members exhibited the abilities required for the task in aggregate, and teams in which the members' tasks matched their respective abilities, performed better than teams with mismatched assignments or teams that had members with the same abilities. That's not unexpected, but what *is* surprising is that while verbal collaboration helped the underperforming teams compensate for poorly assigned roles, it did nothing to help teams with inadequate abilities. Remarkably, verbal collaboration actually *impaired* the performance of the homogenous teams. Apparently, talking things through only helps if your abilities are different.

The implications are stunning. It means that no matter how many players you add to a team and how closely they work together, the results will *never* improve if they are all inadequate to the task. On the other hand, if you team up top-talented people—even if you give them the wrong jobs—they will figure out a way to do a good job. Collaboration will not compensate for an inadequately endowed team. Of course, the most effective teams combine the required aggregate abilities, the proper role assignments, and a lot of talking.

Next, Professor Woolley and her team gave forty-one four-person teams an analytical task to solve.[5] This time, the most effective teams were those that had not only the relevant expertise but also engaged in collaborative planning. That is, the successful teams sat down together and explicitly identified strategies for best using their expertise.

Those strategy meetings were not ad hoc. In fact, research has shown that collaborative planning almost never happens spontaneously. Someone has to run the show; someone has to serve as team leader to foster this type of planning (otherwise, the team needs an outside administrator).[6]

Researchers found that collaborative planning made teams more productive because those meetings led to the more effective integration of information. Team members were able to resolve critical questions early on. This in turn constrained the scope of what the team had to deal with later, and it also helped team members target their analytical resources more effectively. As a result, they weren't overwhelmed by the sheer quantity of information they had to deal with but could prioritize the various aspects of the overall task in the early stages of their work. In other words, by meeting and planning early, the team members knew the scope of the job and the talents of their team members, and could then divide up the work into reasonable assignments.

Researchers also found that collaborative planning proved especially effective when team members gave the task to the least skilled member of the team, which helped raise each team member's awareness of his or her fellow members' expertise and experience—thus helping the team structure and divide up the work appropriately.

A DIVE INSIDE THE HIVE

This is a good place to address the subject of "group minds" or what is called *transactive memory*. This notion has been picked up by popular culture, especially science fiction, as the equivalent in higher-order animals of the "hive mind" found in bees, termites, and other social insects (*Star Trek*'s Borg). In fact, transactive memory is a much more prosaic concept, but one with important possibilities.

First promulgated by the scientist Daniel Wegner in 1985 and elaborated on by other scientists in the years that followed, transactive memory is used by teams to benefit from a collective awareness of who knows what and therefore to both direct incoming knowledge to the appropriate group members and to retrieve vital information from within the group.[7] They do this not through some kind of mind-meld (though it can seem like that to outsiders) but because they communicate a lot. In the process, they gain a common understanding (a "metamemory") of who knows what, and which member has a particular expertise or skill—as well as what the team *doesn't* know. Once again, this process begins with collaborative strategy meetings, and, perfected over time, it can result in a team that can maneuver very quickly and not waste time searching for answers to questions or determining the right person for a job. Research confirms that teams with transactive memory perform better than their counterparts who lack it because the group's members efficiently identify and use relevant knowledge and generate higher-quality solutions.

Most successful large organizations exhibit this transactive memory, whether they know it or not. For example, there is always one person in the organization who knows the company's early history, or how to fill out travel vouchers, or the policy on leaves of absence—and everyone in the company knows who that person is. As an outsider, if you want to find these people, one of the quickest ways is to track the company's internal emails and phone traffic. Wherever they cluster, that person is likely a transactive memory node. Stupid companies will sometimes fire these key employees during layoffs—and then fail to understand why they are losing more productivity than people. Mess with your transactive memory employees at your peril. You're better off giving them lifetime employment.

THE MAGICAL ENERGY OF COGNITIVE DIVERSITY

Confirming what most of us have long suspected, recent research has shown that people think differently from one another. But even if we accept that fact, few of us give it much consideration—sometimes to our regret—when we populate teams. As a result, everything can look good on paper, the team members' talents dovetail neatly, and everyone gets along well, and yet, in action, the team just doesn't work.

Why? Because it is not enough for résumés and personalities to match. In fact, doing so may be the worst thing you can do. Given the choice of a team that is a rainbow of races and cultures but whose members all went to the same Ivy League university, and a team entirely composed of African American women (or Asian men) of different ages, classes, educations, and personality types, you are far more likely to have success with the latter. That is, if you can hold that team together.

When it comes to teams, traditional definitions of "diversity" are meaningless. Cognitive diversity—*how* people think—is all.

Cultural Perspectives

One common source of this cognitive diversity is cultural and is the result of different patterns of socialization. For example, in some cultures, people tend to be holistic thinkers, and in others people tend to be more analytical.

In 2001, the psychologists Richard Nisbett and Takahiko Masuda conducted an experiment with American and Japanese participants.[8] They showed both groups twenty-second animated videos of underwater scenes. When asked what they had observed, the Americans focused on objects in the foreground (brightly colored fish). Meanwhile, the Japanese focused on the background and talked twice as much as the Americans about interdependencies between the foreground and background objects.

As you might imagine, this mix of perspectives can be problematic for a team if its members are assigned tasks without paying heed to their unique cognitive skills. On the other hand, if properly handled, this diversity can be an unequaled source of team strength, with some members focusing on the details and others on the big picture.

Another form of cognitive diversity can be found between *socially contextual* (context-dependent) and *independent* (context-independent) thinkers. This difference can be quickly and easily determined by team leaders by giving the team a simple test: Show your team members a slanted box frame (that is, a box shaped like a parallelogram), give them a rod, and then ask them to align the rod vertically in the box. If the result looks like this . . .

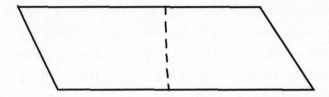

. . . your team member is context-dependent. If the result looks like this . . .

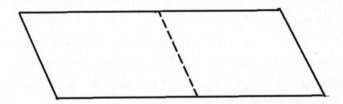

. . . your team member is context-independent.

Howard Weiss and James Shaw, in their 1979 study of eighty-eight male undergraduates, found that context-dependent people are more susceptible to social cues than context-independent people are.[9]

Here's the thing: a team needs both independent and socially attuned thinkers. But leaders also need to know the distribution of the different types of thinkers on the team and manage accordingly. So, go ahead and test potential team members for their thinking style—not to exclude one type or another but to include the right number of each type.

At this point, you may be thinking: Why do I want diversity in thinking styles? Why shouldn't I go just for the independent thinkers—after all, aren't they more creative than the conformists? Won't that increase the likelihood of the team's coming up with something radically new and valuable?

Actually, no. Research on radical-innovation teams shows that adding some conformity to a team may actually drive creativity.

In particular—and counterintuitively—the leavening addition of a conformist can dramatically increase a team's radical innovations. Studies have found that the optimal balance of people on radical-innovation teams requires that 50 percent of the members have the following distribution of personality types:[10]

- Creative—20 to 30 percent. Teams with too many creative types struggle with implementation. That's because (surprise!) creatives are not always practical, are not concerned with rules, and may initiate conflict.
- Conformist—10 to 20 percent. Conformists are the backbone of the team; and their key role is to support the creatives. Conformists help boost cooperation and improve team confidence. They make teams predictable, in a good way.
- Detail-oriented—As much as 10 percent. Detail-oriented people may often be risk-averse, but they help strengthen important team functions such as budgetary control. The detailers make sure that the team is still there each morning.

Brain Differences

The notion of left- and right-brain thinking entered everyday language a couple of decades ago. Even though recent research suggests that there may not be any measurable physiological differences in the two brain hemispheres, most of us do recognize the personality differences between logical and creative types.[11] So-called left-brain thinkers typically engage in more logical and analytical approaches to problem solving. In contrast, right-brain thinkers are more nonlinear and intuitive in their approaches.

This difference (which has obvious connections to the socially contextual and independent thinking we just described) also turns out to be very important in the composition of teams. The goal, whenever possible, is to create, if you will, *whole-brain teams* in which the two brain types are in relative balance.

Whole-brain teams carry with them a wide variety of problem solving and critical thinking approaches that are vital to innovating in dynamic environments. That's why some organizations already make it a practice to create whole-brain teams.

For example, Jerry Hirshberg at Nissan Design ensured intellectual diversity by pairing free-form thinkers with analytical designers.[12] Hirshberg realized that "sometimes the right person for the job is two people." Therefore, when hiring new employees, he worked to create divergent pairs by bringing in two people and coupling them because of their cognitive differences. Hirshberg found that the continuous tension within the pairs, as well as their opposing views, created a more innovative environment, one that led to some of Nissan's most successful vehicles, including the Pathfinder and the Infiniti series of automobiles.

But bolting together left- and right-brained team members is rarely enough. Rather, leaders need to do more than just assemble whole-brain teams; they also need to harness the diversity in those whole-brain teams. They can do this through what is called *creative abrasion*.

Creative abrasion is exactly what it sounds like. It involves eliciting engagement from everyone on a team by having team members' diverse approaches "rub" against each other in productive ways. To foster this creative abrasion, leaders need to:

- Know their own preferences, weaknesses, and strengths, and understand how their own style can stifle creativity.
- Help team members learn and acknowledge their intellectual preferences and differences.
- Keep project goals front and center, and schedule time for *divergent thinking* (generating multiple options) and *convergent thinking* (focusing on a single option and its implementation).

- Devise guidelines in advance for working together. For example, establish a rule (and get team members' agreement) up front that any conflicts on the team will not get personal and that any reasons for disagreements will always be stated.[13]

Creative abrasion can be a challenge, but the payoff is well worth the effort.

For example, Nest Labs—purchased in January 2014 by Google for $3.2 billion—uses creative abrasion to refine the design of its "smart" home products, including its Learning Thermostat and others in the Nest pipeline. When faced with a particularly tricky problem or tough decision, Nest Labs' founder and CEO, Tony Fadell, a former Apple executive, gathers a diverse group of user-experience experts, product managers, software engineers, algorithm analysts, and marketing executives. Some are women, and some are men; their skills differ; and the skin tones and cultural backgrounds vary as well. But it's not about gender, job, or racial representation. Instead, it's about combining so many viewpoints that ideas are bound to collide, resulting in a product that better serves a diverse and demanding customer base.

Teams versus Lone Wolves

In our earlier discussion (and rejection) of the "lone wolf" theory of leadership, we noted that the very human desire to create a simple narrative tends to reinforce the idea of a single actor defining events rather than the idea of more complicated teams. Now here are the scientific underpinnings of that desire.

It all focuses on leaders as the locus of attention. Psychologists have found that the human tendency to attribute success and failure to leaders is so strong that they have even coined a term for it: *leader attribution error*. It is the inclination to assign to the leader credit or blame for the team's success or failure. And it is not just observers, or bosses, who overattribute responsibility to leaders. Team members do it too.[14] The reality, however, proved over and again in studies, is that teams, per member, consistently outperform individuals.

Ben Jones, a professor of management and strategy at the Kellogg School of Management, and his colleagues studied the largest repository of scientific research available—an astonishing 17.9 million research articles across five decades spanning all scientific fields. There they found a nearly universal pattern: highly influential scientific papers (that is, the ones that are the most frequently cited) exhibit novel combinations of interdisciplinary information, at a level of complexity almost impossible for a single individual to achieve. The latest research on the subject has found that teams are 37.7 percent *more* likely than solo authors to introduce novel combinations into familiar knowledge domains.[15] Put simply: teams are more likely to come up with really great new ideas.

In 2010, Lee Fleming, a professor at the University of California, Berkeley, and his colleague Jasjit Singh directly tested the myth of lone inventors. Their analysis of more than half a million patented inventions showed that people working alone, in particular those without affiliations with organizations, were more likely to devise relatively low-impact inventions—and thus were less likely to achieve real breakthroughs. Solitary inventors were also less effective than groups at culling out bad ideas. Finally, collaborations also increased combinatorial opportunities for novelty—that is, different ideas can be mixed and matched to come up with something truly innovative.

In sum, the solitary inventor *may* come up with an earthshaking new idea or invention, but you are better off betting on a team to bring the idea to life.

DIVERSITY: A DOUBLE-EDGED SWORD

It would be nice if we could simply apply a standardized notion of diversity to the recruiting of group members and then get on to the task at hand. Unfortunately, while most researchers agree that diversity is a key contributor to team success, they can't agree on precisely what constitutes that diversity. Indeed, some believe it to be very different from the "diversity" we refer to in everyday language or in government regulation.

In two studies in 2010 involving nearly 700 people, Anita W. Woolley (whom we've already mentioned) and her colleagues examined teams of two to five members working on a wide variety of tasks. They identified a general factor relating to intelligence in groups that explained their performance more than anything else. Interestingly, this intelligence factor was strongly correlated with neither the average intelligence nor the maximum individual intelligence of the group's members. Rather, and this proved especially surprising, they found that the intelligence factor in groups is correlated with:

- The equality in distribution of conversational turn-taking
- The average social sensitivity of group members
- The proportion of females in the group

But not everybody agrees. Scott Page, a professor of complex systems, political science, and economics at the University of Michigan, is the author of *The Difference: How the Power of Diversity Creates Better Groups, Firms, Schools, and Societies*. In it, and in comparison with Woolley, he identifies three causes of cognitive diversity:

- Training
- Experience
- Genes

Page argues that team members' training and experience are the dominant causes of cognitive diversity, while genes are a relatively minor factor. For Page, it is not apparent diversity (such as differences in gender, age, or race) that promotes better group performance, but rather diversity in people's heuristics, perspectives, interpretations, and predictive models—all of which are derived from members' cultural backgrounds, training, and experience. It is this diversity, he argues, that can enable diverse groups to perform better than individuals or homogenous groups. Thus, the role of female members in a team, so important to Woolley, is to Page just another example of different perspectives at work.

Page's conclusion? When managers and organizations build and promote teams with inner (and not necessarily apparent) diversity, they can reap the benefits of group diversity.

So what are these inner factors mentioned above?

- *Heuristics* are quick and simple techniques used for finding solutions. For example, the rule of 72 (72 divided by percent of interest rate is the number of years required for an investment to double).
- *Perspectives* are representations of the set of possible solutions, and they can simplify problems. For example, certain problems are simplified using polar coordinates instead of Cartesian coordinates.
- *Interpretations* are ideas drawn from our observations of events and people. In these observations certain aspects are highlighted and others ignored to draw causal inferences.
- *Predictive models* are models created from a combination of interpretation plus a prediction for each set or category created by an interpretation.

These so-called inner factors are quite a bit different from what we think of as traditional diversity. Indeed, they may be just the opposite. If Page is right, then the standard (and often government-required) "diversity" practice of hiring graduates from a similar set of top universities while ticking off the boxes for race, gender, ethnicity, and so forth may be a misdirected effort. As externally diverse as these new hires may be, their socialization, training, and education may render them very similar to other new hires in terms of the heuristics, perspectives, interpretations, and predictive models they use to solve problems and achieve their goals. In other words, they aren't diverse at all—and filling a team with them will likely prove to be suboptimal.

So just hiring more women as per Woolley works for Page only if those women come from sufficiently unusual backgrounds to *think* differently from their new teammates. Otherwise, if they are merely cut from the same cloth as the male members of the team, they will have only a minor impact (that is, there will be a comparatively small cognitive difference between the sexes). What matters most are differences in culture, class, and aptitudes.

To help explain his model, Page has introduced what he calls the *diversity prediction theorem*:

The squared error of the collective prediction = (average squared error − predictive diversity)

Yeah, that's pretty complicated. But it boils down to this: Teams err when they lack accuracy and diversity. So, *when group diversity is large, the error in the team is small.*

Page goes so far as to warn against using traditional stereotyping in selecting for diversity because it may lead to team members' living down to the expectations imposed on them.

In one classic study, Asian women were judged differently on their mathematical skills based on whether they were primarily described by their gender or their ethnicity.[16] When the participants were described by their gender, they were rated lower ("women are bad at math") than when they were described by their ethnicity ("Asians are good at math"). Even more troubling, the women themselves, when given a math test, performed to those judgments.

The lesson is that diversity is powerful in teams, but only if it is *real* diversity.

That's just the beginning. Even when we can all agree that diversity is critical to team performance, it's still a real-world challenge to figure out how to blend all those ingredients into a high-performing team—much less make all those different personalities get along.

As the research suggests, there's no point in adding new members to a team just because they fit your diversity requirements. If they cannot influence or improve the team's collective decision-making, they have little value. Indeed, being placeholders, they may actually reduce the total intellectual capital of the team.[17]

More than forty years of research on diversity has been conducted by psychologists, sociologists, economists, and organizational scholars. A review of this literature in 1999 by Katherine Y. Williams and Charles A. O'Reilly of Stanford Graduate School of Business underscored that diversity is a double-edged sword.[18]

The good news is that group diversity can enhance performance, because group members bring to bear varied ideas, knowledge, and skills to accomplish tasks. However, in a diverse group, members may view each other through a biased lens of stereotypes based on social categories (the same differences in race, gender, and so forth that are supposed to help). This bias invariably reduces the effectiveness of the group's interaction as group members fail to identify with the group.[19]

Williams and O'Reilly's key insight is that team members maintain their self-esteem by making comparisons with other team members and then classifying themselves using those same salient characteristics of race, gender, and so forth. And when a particular characteristic allows members to assume a positive self-identity, they then look upon those who lack that characteristic as being out-group members—and thus less trustworthy. And it can get ugly: those individuals, now considered out-group members, can face exclusion from intragroup information networks and decision-making processes.[20]

And so we find ourselves with what is, scientifically speaking, the central paradox of teams: the most successful teams exhibit diversity in their ranks, but heterogeneous (that is, diverse) teams face serious structural challenges regarding motivation, integration, and coordination.[21]

Thus it all comes down to the team leader. The more diverse a team, the more volatile it is likely to be. And often the only thing keeping such a team from exploding is the quality of its leadership. Great leaders create team genius by bringing together, and holding together, the most diverse and heterogeneous teams.

And that leadership is needed from the very start. Thus, leaders need to be mindful of how to "activate" the identities of new group members, especially when introducing the new team. And as we will see later in this book, that same quality of leadership is still needed, often years later, when the team is led through its retirement and dissolution. Great leaders make great teams because only *they* can manage them.

Based on those four decades and thousands of research reports, Williams and O'Reilly summarize the different types of diversity, and their distinct challenges, as follows:

- *Tenure diversity* is associated with low social integration, poor communication, and high turnover in groups—all processes that can impair group performance.
- *Functional diversity* improves creative ideas in groups—however, not necessarily the implementation of those ideas.
- *Age diversity* can increase turnover and withdrawal, especially of those individuals most different from the rest of the group.

- *Gender diversity* typically has negative effects on men. Men are less satisfied and less committed when in the minority—even though in female-dominated groups men are likely to be more accepted, less stereotyped, and less likely to be treated with hostility.
- *Racial/ethnic diversity* research is mostly on white-black dynamics, and the results are inconclusive.

GETTING THE BEST FROM DIVERSITY

That's a pretty daunting list.

Is it really worth it? Why not instead just use all the other tools for team building and skip the diversity part? Or just pursue a lesser degree of diversity—one that may enhance the team without exploding it into a nightmare of cliques, accusations, and fights?

The answer lies, like most things, in your own cost-benefit analysis of the importance of the project, your confidence in how well you will recruit your team, and how much risk you are willing to take to achieve your goals.

The bottom line is that your greatest chance to create a successful, productive team involves a diverse membership—but the more diverse that membership becomes, the worse the odds are that the team will survive long enough to produce those results. So you need a strategy to mitigate the cost of that increased diversity. The scientific evidence suggests that this strategy should take two tracks.

First, diverse teams need to be *actively managed*.[22] Abandon now any notion you have that you can build the most powerful team possible, wind it up, and let it run by itself. In fact, the more diverse the team, the more hands-on management it will need.

That means, with larger groups, that you must be very selective about the team leader you choose. You will need a pro, not just, say, someone selected from the team. You will also likely want to relieve that leader of any duties that contribute to the operations of that group and reserve to them the job of full-time management. That, of course, will require increasing that team by one member, with a commensurate jump in the team's budget. It also means that with small teams—that is, pairs and trios—you will not be able to, as usual, leave them be. Rather, an external manager will be required to provide regular oversight.[23]

Besides increasing the quality and participation of direct management, you will also need to be constantly vigilant against a number of threats to the team's continued existence. These threats include the following:

Turnover

Turnover is a problem in groups in which the members perceive each other as too different. The added stress of dealing with the "other" will drive some people to seek the safety of being with people more like themselves in other teams. The best way to counter this centrifugal force is to foster *social identity*—that is, to cultivate the process by which a person's self-concept becomes derived from his or her membership in the group. Social identities—team titles, stories, recognitions, shared adventures, and so forth—build members' loyalty to the team and serve as social glue in groups that would otherwise explode. Experiments show that people who highly identify with their team express a stronger desire to remain in that team despite the presence of an attractive exit option.[24]

Framing

Framing is how a potential challenge or opportunity is presented to team members in relation to their overall project. Thus, how the challenge of workforce diversity is framed by the team leader will affect how team members manage diversity-related tensions and whether this diversity will enhance or detract from the group's functioning effectively. In 2001, the Harvard researchers Robin Ely and David Thomas studied three professional service firms and found that each dealt with diversity with a different way of framing the challenge:

- *The integration and learning perspective*—the first company framed diversity as a mechanism for helping teams enhance their capacity for adaptive change. ("Your differences in experience will help us to react quickly to a rapidly changing marketplace.")
- *The access and legitimacy perspective*—the second company framed diversity as a way to better connect with an increasingly diverse marketplace. ("Your differences in cultural backgrounds will help us understand the global marketplace.")
- *The discrimination and fairness perspective*—the third company framed diversity as a means to ensuring fair and equal treatment of all. ("Our differences ensure that there will be no bias against anyone.")

According to Ely and Thomas, only the integration and learning perspective provided the necessary rationale and guidance for harnessing significant benefits from diversity. By comparison, the discrimination and fairness perspective, while sounding noble, had little effect on performance. And the access and legitimacy perspective actually proved to be destructive, by creating the perception of a status hierarchy. In other words, frame the value of your team's diversity as a matter of staying competitive and emerging victorious. They are in it to win, not to feel better.

Belief

Research has found that teams with prodiversity beliefs are better at harnessing the power of their own diversity. That is, if they believe that their diversity is a competitive advantage, it will usually turn out to be so. Why this self-fulfilling prophecy? Because the believers are willing to engage in more sharing of information and perspectives—and that sharing ultimately pays off.[25]

In a test of this theory, multiple four-person teams (each composed of two men and two women) were persuaded of either the value of diversity or the value of similarity for group performance. They then were provided with either homogenous (every member got the same) information or heterogeneous (everyone got different) information. Each team was then tasked to generate, discuss, and select as many useful items for survival in the desert, based on the information and rules provided to them.

The result? The diversity beliefs of the teams did not affect their performance carrying homogenous information. However, for teams armed with heterogeneous information, those with prodiversity beliefs outperformed those with prosimilarity beliefs. In a rapidly changing global marketplace, which team would you prefer?

Tenure

It turns out that the longer you keep a team together, the fewer the negative effects of its diversity. The laboratory consensus is that more intragroup contact ultimately reduces the usual negative effects of social categorization, such as stereotyping and prejudices.[26]

Field research confirms this. Teams with high degrees of familiarity are better able to take advantage of diverse experiences among team members.[27] Familiarity helps team members not only to coordinate their activities but also to carry over those communication skills from one project to the next. In addition, the more frequently team members work together, the better they become at innovation by integrating each other's knowledge.

In a region known for rapid job-hopping and résumés showing a score of positions at different companies over the course of a dozen years, the senior management of Silicon Valley Bank (SVB) stands out as a true anomaly. In its more than three decades of existence, SVB has been led by five individuals: Roger Smith, Harry Kellogg, John Dean, Ken Wilcox, and Greg Becker. That's not unusual; what *is* unusual is that all five men still remain in close contact and connected with the bank.

This enduring relationship at the top has had some important benefits for SVB. None of its CEO-level intellectual capital, its network of contacts and relationships, or its internal culture has been lost over the course of the bank's entire history. This gives the current CEO, Becker, an enormous resource he can tap at any time to help with decision-making. The result? In 2011, the Export-Import Bank of the United States named SVB its bank of the year. Current deposits have now reached $40 billion.

Or consider San Antonio's professional basketball team, the Spurs, which has been crazily successful for four decades. San Antonio is one of the National Basketball Association's small-market teams. In a glamorous sport with glamorous players like LeBron James and Kobe Bryant, the members of the San Antonio team prefer relative anonymity. Yet their team's organizational methods are remarkably similar to those suggested by the research in this book. The Spurs' coach, Gregg Popovich, is in his middle sixties and has the longest tenure in a league whose rich owners like to fire coaches on a whim. The Spurs also have the greatest diversity of players in the league—both in terms of the nations they represent and in the range of their ages, from the late teens to the late thirties.

All of this is a good argument for not disbanding teams quickly. Instead, the best strategy is, if possible, to keep team members together through more than one project. That will give them a chance to learn about each other and to bond—and in the process, help mitigate the social categorization problems associated with diverse teams.

Congruence

Unfortunately, many organizations don't understand the value of tenure to diversity. Instead, they disperse and reassemble teams under the mistaken assumption that such changes help "freshen up" teams. The truth appears to be that rather than freshening their teams, these organizations are essentially forcing their employees through the same learning curve over and over again—only to break their teams up before they can put their mature harmony to work. The scientific term for this harmony is *interpersonal congruence*—the degree to which team members view others in the group as those others view themselves. It is this interpersonal congruence that moderates the relationship between diversity and group effectiveness.

To understand the nature of interpersonal congruence, one longitudinal study looked at eighty-three work groups of four to six members from an MBA class.[28] Members were assigned to teams in such a way as to maximize the within-team diversity by sex, country of origin, ethnicity, previous job experience (including function and industry), and concentration in their current graduate program.

The result? A powerful discovery. In groups with high interpersonal congruence, the diversity of members actually enhanced creative task performance. By contrast, in groups with low interpersonal congruence, the presence of diversity actually impaired performance. That means that if you can teach a diverse team, through the common goal of competitive success, a belief in the value of diversity, and an extended time working together, to see itself as a successful team, it can achieve superior performance.

Now, even better news: this improved performance can begin almost immediately. In the study of those MBA teams, the researchers decided to push the process. In certain teams, they had members prepare positive self-appraisals to be shared with the other team members. Incredibly, in doing so, the teams achieved enough interpersonal congruence in the first ten minutes of the interaction to continue to benefit the group's outcomes *four months* later.

Team members can harness the benefits of the group's diversity by expressing rather than suppressing their unique characteristics. And leaders who encourage team members to seek congruent, self-verifying appraisals can see immediate, and enduring, positive results.

Integration

Even when they find a measure of harmony, teams still frequently fail to extract, organize, and integrate their members' knowledge and expertise.[29] Instead, they become overwhelmed with data and struggle to make sense of it.[30] Or they fail to make the necessary connections that lead to original ideas.[31] Or they omit pieces of critical information and focus too much on shared information.[32]

This is the best argument for having the unique "diversity" of one of your team members be that of a generalist (or at least someone with a wider-than-usual set of personal skills and experiences). Teams of specialists almost always benefit from members capable of translating discoveries among members with relatively narrow expertise. Without these translators, valuable information can fail to be integrated into the overall effort and be wasted.[33]

Moderation

Group connectivity is important, but it shouldn't be overdone. Comity can be the enemy of complexity. A group whose members are too closely connected can see the benefits of its diversity fade. That's because while dense ties among team members may enhance the team's solidarity, they can also impede creativity. This is particularly true for complex problem solving. Communication networks that are highly efficient at disseminating information typically enhance short-run but not long-run performance. Why? Because inefficient communication networks maintain diversity. They are also better for exploration (they free the "mavericks") and the long-run search for solutions.[34]

Obviously, this creates a paradox: you need to promote intra-group communications to overcome the obstacles created by diversity, but at the same time, if you draw the team too close together through overcommunicating, you will stifle that same diversity that is so valuable to the team's success. The only real answer, we believe, is to *communicate regularly, but not constantly*, and to use that communication for the dissemination of new information, not for setting boundaries on members' efforts.

Dissent

All of us have been through brainstorming sessions in which we've been told that we are not to judge or criticize our own or others' ideas—at least not in the creative phase. In the real life of teams, exactly the opposite appears to be true. Experimental research on teams has shown that debate and the presence of competing views actually *stimulate* divergent and creative thought. Furthermore, permission to criticize and to debate is also conducive to idea generation. As an aside, it has been found that groups instructed to criticize and debate even in brainstorming activities did better than the groups instructed not to criticize.[35]

Creativity

The sociologists Brian Uzzi of Northwestern University and Jarrett Spiro of INSEAD set out to discover the ideal composition of the teams behind Broadway musicals. To do so, they studied every musical produced on Broadway between 1945 and 1989. They also tracked the names of every known collaborator on those shows. The eventual list numbered 2,092 people who had worked on 474 musicals of new material produced during that era.

In particular, Uzzi and Spiro wanted to understand whether it was better to have a team composed of close friends who had worked together before or to have a team of strangers. An incumbent team exhibited an extremely high Q rating and a team of strangers had a low Q rating, where Q was a measurement of the density of connections in that production team.

What the two researchers found was that the relationship between Q and musical success was *curvilinear*—that is, it was thickest in the middle. Thus, when the Q was low (less than 1.7), team members did not know one another and struggled to exchange ideas and truly collaborate. By the same token, when the Q was too high (above 3.2), team members thought in too-similar ways and, as a result, stifled creativity.

They found that the best Broadway shows were produced by teams with an intermediate level of social intimacy. This ideal level of Q—called the *bliss point*—was between 2.4 and 2.6. Within this range, a musical was *three* times more likely to be a commercial success and *three* times more likely to receive critical acclaim than a musical produced by a team with a low Q or a high Q.

This suggests that the best teams enjoy a mix of old friends and newcomers. In this way, the team members are comfortable with each other and readily exchange ideas, but they are not so comfortable that they stifle creativity in each other.[36]

Divergence

What is the best strategy for new members when entering a team? *Conform early, diverge later.* We humans are neurologically predisposed to see new people and new ideas as potential threats. So it's not surprising that social psychologists have found that new group members, who invariably present new information to their teams, are often perceived as threats. And because of that, their feedback is typically dismissed, ignored, or rejected out of hand. It is only after a sufficient number of positive experiences that cement a new arrival's status as a group member that this person's divergent feedback is perceived as nonthreatening. Until then, the new member's often valuable knowledge is lost.

This loss can be costly—yet solutions don't come easily. The group members resist, reject, or ignore criticism from newcomers because it represents a threat to the group's collective self-concept. As such, they are obliged to challenge the integrity of the message.[37] As long as a person is considered by the group to be an outsider, his or her criticism is likely to be rejected even if that criticism is appropriate, well justified, and well argued.[38] Not surprisingly, the same criticism made be someone considered an insider is likely to be accepted by the team.

So, what's the answer? *Preparation.* New team members need to be taught that entering a new group and introducing divergent thoughts without having gained the group's trust may backfire. The key, new members must be told, is to first gain group trust by conforming—and only later, when that trust has been earned, should they dissent. Obviously, this doesn't entirely solve the problem of lost contributions at the beginning of a new member's inclusion, but it may shorten its duration.

Experience

Cognitive abilities do not necessarily become impaired with age.[39] "Cognitive fitness" is a state of optimized ability to reason, remember, learn, plan, and adapt that is enhanced by certain attitudes, lifestyle choices, and exercises. Cognitive fitness enhances people's decision-making, problem solving, ability to manage stress and change, and openness to new ideas and alternative perspectives.

Depending on how you live your life, your brain's anatomy, neural networks, and cognitive abilities can actually improve through experiences. Contrary to the selection for youth in places such as Silicon Valley, older members can be crucial team participants.

Proximity

The final challenge to maintaining teams' effectiveness may come as a surprise in this age of global work teams, telepresence, and remote collaboration. An analysis of 35,000 articles across 2,000 journals by 200,000 authors for the years 1999 through 2003 shows that proximity among team members is a predictor of the quality of team outcomes.[40] The researchers mapped the location of co-authors and the quality of research based on the number of subsequent citations. Physical proximity proved to be an important predictor of publication impact.[41]

What does this mean in light of modern telecommunications, international teams, and a global marketplace? Much depends on the definition of "proximity." A virtual work team living on four different continents and handing off their work across twenty-four time zones and communicating via email and text is almost the embodiment of the *lack* of proximity. So the challenge in such a case is to replace traditional physical proximity with something else: regular online meetings, enhanced communications tools (such as telepresence technology), team rituals, nonwork activities, and, whenever possible, actually getting the team physically together in a single place.

THE SIZE QUESTION, AGAIN

This brings us, inevitably, to the question of team size. We have already discussed this topic extensively—and we will go into even more depth later. For now, we want to devote ourselves to what the latest scientific research tells us about how teams should be created in terms of the number of members.

Here are some of the most interesting recent findings:

First, *team boundaries become a problem as team size increases.* In a well-bounded team, people know who is and who is not on the team. But as the team grows in size, this sense of "boundedness" becomes less clear.

Corporate management teams, as a rule, tend to be especially underbounded and overlarge. In a study of 120 top management teams, only 11 of those teams (9 percent) had a common agreement on the precise number of members on their team. This is not a minor matter: as we've just seen, knowledge of who is and who is not on the team is vitally important, because it enables team members to make an accurate assessment of all the available resources when developing the team's goals. Without it, they can only make a rough, and usually inaccurate, estimate.

But that isn't the last word on the matter, because *increasing team size does offer a range of performance benefits.* Here are some examples:

- Having more members creates the opportunity for a greater division of labor; this in turn allows for more task specialization.[42]
- Having more members also creates a larger pool of aggregate team knowledge and experience.[43]
- The larger the inventory of slack resources at hand, the more the team is prepared to deal with changing circumstances.[44]

Increasing team size, however, can also impair performance: As a team's size increases, its functional size—that is, the number of people who are actually contributing to the team's work—usually does not increase accordingly.[45] There are no guarantees that the larger knowledge and experience pool of the expanded team will be effectively utilized.

And don't forget the networking problem—six communication links in a four-person team and forty-five in a ten-person team. As team size increases, the need for coordination multiplies.[46] And at the same time, any sharing of the technical and coordinative information needed to maintain those networks also becomes more difficult.[47]

There are also integration costs associated with increasing team size. It takes time and effort to incorporate new members into a team. While this happens, the team may slow, or even stop.[48]

And don't forget the lesson of tugs-of-war. In groups in which individual and collective performance is inextricably tied, and individual contributions are difficult to assess, individuals—knowing that their efforts can't be isolated—will often slack off and contribute less than their best efforts. In psychology, this phenomenon is known as *social loafing*; in economics it's *free riding*. Experiments by the French psychologist Max Ringelmann back in 1913 showed a sharp decline in the individual efforts of men engaged in a tug-of-war.[49] On average, one person pulled 139 pounds, groups of three pulled 353 pounds (that is, 15 percent less per person), and groups of eight pulled 547 pounds (51 percent less per person). Ringelmann wisely chose the tug-of-war because it presented no coordination problems—the only task was for everyone to pull hard. So, the difference in performance came down to one thing: decreased effort.[50]

Finally, increasing team size can also cause relational losses in knowledge-based teams. Studies have found that as team size increases, its members' perceptions of available support diminish even when that support is available. This is important, because the belief that support and multiple high-quality relationships are available plays an important role as a buffer to stressful job experiences.[51]

One of the leading social scientists in the study of team size is Bibb Latané of the Center for Human Science. A pioneer of social impact theory, Latané has made a number of important discoveries on the implications of increasing team size on team dynamics, on how order is spontaneously created in large groups, and the spread of social influence in populations. Among his findings:

- *As team size increases, individual responsibility dilutes.* Latané's work on the "bystander effect" with John Darley shows that people are less likely to help someone in an emergency if there are others around, because the responsibility to help is distributed over many people.

- *As a group's size increases, adding people yields diminishing returns on individual contributions.* The greater the number of people present, the greater will be their influence on each individual. For example, one person added to a group of two is likely to have more impact on the group than one person added to a group of twenty. Thus, the influence of unique expertise and skills in a team diminishes as team size increases. There is a trade-off between creating a thoroughly diverse team and creating a small team in which individual contributions are more easily harnessed.

- *Managers and leaders tend to overestimate the benefits of larger teams.* One reason we often see teams with more than five members when a pair or trio would be obviously more effective is that managers fall for the belief that, in teams, the more, the better. In 2012, after finding field evidence for this, researchers Bradley Staats, Katherine Milkman, and Craig Fox named one version of this phenomenon, the tendency to increasingly underestimate task completion time as team size grows, the *team scaling fallacy.*

Following Latané's lead, other scientists have taken up the quest to find the optimal team size. Unfortunately, it's too early to come to conclusions. However, there is some research on both how to mitigate the negative effects of large teams as well as on how to keep team size small even when projects demand a large number of people:

- It is important to help team members perceive their task and goals as significant and meaningful. This helps mitigate social loafing. If that fails, encourage team members (through team pride) to compensate for substandard contributions from their coworkers.[52]
- To keep team size small, managers should create multiteam projects. They can also build core and extended teams, or outsource certain tasks.[53]
- In large teams, not all team members have to be involved all the time—team members can be brought in for specific tasks.[54]

Now that you've built your team and populated it with a diverse group of members, your final challenge to keep it running at its full potential is not just to drive it to full productivity but to keep it running at that pace by minimizing its long-term losses.

Managing Teams to Genius

Fortunately, there is more than one path to team success. Fully armed with this knowledge, you should be able to find the team for you—as well as a leadership style that suits your personality and your organization's culture.

Here again, research in the last decade has revealed some interesting discoveries. One of them is that the values instilled in a team at its formation will shape the way its members approach tasks and their social interactions, and that over time those attitudes will solidify as a feature of the group's structure. That means that how your team begins will determine how it ends, and how it will perform during its existence.

Scientists have looked at these life cycles and found that:

- Group members who share egalitarian values form highly interdependent task structures and social patterns. They typically perform well.

- Group members who share meritocratic values tend to form fewer interdependent approaches and social patterns. They also can perform well.
- Groups with mixed values, by comparison, end up lacking consistent approaches to tasks and group processes. Compared with the egalitarian and meritocratic groups, they significantly underperform.[1]

These findings help explain the paradox of how different companies, with very different, even antithetical, cultures, can enjoy continuous, long-term success, while other companies with cultures in the "middle," even featuring the best of the two extreme cases, are not as successful.

As we were writing this book, Rich sat in on a fascinating conversation between Jim Davis, a senior vice president and CMO at SAS, and the CEO of a start-up company who had once worked at Amazon. SAS, a private corporation, is regularly listed as one of the world's best places to work. Employees enjoy a beautiful corporate campus, free child care, fabulous food, doctors on staff, salons, and so forth. Not surprisingly, it has 3 percent turnover per year.

Amazon, said the CEO and ex-Amazon employee, is the opposite. It "works the shit" out of its people and retains them for an average of one year. Yet, by any measure, Amazon is hugely successful—arguably even more successful than SAS.

If SAS is successful with a nourishing culture, and Amazon with a harshly meritocratic one, why do both work?

The answer is that both SAS and Amazon are clear about their culture. There is no confusion or dishonesty—but rather authenticity and trust—to both companies. SAS's message is: *spend a career with us.* Amazon's is: *challenge yourself with us.* By comparison, mediocre teams and companies don't know what they are. They say one thing and then do another. They blow around like the wind, and they destroy authenticity and trust.

It all begins at the beginning. Effective leaders, in their own way, achieve three tasks at team launch:

- Clarify and give meaning to the team's task
- Bound the team as one performing unit
- Establish norms of conduct

This helps explain why *both* independent and interdependent group work can be effective. Research shows that groups perform best when their task and outcomes are either purely the product of group work or purely the product of individual effort. Hybrid groups—once again, the in-between position, in which tasks and rewards have individual as well as group elements—inevitably struggle with interactions, group stability, and member satisfaction. In hybrid groups, cooperation norms are weak.[2]

As usual, it comes down to leadership, with the biggest penalties going to team leaders who are neither decisive nor consistent. Michael Dell made a mistake common to successful tech entrepreneurs who find, after a run of great success, their growth flattening and their stock price falling back to earth. During the 1990s, Dell was the fastest-growing stock among more than 5,000 traded in the United States. One thousand dollars of Dell stock purchased in January 1990 was worth a million dollars by December 1999.

But this good fortune eventually led to a bad outcome. After the tech stock crash of 2000 and 2001, Dell's stock never recovered to its all-time highs. Even though Dell's revenues continued to grow for the next thirteen years, the company's performance disappointed Wall Street. When Apple's market value raced past Dell's in 2006, Dell was seen as a loser, even though it was still growing and profitable. The effect on Dell's culture and on Michael Dell himself was devastating. Leadership at Dell seemed almost to give up. It was neither consistent nor decisive.

Finally, in late 2013, the company did a leveraged buyout and took itself off the NASDAQ stock exchange. The very day Dell went private, Michael Dell did something equally important. He dumped the employee forced-ranking system within Dell. The forced-ranking system, which pitted every employee against each other on a bell curve of performance, had turned good employees into politicians, bad employees into backstabbers, colleagues into enemies, and the entire Dell culture into a sort of *Lord of the Flies* drama. We exaggerate—but you get the point. More important, so did Michael Dell. In just a year of the company's being private, Michael Dell brought deep cultural values and consistent, decisive leadership back to his company.

Often, poor team leaders tend to have control issues. They are either overcontrolling tyrants (not asking for or ignoring input from team members) or undercontrolling weaklings (so laissez-faire that team members end up with little clarity on how to operate). The very worst leaders manage to be both, unpredictably vacillating between the two extremes and in the process incapacitating team members from doing their work.[3]

J. Richard Hackman, an esteemed expert on teams, summarizes the leadership challenge most aptly. He notes that you cannot guarantee team success but you can increase the probability of it by managing at the margins and setting up the right conditions.[4]

According to Hackman, these "right conditions" are:

- The team has a compelling direction: the team task is clear, challenging, and consequential.
- The team is bounded (it is clear who is and who is not on the team) and stable (the team's membership is not constantly fluctuating), and its members are interdependent (that is, they interact with one another to accomplish the team's work).
- The team is set up with the right mix of members, who have norms of conduct that guide their behavior. Team members are different but not so different that they cannot work with each

other. Team members have the right set of skills and expertise for the team task.

- The team has a supportive organizational context that provides team members with access to resources, information, and training to help accomplish their task.
- The team receives coaching from experts, peers, and leaders.[5]

CUTTING YOUR LOSSES

In 1972, the social psychologist Ivan Steiner proposed the following, now widely cited, equation:

Actual group productivity = Potential productivity − Process losses

Where:

- *Potential productivity* is what the team can theoretically achieve, given its resources.
- *Process losses* are what the team loses through coordination and motivation problems.

Steiner went on to say that group size and group productivity are related to group tasks.[6] These tasks, he continued, can be differentiated based on three categories: component, focus, and interdependence.

Component. This is the type of team task ("divisible") that can be easily divided into subtasks that can be assigned to specific team members. Or it is the team task ("unitary") that cannot be divided into subtasks and either all the team members must work together or one group member must complete the task while the others observe as bystanders.

Focus. This is the direction of the team's efforts. At the heart of focus is the question "Is the quantity or the quality of the team's output most important?" When the team is focused on *quantity*, it is performing a maximizing task—team members are focused on producing as much as possible. When the team is focused on *quality*, it is performing an optimizing task, and the group members are seeking the optimal solution because high-quality performance is rewarded and poor-quality performance is penalized.

Interdependence. The interdependence of team tasks refers to how the individual contributions of team members are combined or integrated. There are six types of task interdependence—and each produces its own type of process loss.

Additive tasks are completed by combining individual contributions into the final team output. For example, a tug-of-war, an assembly line, and a relay race are additive tasks. In this type of task, process losses occur due to logistical problems, social loafing, and coordination issues. Productivity rises with group size at a decreasing rate because the number of functional links increases rapidly with group size: $n(n-1)$.

Disjunctive tasks require the group to solve a single problem (for example, a crossword puzzle or a brain teaser) and perform at the level of its most competent member. A larger group size increases the likelihood of competent members being in the group, but it doesn't guarantee it. Productivity also increases with group size up to a certain extent, after which process losses may creep in. Process losses are typically due to self-censorship, social loafing, group members not listening to the most competent people in the group, or the lack of a group process in which all voices are heard. These losses can be mitigated by selecting people with the right expertise, by fostering norms and shared beliefs that reduce self-censorship, and by fostering a nonthreatening interpersonal climate in which people are comfortable speaking up.[7] Meanwhile, making the team's task compelling and consequential can also help diminish social loafing.[8]

Conjunctive tasks require that all group members work to accomplish the team's task. Now, unlike disjunctive tasks, the group performs conjunctive tasks (in terms of speed and quality of work) at the level of its least competent member (or its weakest link). Examples of groups working on a conjunctive task include a musical band and a rock-climbing team.

Because a few members can bring down the entire team in conjunctive tasks, the key is to assign team members tasks they enjoy. It is almost as important to increase interdependence and feedback within the team, because they strengthen the sense of personal contribution and social indispensability among team members, which in turn promotes team members' efforts.[9]

Why does this work? The *Köhler effect*, first formulated in 1926, explains it: Weaker individuals in teams strive to keep up with other group members. They do not want to hold the group back, especially when the group is working on a conjunctive task.[10] Recently, experimental studies have found that, in comparison with working alone, team members show as much as a 50 percent increase in performance during teamwork because they do not want to let their teammates down.[11] The effect is even stronger when team members are working on tasks they enjoy.[12]

This finding underscores what most of us know from our own lives: being part of a team taking on a task in which our own participation makes an obvious contribution can bring out the best in us.

Compensatory tasks feature group members who average their individual contributions. For example, consider a group task of estimating the value of a stock. Each member offers an estimate; and the group estimate is the average. Or, consider a process of selecting a job candidate in which everyone on a committee assigns a score to each candidate in the pool.

Here, the process losses occur from having any discussions before the decision. The biggest advantage of compensatory tasks is that systematic biases are corrected by the multiple contributions.

However, if the group engages in a discussion, or if the members try to influence one another, this advantage is lost. This can be compensated for by weighting voters based on their knowledge and expertise. Unfortunately, in real life other factors such as seniority or status or popularity are often used to weight individual estimates—which only makes things worse.

Rich recently interviewed a Navy Blue Angels jet formation instructor. The stakes in aerobatic formation flying are life-and-death. The pilots fly wingtip-to-wingtip, eighteen inches apart, at speeds of up to 400 miles per hour. Every pilot has to be at his top game, within team formations, all the time, or someone will die.

So how do the Blue Angels do it? They start by videotaping every performance and practice. Then they rigorously debrief the performance. To keep service rank, seniority, and popularity from skewing the debriefing, the pilots first walk into the debriefing room and remove their name tags and service rank. They begin with a team saying: "There are no perfect performances. We're here to talk about what was imperfect." Then they begin. What follows is almost like a twelve-step recovery meeting, with everyone saying what he or she could have done better.

Discretionary tasks allow group members to determine how to integrate their individual contributions. In other words, the means by which the team will accomplish a group task is up to the discretion of the team itself. The result can be very successful, as the path to completion is customized by the individual members. But process losses, even failure, can occur when teams adopt an inappropriate performance strategy—as when members put their own motives and ambitions ahead of the team.

Configural tasks, last but not least, are a mix of the above. Needless to say, it would be impossible to do all five task types at the same time—indeed, many are contradictory. However, some teams may institute these different tasks sequentially, say, working together at one point, then each in turn at another.

That brings you up-to-date with the latest discoveries and insights regarding teams, their members, and their operation. In the pages to come, we'll look into the world of different team types—a taxonomy of teams, if you will. As you read about the many different forms that pairs, trios, and larger teams take, please keep in mind that behind these labels and narrative descriptions lie all the psychological and sociological forces about which you've just learned.

We've just looked at the *inside* of teams. Now, in the next chapter, you'll begin looking at teams from the *outside*—from the perspective of a manager assigned to build them and ensure their success.

The Power of Pairs

n the early 1990s, one of the most driven entrepreneurs of his generation hit a rough patch. Howard Schultz was trying to expand his business, Starbucks Coffee, around the United States, but after opening a few hundred stores, he found that his rapid expansion model had begun to break down. Reports came back that customer service—an ingredient perhaps even more important to his success than the coffee itself—was dropping. Maybe the critics were right. It's damn near impossible to scale up a cult brand like Starbucks nationally, let alone worldwide, because the intangibles, which include great customer service, don't always respond to size and scale.

Schultz soon realized that what Starbucks needed most was someone with a deep empathy for employees and an appreciation for the art of customer service. Someone quite unlike Schultz, who was one of those type A, hypercompetitive, poor-kid-who-went-to-college-on-a-sports-scholarship, successful-at-everything-he-touches kind of guys.

So in 1994, Schultz did something unusual. He promoted his exact opposite in temperament, to strengthen employee morale and customer service at Starbucks. By the oddest of coincidences, the outsider also happened to be named Howard, Howard Behar.

"We were so unalike that it was funny," recalls Behar. "We look different. He's tall, athletic, hawkish. I'm short and round. We see the world differently, too. Hell, we argued and fought for three years about how important employee culture was to Starbucks' ability to scale nationally and then worldwide. For Schultz, culture was maybe important, but not primary. For me, it was the whole game."

The Howard-Howard relationship had a rocky start. But the two protagonists stuck to it. Indeed, Howard Behar became the president of Starbucks and served in that position for eight years under Howard Schultz.

In today's tough and competitive economy, the demands of daily life at work and play are almost impossible to manage by oneself. What's needed instead are people with complementary skills. And we find such pairs almost everywhere: the engineer who teams with the technical writer, the trial lawyer with the researcher, the executive with the operations expert, the inventor with the entrepreneur, the tale of the two Howards . . . the list is almost endless.

In fact, the more you study pairs, the less you find that the stereotypical combination of two nearly identical individuals—call them "Castor and Pollux pairs"—appears to exist in real life. Instead, as we will now see, pairs most often take on a wide and colorful array of forms, some of them quite unlikely at first glance. Not only is the success of these teams *not* correlated with compatibility but some of the most successful pairs consist of two people who have *nothing* in common and may actually despise each other. Stranger still are the pairs in which one member may be long dead—or have never even existed.

Needless to say, this is not the way we normally think of pairs, nor how we typically assemble them in business, government, or academia. Rather, we tend either to team up people who we think will work well together, or simply stick together the two best individuals for the job we can find. That this selection process remains so crude even into the twenty-first century is shocking. After all, companies today spend billions, using everything from headhunters to trade shows to Big Data analytics, to winnow out those few individuals determined to be the best possible recruits from the mass of potential employees in the workforce (or from those just graduating from college). And yet, when those talented individuals are finally hired and put to work, they are paired with others, or put into larger teams, through a process that hasn't changed in millennia: perceived compatibility, common interests, similar personalities, intuition, and more often than not, proximity and expediency.

Is it any wonder that, for all the empirical tools that are now brought to bear on corporate HR functions, we still have almost no ability to predict whether a given pair will actually get the job done? And if we can't do it with pairs, the basic building block of all larger teams, how can we ever expect to make such predictions about teams of 50 or 1,500?

This cannot continue—nor will it for long. Just as the sciences of management information, supply chain management, and new-employee profiling have emerged in turn in response to past challenges to organizational efficiency, so too is it inevitable that a new discipline will soon emerge to bring computational power and empirical techniques to enterprise team-building. For those of us who have found ourselves in failed or dysfunctional teams—that is, most of us—that day can't come soon enough.

And when it does, as has been the case with one technology-driven revolution in corporate operations after another, the first adopter in each industry will find itself with a powerful competitive advantage that will enable it to accelerate away from its competitors. Imagine a company or an institution in which every one of its operating units, large and small, works with an efficiency that today is found only among its "superstar" teams.

When that revolution in team construction and management finally arrives, it will no doubt start with the very foundation of all teams: pairs. After all, pairs are not only the most common of human (and animal) teams, but they are also the basic bricks from which the edifices of larger teams are built.

POWERHOUSE PAIR ON THE PRAIRIE

On a warm Southern California evening in 2012, in the eastern Los Angeles suburb of Arcadia, thirty-one skinny high school–age boys lined up on the Arcadia High School track to run the eight laps of the 3,200 meters—the metric version of the classic two-mile run. The boys' 3,200 is the showcase race each year at April's Arcadia Invitational. The race is held under the lights, in prime time.

In high school track, nine minutes for the 3,200 is considered to be national class for a boy. Most of the thirty-one boys toeing the start line of the 2012 Arcadia 3,200 had a chance at breaking nine minutes.

Halfway through the race, at the 1,600-meter mark, a tight bunch of twenty runners came through in 4:31. This pack of boys elbowed and jostled for two more laps. Then four runners, led by a senior from Houston, Texas, suddenly broke out and set a terrific pace. The top four had a different look from the rest, flying like seasoned Olympians. They would run faster for the last two minutes, covering the final 800 meters at a sub-four-minute-mile pace to finish a race that ESPN called the greatest high school boys' 3,200-meter race in history.

Finishing fourth, with a time of 8:51, was a small kid with sandy hair and black socks halfway up to his knees. The first three runners were seniors, but the little fellow in fourth was a junior: Jake Leingang from Bismarck High School in North Dakota. Though sixteen years old, at a wispy five foot eight and 120 pounds, Jake looked like a seventh-grader.

That such an unlikely kid from the sparse plains of North Dakota had found his way to the glitzy Arcadia Invitational track meet near Los Angeles, and then finished fourth in the greatest boys' 3,200 meters ever run, was astonishing. Good distance runners must train year-round, a near impossibility in North Dakota. Most days in December, January, and February are below freezing; many are below zero. March is melting snow that freezes overnight and turns roads into skating rinks. Needless to say, Jake Leingang, coming straight off a North Dakota winter, was at a huge disadvantage competing in April against the tanned runners from Texas, California, and Arizona.

But Jake had an advantage the other runners didn't: he had been trained by the foremost pair of high school distance running coaches in the United States.

Mighty Mouse

Back in August 1970, when a high school sophomore named Darrell Anderson showed up for his first week of cross-country practice at Bismarck High, he stood five feet three inches tall and weighed 105 pounds. Cross-country races are three miles long and take place on hilly trails in public parks or on golf courses. A football player's weight is a burden. So it is typical for distance runners, then and now, to be on the slight side. But Darrell A. was puny even in this crowd.

The most famous American runners of the early 1970s were sinewy men like Frank Shorter, the Yale graduate who in 1972 would become the second American to win the Olympic marathon race, and Steve Prefontaine ("Pre"), the mythical Oregon phenom who would die in a car accident in 1975 and become the presiding spirit of the Nike running shoe brand. The aristocratic-looking Shorter was five feet ten inches and 135 pounds, a self-described ectomorph. Working-class kid Prefontaine from the logging town of Coos Bay, Oregon, was five feet nine inches and 140 pounds. Pre was considered to be on the muscular side.

But little Darrell A. was a runt even for a fifteen-year-old cross-country runner. A Bismarck High cross-country team photo shows Darrell A. with his bowl haircut standing at attention, chest out and hands behind his waist. "I was holding up my running shorts in the back," he says. "They were too big." He was often needled and teased by teammates and coaches alike for his short stature and his unfashionable haircut—and labeled with unfortunate nicknames.

So how did little Darrell A. do when competition started?

Not bad, considering. He discovered that he could do something essential in cross-country running: he could bear the pain of effort just as his idol Steve Prefontaine could. Indeed, during training sessions, Darrell A. would sometimes run so hard that he'd suffer chronic diarrhea for the rest of the day.

By the time Darrell A. was a senior, he had grown to five feet eight inches and 125 pounds and was among the top five high school runners in the state. But then he contracted mononucleosis, and his high school running career was over. Once he recovered, he enrolled in a local junior college and soon captained its cross-country team. After two years, Darrell A. transferred to North Dakota State University, an NCAA Division II powerhouse at the time in cross-country and track. Darrell A., now at his full height of five feet ten inches, became a solid member of that team, able to run ten thousand meters in less than thirty minutes.

But he never forgot high school and his treatment there. Darrell A.'s resentment about those years gnawed at him well into middle age. He asked himself: Did I ever really reach my full potential as a runner? What if I had been more physically mature in high school?

What if I'd had more confidence? What if the coaches had seen my potential instead of calling me stupid names?

What Could Have Been

Across the Missouri River from Bismarck lies its smaller sister city, Mandan. The town of Mandan is best known for an event that happened nearly 140 years ago, in the spring of 1876. That's when George Armstrong Custer mustered his Seventh Cavalry at nearby Fort Abraham Lincoln—and rode westward toward the Montana Territory and his fatal encounter at the Little Bighorn a month later.

That's pretty much the whole story for Mandan. Today it is the poor twin sister of Bismarck. The athletic teams at Mandan High School are spotty. As in many hardscrabble towns, the teenage athletes with the most potential often never show up. They have long since been diverted by after-school jobs, parental neglect, drugs, or dropping out.

The coaches and sports facilities at Mandan High School were, and still are, in a shabby state compared with those of richer Bismarck across the river. Whereas Bismarck High's football teams play in a multimillion-dollar bowl on fancy artificial turf, Mandan football teams play on a soggy and chewed-up grass field in the floodplain of a nearby river. Around that sodden field and its old spectator stands is a 400-meter running track. It is a far cry from the $300,000 tangerine-colored tartan job at the Bismarck Community Bowl. Rather, Mandan's running track is a black asphalt road with a bit of rubber mixed in for only a touch of softening.

With these low-rent attractions, it is hardly a surprise that Mandan High has always had trouble attracting good-quality high school coaches. That rule applied in the 1980s, when Dave Zittleman ran the half mile for Mandan High.

In the boys' half mile (now 800 meters), two minutes is a standard that separates a decent high school runner from the rest.

The better half-milers are five seconds faster, at 1:55, and nationally ranked boys can dip under 1:50. Dave Zittleman looked like a kid capable of breaking 1:55, which is a good time and is often good enough to win the North Dakota state championship meet. Dave Z. stood five feet eleven and weighed a lean and muscular 155 pounds—the perfect build for a half-miler.

Dave Z. may have had the physical goods to break 1:55, but he always seemed stuck on the slow side of two minutes. His coaches were of little help. They didn't motivate Dave, and they possessed no special knowledge about training or tactics. To Dave Z., they seemed lazy.

Like Darrell Anderson, Dave Zittleman began to realize his potential as a runner only after finishing high school. At eighteen, he crossed the Missouri River and enrolled at the University of Mary in Bismarck. A Catholic liberal arts university of 3,000 undergrads, U. of Mary had a decent small college track team. The coaches were several cuts above his coaches in Mandan. Dave Z. took advantage of his new circumstances and completed his University of Mary track career with a personal best of 1:54 for the half mile. Considering North Dakota's lousy spring weather, 1:54 is quite good. Dave Z. had clearly improved as a runner during his college career.

But had he improved enough? Dave Z. would question that for years. It gnawed at him. Like Darrell A., Dave Z. finished his high school and college track careers with a sense of dissatisfaction and unfulfilled promise. Moreover, Dave Z. had a smoldering resentment for his misinformed coaches.

Champions from A to Z

Today Darrell Anderson and Dave Zittleman are the co-coaches of Bismarck High's powerful cross-country and track and field dynasty. The Bismarck High boys have won eleven straight cross-country team championships at the state level, and another eight straight in track and field. One team member was the aforementioned Jake Leingang, the nationally ranked 3,200-meter runner.

In August 2012, the pope of long-distance running came to Bismarck to see what it was all about. In the American distance running hierarchy, the inner sanctum of power and wisdom resides in Eugene, Oregon, home to the University of Oregon. The Oregon Ducks are the most famous men's and women's distance running program in the country. The legendary Steve Prefontaine was an Oregon Duck. The founder of Nike, Phil Knight, was an Oregon Duck mile-runner in the early 1960s. The Olympic trials for track and field are almost always held at Eugene's Hayward Field, sometimes called the Vatican of track and field.

The "pope" of American long-distance running is, therefore, whoever is coach of the University of Oregon's men's and women's distance running programs. Andy Powell is the latest—and there is hardly a serious high school runner, boy or girl, who doesn't dream of running in the green and yellow colors of the Oregon Ducks, on Hayward Field's track, for coach Andy Powell. Conversely, to get Coach Powell to take notice of you in high school is a high hurdle indeed.

Yet there he was, Oregon's Andy Powell, in Bismarck. Powell had flown halfway across the country to take a look at Jake Leingang as a potential Oregon Duck recruit. Decked out in a lime green Oregon Nike golf shirt and khaki pants, Powell was all business—and sitting in a small office in Bismarck High's basement physical education wing with Darrell A. and Dave Z. The Bismarck High coaches were dressed as usual in ratty cargo shorts and faded golf shirts. Immediately, Darrell A. tried to disarm Powell with his shambling low-key prairie humor, a mix of Garrison Keillor and Rick Moranis's Canadian beer swiller Bob McKenzie. Dave Z. was a bit embarrassed by Darrell A.'s shtick. He said nothing but pulled his cap down, as if trying to disappear.

And therein lies a clue to why Darrell A. and Dave Z. form such a powerful pair. Though driven by identical dreams of glory and fueled by a shared resentment of stupid coaching, Darrell A. and Dave Z. are different people at their cores. For one thing, Darrell is an extrovert, Dave Z. an introvert. Darrell also operates by feeling, while Dave Z. operates by numbers. On practice days, Darrell walks around and talks to each of the runners. How are you feeling? Feeling okay? Everything cool at home? School okay? Girl problems?

Off to the side stands Dave Z., head down, cap pulled tight, consulting his index cards. To hell with how anyone feels, he thinks. The calendar says Jake needs some brisk intervals today, at a one-mile-race pace.

It's important to note that Dave Z. has not copied Jake's daily workout from the Internet or from a book. He has calculated the numbers himself, from his own deep study of running theory, the time of year, and from the records he keeps on Jake's progress. Dave Z. keeps meticulous records, and he revisits them almost daily. In the late hours at his apartment, alone, he works the numbers, makes his decisions, and prepares his index cards.

For Darrell A., principles are sacred but details are malleable, subject to feelings and gut instincts. He feels it is important to walk around, schmooze his athletes, and buck them up. Running isn't just training and workouts; it is also about character. And it doesn't end with graduation: Darrell A. has also developed a network of former Bismarck High track stars who have become successful in business and now donate money to the Bismarck program. One, a former high-jump state champion, is an oil developer worth more than $100 million. Another is a former sprint state champion who is now a nationally famous child psychiatrist. Like a good college athletic fundraiser, Darrell A. keeps close to his network of donors so that his Bismarck runners can get the best shoes and physical therapy, go to high-altitude training camps in Montana during the summer, and fly to races all around the country in the fall and spring.

Dave Z. could never do that, one suspects, even if he wanted to. It would kill him to ask anyone for money. The single Dave Z. is so introverted he has trouble asking women on dates, though women find him attractive. Dave Z.'s monkish behavior has even become an ongoing joke among the other coaches. The night that Bismarck won its seventh straight boys' track state championship, Darrell A. held a party for coaches and donors at his house. The beer and whiskey flowed while Darrell A.'s wife unloaded pizza from the oven. Darrell A. presented each donor with a gift.

Dave Z. attended the party too, but the next day few could recall seeing him there. It turned out that Dave Z. had sneaked off to a quiet room in Darrell's house to analyze video from the state meet. He was already thinking about next year. He was, and is, determined to be everything he wishes he had had in high school: a really smart coach. By comparison, Darrell has become the coach he wishes he'd had in high school: a faithful believer.

The differences between Darrell A. and Dave Z. are marked and noticeable within minutes of meeting them. But what unites them runs deeper. It is the need for exoneration. Dave Z. is convinced that his own high school running career was wrecked by lackadaisical small-town coaches, and he wants revenge in the best possible way. He wants to produce great runners. And he is willing to outplan, outcoach, and outthink any other high school track coach in the country to do this. Even if it means sneaking out to watch videos during a party.

Darrell A. had smart coaches in high school, but they were arrogant, bullying, old-school, and they disrespected the nonelite runner. They overlooked the brave heart of the small kid. Darrell A.'s life mission is to nourish every runner on the team, not just the best ones. He wants to motivate them all, and shine a light on their potential. Darrell A. knows that the top runners will emerge in time . . . and that they sometimes prove to be little wispy kids like Jake Leingang.

Darrell A. and Dave Z. are friendly toward each other, but not friends. Darrell A., married for thirty years, is comfortable with men and women, old and young, rich and poor, and though he would never say so, he tires of Dave Z.'s social awkwardness. Dave Z. gets bored, and sometimes irritated, with Darrell's lightheartedness, his seeming to not take things seriously.

In July 2012, Darrell Anderson, the older of the pair, won the national high school coach of the year for boys' track and field. Receiving the award, Darrell A. said his only goal now was to be in the audience when the younger and equally deserving Dave Z. got his award.

PAIRS COME IN MANY FORMS

Pairs are the most fundamental human teams. Indeed, pairing is so common to human existence that we often forget that it is not the case for other animals. For example, many predators pair during their mating periods but often operate solo the rest of the time. Some—like most cats, big and small—barely do even that. Others, like foxes and hawks, may pair up for a season, until the babies are grown, then go their separate ways. Other predators, especially mammals, such as hyenas, wolves, orcas, dolphins, and the family dog, operate in packs, as do crocodiles, army ants, and, the fossil record suggests, certain dinosaurs. Other animals, especially herbivores, form herds, flocks, or colonies, sometimes of enormous size.

By the same token, some other animals—gibbons, wolves, and eagles among them—will mate for life even as they exist within a larger grouping. These are some of the most enduring "teams" in the animal kingdom, though they are almost always based on reproduction and rearing rather than efficiency or productivity. That said, a phenomenon that looks very much like human "friendship" between two individuals can be found across the animal kingdom—and even across species.

The classic example of this behavior is the abandoned infant creature of one species being taken up by the nursing mother of another. But there are also well-documented examples of animals, often merely because of proximity, taking up close and enduring "friendships"—the thoroughbred race horse with a goat or dog; a dog and cat living in the same house; pigs with household pets; and so forth. Sometimes these animal friendships result in what can only be described as "teamwork"—like the dog nosing open the bedroom door so that the cat can jump on the bed and awaken the owners—but with the exception of human beings, there are almost no examples of such pairs forming specifically for instrumental purposes.

But humans constantly form teams—usually first as pairs that coalesce into larger groupings—but, in emergencies, we have been known to form coordinating, effective, and trusting pairs in seconds. Think of the everyday folks who pair up to rescue others in burning buildings or to defend themselves in firefights or who rush to save an individual trapped down a cliff. That we have this ability, uniquely among all living things, cannot be a coincidence. Arguably, even more than language (after all, spontaneous pairs and teams can form without a word), it is this talent that singles out our species—that is, a talent that is not just a sense of self (once falsely assigned solely to humans) but a sense of the selfhood of *others*, and an innate understanding that by partnering with another person, we can accomplish things we cannot do by ourselves.

While our capacity to quickly, instrumentally, and effectively form teams argues for team-building as fundamental to human nature and society, the astonishing range of *types* of teams, beginning with pairs, shows the universality and flexibility of this phenomenon in daily life.

As far as we can determine, there has never been a listing—a taxonomy—of the various types of human pairs. So we decided to create one, and before we were done, even we were astonished by how many different forms pairs can take. And these are just professional pairings: if we were to add the many types of pairs that appear in private and social life, this list might double or triple.

For now, though, we believe it might be of immediate assistance to the reader in forming, identifying, and managing teams in their own enterprises. Let's begin in the next chapter.

Successful Pairing

THE BUILDING BLOCKS OF TEAMS

We like to think of ourselves as individuals. And in one respect that is certainly the case: our consciousness is locked into our individual brains, forever isolating us—Descartes's "ghost in a machine"—from ever fully merging our identities with those of others.

And yet, if we were to track every second of our waking lives, we would probably find that we are interacting with others at least as often as we are alone. And no other type of interaction takes place more often in our daily existence than an interaction with a single other person. As solitary as we imagine ourselves to be, we are just as much binary. One reason is biological: We mate with one person at a time; we typically speak with only one person at a time (even if we are addressing thousands); and we even smell each other's pheromones as individuals. The archaeological evidence suggests that this has always been so, and that the breeding pair pair-bond has been the single most dominant cultural phenomenon for most of the million years that hominids have walked the earth—and certainly for the 20,000-year history of modern humankind.

In other words, to be human is to be a member, both serially and in parallel, with a succession of pairs—numbering perhaps in the hundreds—over the course of a lifetime. Nothing that consumes so much of our existence on earth can be anything less than genetically advantageous . . . and indeed, statistically speaking, being married (that most common and enduring pairing) confers distinct advantages over being single in terms of one's overall health, income, and life expectancy. The following is a taxonomy—a classification—of the twelve different forms, in four categories (occasion, similarity, inequality, and difference) that professional pairings can take. It is based on both research and our own careers as journalists dealing with every manner of Silicon Valley start-up pairs.

PAIRS DEFINED BY OCCASION

1.0–GOT YOUR SIX: We put this type of pair first because it is different from all the others. It is the most spontaneous, the shortest lived, and likely the oldest. Thus it is probably the most fundamental of all teams. The term comes from the military: if twelve o'clock is directly in front of us, then six o'clock is directly behind, the direction from which we are most vulnerable. "I've got your six" meaning "I've got your back" is a modern phrase, but it was surely stated in some form before the walls of Troy, and certainly among the Spartans at Thermopylae. Its most mythical American moment occurs at the O.K. Corral, where Doc Holliday backs up Wyatt Earp (the phrase from the movie, "I'm your huckleberry," echoes the most famous fictional team of this type). Among the most celebrated examples of this kind of partnership are those of the explorers Meriwether Lewis and William Clark, and the frontiersmen John C. Frémont and Kit Carson.

Note that this kind of pairing typically exists during crises and emergencies. The two individuals involved may not even know each other. It is only when facing a threat that such pairings are created—and when that threat is removed, the members of the pair usually go their separate ways again. For all of their evanescence, Got Your Six teams have some extraordinary attributes—none more so than the complete trust each member of the pair puts in the other. The implied message is "Focus on what is in front of you, I'll take of whatever comes from behind—even if I die in the process." This is humanity at its most selfless, which means it is both rare and short-lived.

Because of the intensity of this relationship—there is no greater commitment two people can make to each other than to put their lives in each other's hands—the Got Your Six relationship may be the strongest of all teams. The almost superhuman strength of such a relationship is a force multiplier over the individual fighting alone or even with another person at a lower level of trust. It is also a reason Got Your Six teams are usually short-lived—human beings can maintain that kind of intensity for only so long—and quickly devolve, once the challenge is met, either to friendship or mere acquaintanceship. It is also a very narrow form of partnership, targeted at one type of challenge, and one not really adaptable for other tasks.

2.0–THIS MAGIC MOMENT: "Magical" pair-teams resemble Castor and Pollux teams (see page 126) in almost every way but two:

- The two members may have accomplished little without the other, but together they accomplish extraordinary things.
- Unlike the perfect pairs, these duos typically exist for a much briefer duration.

Magic Moment pairs exhibit behavior similar to that of a brief but intense love affair. Their members often know they have met their perfect partner almost from the moment of their first encounter—the equivalent in professional life of love at first sight.

Magic Moment pairs are most visible in the performing arts, especially music, in which the fruits of collaboration are almost instantly apparent. Musical duets can form almost instantly and produce astonishing results: Lester Flatt and Earl Scruggs, Louis Armstrong and Earl Hines, Billie Holiday and Lester Young, Paul Desmond and Dave Brubeck, Dizzy Gillespie and Charlie Parker. In cinema, the magic of such duos—often romantic pairs—can be almost instantly apparent: Mickey Rooney and Judy Garland, William Powell and Myrna Loy, John Wayne and Maureen O'Hara, John Gilbert and Greta Garbo.

The most successful—and certainly the most famous—of these musical magic duos is John Lennon and Paul McCartney. They are listed as a magical pair instead of a perfect Castor and Pollux because their partnership, despite beginning in childhood, was comparatively short, ending in their early twenties; and because their collaboration was even shorter—they were essentially solo artists by the time of *Sgt. Pepper's*. Yet in the brief interval from Hamburg at the beginning of the 1960s to global superstardom at the end of that decade, Lennon and McCartney produced the most valuable and influential corpus of popular music of all time. The zenith of this collaboration was probably "A Day in the Life" on *Sgt. Pepper's*, in which Lennon's social commentary and modernist anomie in the writing and singing of the primary lyrics is perfectly countered by McCartney's chugging urban proletarian ditty in the bridge. In retrospect, and based on their later solo careers, neither John nor Paul could have written this song alone.

In the business world, the best place to find the traces of these magical partnerships is in patent filings. Much of modern technology and science is multidisciplinary; thus, outside of a few Renaissance men and women, it is typically the product of electrical engineering and software code, or solid-state physics and inorganic chemistry, or microwave and semiconductor technology—and lately, computer science and biotechnology. This almost always requires a collaboration, often for just a matter of months, between two innovators in different fields. In the Internet age, these fundamental partnerships now extend to between code writers and marketers and other seemingly incompatible combinations. Pierre Omidyar was a code writer when he founded eBay (as AuctionWeb) and hired as his first employee and CEO Jeff Skoll, a Stanford MBA with a background in the Internet. Google's Sergey Brin and Larry Page were both computer science graduate students at Stanford.

Perhaps the most famous contemporary example of a Magic Moment pair is that of Steve Jobs and Steve Wozniak. The authors of this book were in a position to see this pair (along with Omidyar-Skoll and Brin-Page) almost from the day of its creation. The popular myth is that the two young men, who met in high school, were close to being a perfect pair, as discussed in the previous section. The reality was much different. For one thing, the famous pair were not really childhood friends. Their age difference was such that they really only overlapped for a year of high school, when Wozniak was already a celebrated young technologist (he'd earned his first media attention for a junior high school science project, and later for planting a fake bomb at his high school). At that point, Steve Jobs was just a little kid.

In person at that young age, the two young men were very different from their later personas. Wozniak was the voluble one, the one with a job and career, and something of a jock. Jobs, the future charismatic idol of millions, was shy, mercurial to the point of being obnoxious, and comparatively antisocial. Different as they were, they had a spark between them that was obvious from almost the first moment they met. Wozniak saw in the younger boy an enthusiast for his work, a visionary, and, most important, someone with a plan. Jobs brought a sense of destiny, and he made Woz's life thrilling. And though their names will be tied together forever, in reality they worked together closely for less than a decade, and only a couple of years into Apple.

Had Wozniak never met Steve Jobs, it is highly likely that he would have stayed at HP—and been part of its ill-fated move to Corvallis, Oregon. Like many others, he would have probably come back to the Valley . . . and been yet another bit player in the Homebrew Computer Club. The personal revolution would have happened with or without Apple; it just would have started a couple years later, and might never have had the galvanizing event that was the Apple II's introduction. These days, if he had survived the many layoffs, Woz would likely be an aging and anonymous HP engineer with a few patents under his belt, putting in a last couple of years before retirement. As for Steve Jobs, his type of genius would have had a hard time finding purchase, even among the start-ups of Silicon Valley, where he likely would have jumped from one failure to another. His personality would have been a deal-breaker in any company he didn't run; and he was too harsh to have eventually become a venture capitalist. In the end, he would have probably left Silicon Valley.

But none of that happened, because Woz and Jobs had their "magic moment." Such Magic Moment pairs are among the most creative phenomena in human existence; they are supernova events. The fact that two very different individuals can, even briefly, join together in such a way that both can work at the absolute peak of their abilities is a kind of miracle. Think Edison and William J. Tanner working on the incandescent lightbulb; or John Bardeen and Walter Brattain on the semiconductor transistor. One of the oddest business Magic Moment pairs was that of the high-rolling playboy William Durant and the sober, hyper-rationalist Alfred Sloan—a short-lived combination that set General Motors on the path to being the world's most valuable company of its day.

In the arts, probably the most famous and influential such partnership was that between Pablo Picasso and Georges Braque. The two worked together only briefly, and rarely encountered each other in the decades that followed. But during their legendary few months as a team they developed cubism—and set the direction of modern art. A comparable, though much more volatile, pairing took place twenty years earlier between Vincent van Gogh and Paul Gauguin.

3.0-CHAINED TOGETHER BY SUCCESS: These are "antagonistic partnerships" . . . and they can be the strangest, scariest, and most remarkable of any pair type. In particular, "Chained" pairs feature a duo of people who are hugely successful together, but for various reasons—lifestyle, personality, stage of career, and so forth—simply do not get along with each other. Indeed, this antagonism can often lead to outright hatred . . . and end in loud, sometimes violent, and often legendary breakups.

The most famous example—indeed, it is the archetype, and even the subject of a film (*Topsy-Turvy*)—is the legendary Victorian operetta team of William Gilbert and Arthur Sullivan. The two men appeared not just to despise each other but also to hate the predicament in which they eventually found themselves: solo, their careers went nowhere; together, they produced immortal work. Being trapped in such a partnership must be its own particular hell—the world is forever pressing you together, seeing you as perfect partners, sometimes even seeing you as one person indivisible. Meanwhile, if you break up the team, all your success and fame could just fade away—though some Chained team members become so unhappy that they risk it anyway.

Chained teams are typically well known precisely because of their volatile nature. For one thing, if they weren't wildly successful, they would have happily split up. And, of course, these teams also feed certain human perversities: both the schadenfreude of knowing that their great success has come with equally great frustration, and the excitement of waiting for the inevitable explosion.

And when that explosion does come, it usually makes for good copy and bestselling memoirs.

Chained teams can be found almost everywhere. Richard Rodgers and Lorenz Hart—the latter so bad a drunk that Rodgers dumped him at the height of their success to take a risk with Oscar Hammerstein. The Beach Boys' Mike Love and Brian Wilson, who recently reunited after decades—only to split up again. Gene Siskel and Roger Ebert, by both temperament and employment natural competitors, who found their greatest fame paired as movie reviewers. Intel founders Bob Noyce and Andrew Grove, who feuded (at least on the part of the inflammatory Grove toward the indifferent Noyce) even as they built one of the world's most valuable companies.

We'll discuss the Everly Brothers in the Castor and Pollux section—and, to a degree, they belong here as well. But their Chained relationship pales next to, say, Sam and Dave, whose breakup reportedly involved knives. The Lennon-McCartney pairing also began to look chained by the time of *The White Album*. Rod Stewart being fired by Jeff Beck, and Dizzy Gillespie stabbing Cab Calloway are also classic examples. Bob Hope and Bing Crosby created perhaps the most successful duo in film history but rarely saw each other off the set; and Dean Martin and Jerry Lewis didn't speak to each other for decades after they broke up. Neil Simon famously captured the complicated love-hate (mostly hate) nature of one of these pairs in his comedy of old vaudeville partners, *The Sunshine Boys*.

Chained teams aren't *always* at each other's throats. Indeed, at the beginning, if there weren't some chemistry, they would never have teamed up. But even then, the fault lines are usually obvious. Such teams often emerge because the extraordinary opportunities presented by their harmonious talents overwhelm the differences in character, attitude, or temperament—at least at the beginning. But, as great as the fame that follows may be, it never completely resolves those differences . . . and more often than not, it amplifies them. Thus, what began as areas of friction that could be ignored in the excitement of early success can grow in time to a chasm that isn't reduced with each new victory but widened.

How long it takes for these Chained pairs to finally snap is anyone's guess. Like marriages, some Chained pairs can seem doomed from the start yet last decades, the partners squabbling all the way. Others can seem much calmer, and in little peril . . . only to have one member awaken some morning and decide that he or she can never work with the other again. All that can be done is to take full advantage of the power of one of these unlikely and incompatible pairs for as long as it lasts, be prepared for it to shatter without notice, and get out of the way when the blast occurs . . . and start planning for the inevitable reunion tour a quarter century from now.

It is interesting to speculate that one reason such pairs seem so (temporarily) successful is that the available pool of potential partners is almost infinite, because they don't have to be compatible—as opposed to the limited number of compatible pairs in the other pair-team types. But that success is also something of an illusion: you don't see a lot of mediocre Chained pairs, because they split up quickly. It takes real success to stick together day-to-day with someone you hate or despise.

Another reason for the success of these partnerships is not so obvious. It is that the members of the pair usually enter the relationship with a pretty good idea of not just the strengths of the other party but also his or her weaknesses. That doesn't mean they don't often delude each other that they can make it work (again, the similarity to marriage is obvious), but at least they know those differences exist and can develop work-arounds or other strategies for dealing with them.

Ultimately, even after they fail and split up, Chained teams are often unforgettable, the stuff of legend. Certainly their achievements are part of it. But just as memorable is how they did it: two people, often at each other's throats, resentful and jealous of any credit earned by the other, each feeling trapped in a miserable relationship, their names forever linked, and any memory of one inextricable from that of the other . . . and yet, somehow, they create magic, some of it immortal. Who could ever forget encountering a relationship like that? It's the stuff of memoirs—which only make that Chained pair even more famous.

4.0-HERE AND THERE: "Here and There" duos are really a twenty-first-century phenomenon, the product of the Internet-enabled global economy, of the arrival of those two billion new consumers from the developing world into that economy, and of the competitive need to create customized solutions for all customers, new and old. The solution has been to create a pair-team that includes one member from a home office or headquarters and one member from the international front where the company is targeting its next marketing thrust. The headquarters partner represents the institutional memory and the culture of the company, and the field partner brings an understanding of the consumers, market, and community or country being targeted. In operation, the field partner provides the momentum of entering the market, while the headquarters partner guides that effort, making sure it is congruent with the company's products and services, resources, and rules—and when it isn't, making the case for the field partner's strategy with the senior management. What ties them together and makes such a team possible is technology: the emergence of the Web, global communications, the cloud, and teleconferencing and telepresence.

PAIRS DEFINED BY SIMILARITY

5.0-TOGETHER, WE'RE MORE THAN TWO: This is the first pair-team type that can be intentionally created. Indeed, given the low odds of two appropriate individuals finding each other, this pairing almost demands outside influence.

"Together, We're More Than Two" teams are *fulfillment partnerships*; that is, these are pairs composed of two individuals whose lives or careers have remained incomplete and unfulfilled until they team up. These individuals are typically late bloomers who have certain limitations in their personalities or skills that they have little chance of overcoming through their own actions. Sometimes a limitation can be as simple as risk-aversion, anxiety, or a lack of nerve—which a partnership helps them overcome. The unlikely pairing of Darrell A. and Dave Z., those two obscure North Dakota high school track coaches who teamed up to set new records, is a paradigmatic example of such a fulfillment partnership.

It is crucial to note—to distinguish it from some of the other teams to follow—that this type of partnership consists of two individuals of comparable traits and attributes, . . . and who on their own have failed to reach their full potential. This is among the most homogenous of pairs.

Together, We're More Than Two partnerships appear throughout history. Stan Laurel and Oliver Hardy had mediocre solo careers in silent films until they teamed up and created one of the greatest comedy duos in cinema history. Bill Gates and Paul Allen were both computer nerds from a Seattle prep school, and all but indistinguishable at the start of Microsoft.

This type of partnership enables each partner to accomplish more than he or she could do alone. The return on the investment of time and energy required to create such duos can be enormous. After all, you are taking two "failures"—or, more accurately, employees who have fallen short of their potential—and turning both into top achievers. That's a whole lot cheaper than going out and recruiting two superstars. Moreover, because these pairs really succeed only together, their members are drawn to maintain their relationship—or risk falling back to their old ways.

The biggest and inevitable risk for this type of team is the resentments and jealousies that may crop up as each member starts to grow and change over time.

6.0–CASTOR AND POLLUX: These are the "perfect partnerships," the ideal teaming of individuals who are so much alike that they each can take on the other's duties with barely a hitch.

The name comes from Greek mythology. Castor and Pollux (known in Latin as the Gemini) were twins who were so close that when the mortal Castor was dying, Zeus allowed Pollux to share his immortality, such that each spent alternate days on Mount Olympus and in Hades. Castor and Pollux pair-teams are the organizational version of soul mates—and they are just as desirable and just as rare. These partnerships can range from near clones—often taking the form of siblings, such as Orville and Wilbur Wright or George and Ira Gershwin—or very different people who still match each other in the details of their joint efforts, such as Bill Hewlett and David Packard, and Warren Buffett and Charlie Munger.

Such sibling or best friend pairs are the ultimate Castor and Pollux form. But more interesting are the less rare cases of duos that begin in one of the other pair-teams (such as a Yin and Yang) and then evolve to this higher level. So complete and mutually actualizing can these pairs become that they resemble less a partnership than a love affair or a long and happy marriage. Like lovers, these perfect duos, whatever their differences in personalities and behavior, exhibit (and, conversely, earn) an almost perfect trust in each other. A classic example of this was the partnership of Tom Perkins (flamboyant, mercurial) and Eugene Kleiner (humble and courtly), who together created the world's most influential venture capital firm.

Castor and Pollux pairs, because they essentially erase all the natural friction between two individuals, can be uniquely powerful and effective. It isn't just like doubling the intellectual attributes, talents, and capabilities found in a single individual, but instead like multiplying them. Such pairs can be remarkably creative and decisive, and because (like the mythical twins) they can alternate focus and energy, they can also seem tireless.

Sometimes, depending on the nature of the work, Castor and Pollux pairs can be superfluous. You don't necessarily need or want them on the loading dock or even in a sales office, but you probably very much want them in R&D or marketing or IT. On executive row? Probably not. But as chairman and CEO? Absolutely—such pairs may be the single best executive combination imaginable . . . and the names of these pairs would fill a hall of fame of American business: the aforementioned Hewlett and Packard, Larry Ellison and Ray Lane, Walt and Roy Disney, Andrew Carnegie and Henry Clay Frick, Ulysses S. Grant and William Tecumseh Sherman, and so on.

Probably one reason these "executive-level" teams work so well is that the demands placed on leaders at the top of both fast-moving young start-ups and large public corporations are so great and so wide-ranging—strategy, day-to-day management, public relations, and so forth—that they are better handled by two individuals rather than one, especially if those two individuals are consistently of one mind, and have complete faith in each other's judgment when they are not. Moreover, in the face of such extreme demands on their time and energy, these individuals can also occasionally spell each other without losing a step. Thus, when Packard was asked to go to Washington to serve as deputy secretary of defense, Hewlett stepped up to run the company solo—and HP's employees, customers, and shareholders barely noticed the change. (Tellingly, and providing a glimpse into the emotional depth of these remarkable relationships, Hewlett broke down and wept in front of the company's thousands of employees in making the announcement of Packard's temporary departure.)

All of that said, Castor and Pollux teams aren't flawless. For one thing, they can become hermetic—like the happily married couple whose relationship is so fulfilling and harmonious that they even withdraw from past friendships and affiliations. Finally, the breakup of these perfect teams—through death or outside events—can be devastating. Just as the effectiveness of such pairs is not a consequence of the addition, but the multiplication, of the two personalities, so too is a breakup not a subtraction, but a division. The surviving member can experience something close to being divorced, even widowed, with long periods spent in depression, involving low productivity and a (usually failed) search for a replacement.

Probably the ultimate Castor and Pollux example, in all of its ups and downs and extraordinary achievements, is that of the Everly Brothers. Phil and Don Everly were children when they began to sing together on their parents' country music radio show. By age twenty, they were already among the most successful singing duos in popular music history. It wasn't just their legendary harmonies, or the remarkable songs by the likes of Boudleaux and Felice Bryant (another perfect pair; she actually dreamed of her future husband before she met him)—the Everlys looked alike and dressed alike, and for most of their first thirty years in this world they were all but inseparable.

As any rock or country music fan knows, that perfect partnership ended on July 14, 1973, at Knott's Berry Farm in California, when, in a combination of drug abuse, exhaustion, and weariness of each other's perpetual company, the Everlys broke up in the most public way imaginable—Don smashed his guitar on the stage and stormed off, leaving Phil to complete the show. Reportedly, the only time the two men spoke again over the next decade was at their father's funeral. During those years, both men seemed lost and in a perpetual and sad search for a new partner. Finally, on September 23, 1983, in one of the most moving reunions in pop music history, the brothers settled their differences and appeared again as a duo at Royal Albert Hall—and restarted their partnership as if it had never ended.[1]

7.0-LIFEBOATS: These are "rescue" partnerships. That is, they consist of pairs whose teaming up is perhaps each individual's last chance at a career or personal survival. "Lifeboat" partnerships are a common trope in movies because of their inherent drama and their natural plot climax of success and redemption—think of the Sylvester Stallone and Burgess Meredith characters in the Rocky movies. When you hear the phrase "I've got no place left to go" or "You're my last hope," you are probably watching a Lifeboat movie.

In fiction, Lifeboat stories are almost always uplifting. That's somewhat true in real life as well—though that is in part because we rarely hear about failed such partnerships. The most famous, or at least the most influential, Lifeboat story of modern times is probably that of Bill Wilson and Robert Smith, the founders of Alcoholics Anonymous. As the story goes, Bill Wilson ("Bill W.") was struggling to stay sober while on a business trip to Akron, Ohio, in January 1935. In desperation, Wilson called some local ministers who might know of any alcoholics. Wilson was put in touch with Dr. Robert Smith ("Dr. Bob"), a notorious Akron drunk who hadn't yet achieved sobriety. The two met at Smith's house, and from that first encounter, the two men—both of whom had nearly lost their families and careers to drink—teamed up to create Alcoholics Anonymous. Together, the two men not only established the most successful sobriety program ever, one that is now found in almost every country around the world, but also stayed sober the rest of their lives.

Lifeboat pairs present an interesting problem. On the one hand, they can produce impressive results—certainly greater than the sum of their two busted parts. But, on the other hand, since the starting point is so low, their results may not be, in the end, that impressive of an achievement—especially if you end up paying two salaries to get what you might find with just one person without black marks on his or her résumé, and posing much less of a risk.

Of course, you may get lucky. The deep loyalty that characterizes "Lifeboat" pairs—after all, they have often literally saved each other from certain death—can make them a formidable force: Got Your Six taken to the nth degree. In that earlier section we mentioned Grant and Sherman—and indeed, they famously covered for each other. But they also, at least at the beginning of the Civil War, even better fit the Lifeboat team model—remember Sherman's statement: "[Grant] stood by me when I was crazy, and I stood by him when he was drunk; and now we stand by each other always."

The two men hit bottom in their lives in the lonely antebellum years after the Mexican War. Sherman had missed that war, stuck in various failed commands in the West. Then, obtaining a command at the beginning of the Civil War, and placed in the thankless command of the army in Kentucky, he had a nervous breakdown and was relieved of duty.

Grant, by comparison, was a hero of the earlier war, but also in a lonely posting out West began to show a pattern with which he would be associated in the years to come—becoming depressed at being apart from his wife and taking to drink. In time, this led to a forced resignation from the army. This was followed by seven years of poverty for his family, as Grant failed at one business after another.

In other words, Sherman wasn't exaggerating with his remark. It was only the desperate shortage of experienced officers that led the Union army to give the two men one more chance. They soon proved their worth, both individually and as a team, on the second day of the Battle of Shiloh.

Because a Lifeboat partnership is built on the mutual rescue of two individuals who have reached rock bottom, it typically features an almost superhuman level of commitment to that relationship by both partners. That commitment can be a formidable force—especially if beyond the obvious failures of the two individuals there lie impressive but unrealized gifts. If you can find them, hiring these "failures" can be a steal: no one else wants them, they are cheap to hire, and they will be almost as loyal to the organization that "saves" them as they will be to each other. But keep in mind that if one slips, he or she is likely to also pull down the other.

PAIRS DEFINED BY DIFFERENCE

8.0-YIN AND YANG: "Yin and Yang" pairs are teams of two individuals whose different skills combine to produce a complete and competitive force. These pair-teams are typically found among salespeople, educators, and law enforcement officers (and criminals), and in the creative business professions such as advertising, art design, and copywriting.

In the classic Yin and Yang teams, one individual is artistic, the other empirical; or one brings the verbal skills, the other the non-verbal; or one is the extrovert, the other the introvert. This combination often appears in the entertainment business. Think of the many songwriters and lyricists, from Rodgers and Hart (or Hammerstein) to Jerome Kern and Dorothy Fields all the way up to Elton John and Bernie Taupin; or performer-producer combinations such as Michael Jackson and Quincy Jones or Frank Sinatra and Nelson Riddle. And it can also be found in pairings of performers and business managers (Johnny Carson and Henry Bushkin, Louis Armstrong and Joe Glaser, and hundreds of others).

In the business world, Yin and Yang teams take several common forms: businessperson and scientist/engineer, salesperson and contract specialist, and marketer and manufacturer. In small companies, the operator-and-silent-partner duo is one of the most common. In high-tech start-ups, the combination of the entrepreneur and the techie (Jobs and Wozniak being the most famous) is so ubiquitous that new companies that lack this combination are looked upon by investors and potential hires as suspect.

In daily life, across all professions, one of the most common and yet least celebrated Yin and Yang teams is that of the innovator and the communicator. Most highly successful individuals combine high skill levels with decisiveness and action. That combination is rare enough, so to expect an individual to also be a great communicator is usually a bridge too far, the convergence of all of those attributes too rare. Conversely, there are a number of people with superior communication skills—in particular, the ability to convert complex concepts into easy-to-understand narratives and powerful and intuitive metaphors. Bringing together these two types of individuals can lead to extraordinary results that only grow better with time, as the individual serving as the scribe/speechwriter/ghostwriter learns his or her subject's voice and thought processes. At the highest levels (Peter Robinson writing Ronald Reagan's Berlin Wall speech) this kind of partnership can change the world. But even at a lesser degree, it can still have a valuable effect at the corporate, divisional, or even departmental level of an organization.

That said, Yin and Yang teams are naturally volatile; a chimera of two very different species of human personalities that will always be fundamentally incompatible at some level. The extended failure of such a pairing will almost always lead to a breakup and mutual recriminations. But success can also lead to an early split, as each party, not fully appreciating the value or the contribution of the other, comes to believe that he or she is the real source of success, is insufficiently credited for that achievement, and can be even more successful on his or her own. This is the story of an endless number of musical duos or lead singers in larger groups, songwriting teams, and comic teams (Martin and Lewis). It also takes place in creative teams (Walt Disney and Ub Iwerks), and most of all, in business partnerships.

Unfortunately, the cracks in this type of team often start very early—and great success can lead to fissures so huge that they simply can't be mended . . . except for some hollow "reunion" years hence that exhibit little of the power of the original pairing.

A classic form of the Yin and Yang relationship is:

8.1—THE ARTIST AND THE ANGEL: These are "investment" partnerships. The analogy is to the venture capitalist and the entrepreneur. These are pair-teams in which the individual members exhibit very different skill sets, and they enter into the partnership with not only very different interests and needs, but also different—but symbiotic—notions of success.

A classic example of such an "Artist-Angel" pair is the brothers Vincent and Theo van Gogh. As you may know, younger brother Theo financially and emotionally supported the work of his more famous artist brother. Indeed, in Vincent's short lifetime, brother Theo was the only buyer of his works. Theo, himself a successful art dealer and a key figure in the public acceptance of Impressionism, stood by Vincent even as the artist's mind deteriorated, providing him with money, helping check him into hospitals, and being there, without questioning, to the very end. It can certainly be said that without Theo van Gogh, the world would never know Vincent's late masterpieces, some of the most valuable works of art ever created.

Tragically—but also offering a glimpse into the intensity that can characterize these odd couples—Theo lived only six months longer than his brother, dying of a dementia that could have been due to syphilis, but was just as likely, as his death certificate noted, owing to "heredity, chronic disease, overwork, sadness."

Artist-Angel pairs are, not surprisingly, most often found in the creative arts. That's been the case throughout history—think of the many court painters (like Leonardo, Goya, Holbein), papal artists (Raphael, Michelangelo, Bernini), writers (Machiavelli, Milton,

Bacon), and composers (Handel, Mozart, Beethoven) throughout history who have dedicated their work to patrons.

And these relationships don't just characterize an earlier era—in the more recent centuries, the allegiance has merely shifted to other types of wealthy patrons; for example, Rilke with his rich mistresses and the Swiss industrialist patron Werner Reinhart, or, conversely, Peggy Guggenheim with Kandinsky, Duchamp, and Pollock. Artists these days often find their patronage from the government (for example, from the National Endowment for the Arts), or from traditional patrons now filtered through their foundations.

In the modern world, the Artist-Angel pairing has also found other, equally influential, outlets. One is the top corporate executive who develops a close relationship with the company's top creative person. The automotive industry has long been characterized by executive-designer teams, from Lawrence Fisher with Harley Earl at General Motors, to Virgil Exner and Raymond Loewy at Studebaker (Loewy, probably the premier designer of the twentieth century, developed similar relationships with executives at numerous other corporations).

Fashion designers are also noted for their Artist-Angel pairings, typically with a business manager (and sometimes life partner) who, more often than not, remains in the shadows. This has been the case at least as far back as Pierre Wertheimer and Coco Chanel, and it has certainly been the case with the likes of such legends as Yves Saint Laurent, Giorgio Armani, and Christian Dior.

But, for all the success of those pair-teams, arguably the most powerful Artist-Angel pairings in modern life are between angel investors and innovative entrepreneurs. Because angel investors typically work with start-up companies in their earliest days, funding them as they develop products and services in preparation for their first ("series A") injection of big venture capital money, they usually work very closely with their entrepreneur counterparts.

Without angels, most new start-ups would never even make it to the starting line.

Artist-Angel pair-teams represent the ultimate utilitarian relationships, in that the members of the pair have almost no overlap in skills or interests. Because of that, these teams are among the most pragmatic of all teams, and the least subject to the storms of emotion, competitiveness, and jealousy found in some of the other partnership types. Indeed, of all the pair-teams, Artist-Angel partners are the most likely to have found the partners motivated to maximize each other's success, not least because that success is measured differently for each of them.

Such pairings, because the relationship is highly practical and instrumental, typically exhibit equally pragmatic life cycles. The pairs are usually formed to tackle a particular business or creative challenge, and they are dissolved when that challenge is met—no hanging on because of residual emotional ties. That precision usually means that these teams operate only during the period of highest productivity, and thus produce the best possible bottom-line results. The only real danger is if the angel in this pair begins to exploit the artist, Svengali-like. Think of "Colonel" Tom Parker and Elvis Presley, or Don King with his various boxers.

9.0–COUNTERWEIGHTS: These partnerships resemble Yin and Yang pairs, but rather than being about skills, they are instead about character and personality traits. Yin and Yangs need each other on a professional basis; Counterweights need each other also on a personal—and ultimately, often unhealthy—basis.

Even more than Yin and Yangs, Counterweight pairs often crack from the twin wedges of pride and resentment. But to these threats can be added both dependence and disgust. This kind of partnership is often the subject of fiction, as its weird chemistry holds the potential for both great achievements and bitter divorces—even violence.

The various forms that Counterweight pair-teams take are all celebrated, and are thus the subject of endless curiosity and speculation. As with any marriage of opposites, it is constantly asked how these two people ever found each other, whether they have anything at all in common, and what keeps them together. Thus, the shy person with the showman, the coward with the hero, the technical genius with the natural leader, the playboy with the clerk.

Perhaps the most famous example of such a Counterweight partnership in popular culture is that of Captain Kirk with Mr. Spock. But again, these pairs are found everywhere, such as Facebook's young founder, Mark Zuckerberg, and his "adult supervisor," Sheryl Sandberg, or Oracle's chairman, Larry Ellison, and CEO, Safra Catz. Pairs of explorers often show this combination, including Lewis (depressive) and Clark (optimist), and Robert Peary (promoter) and "Arctic Eagle" Paul Siple (quiet competence). Even Orville and Wilbur Wright seem to have exhibited some Counterweight characteristics.

The best Mormon missionary teams, experience has shown, are often Counterweight pairs, their emotional completeness enabling them to cope with the hugely stressful experience of being thrown into an alien environment while still expected to do their job. That fact offers a window into how Counterweight pairs work best: When facing huge, stressful, and sometimes even dangerous challenges—especially one that requires both risk-taking and a cool appraisal of the facts—most individuals lack one or both traits and are quickly overwhelmed. But a pair with supplementary traits has a much better chance of bringing all the requisite perspectives and attitudes to the challenge.

Because Counterweight teams operate at the very heart of the human psyche, they can be incredibly strong—to the point where they can overcome almost any differences in personalities, background, and lifestyle. That's because the experience of being made "complete" by another is so comforting and satisfying—and ultimately successful—that it creates the most powerful positive feedback loop imaginable. The result is a partnership that is so unlikely that it leaves outside observers scratching their heads: the casual player who never takes anything seriously teamed with the uptight grind with no apparent sense of humor; the borderline criminal with the by-the-book straight man; the deeply religious person with the godless rule-breaker; the family man with the rake; the archradical with the archreactionary . . . it doesn't take much searching to find successful examples of each of those types of Counterweight pairs. Think of senators Orrin Hatch and Ted Kennedy or actors Wally Cox and Marlon Brando. The danger is that Counterweight pairs can create a dependency that, at its worst, can lead to devastating breakups or even violence.

It's not surprising, then, that one of the most prominent features of Counterweight duos is their compartmentalization. For even with all the chemistry between the members' personalities, the differences between the two are sometimes so great that they simply choose to overlook those differences—and if that's insufficient, to keep parts of their personal (and rarely, even business) lives from each other. In fact, this is a measure of the power of a "Counterweight" partnership: its members are willing to accept characteristics, attitudes, beliefs, and behaviors of their counterpart that they would never accept in any other human being.

As we'll see, the three early leaders of Intel Corp. created one of the most successful business trios of all time. But before there were three, there were two: Robert Noyce and Gordon Moore, two men of very different personalities and lifestyles, but whose mutual trust and admiration were complete—and their melded personalities built two of the most important companies of the twentieth century, Fairchild and Intel.

One the of most successful, and least celebrated, Counterweight partnerships in Silicon Valley history was that between Paul Baran and Steve Millard. Baran was one of the greatest inventors of the age: his packet-switching technology is generally credited with playing the key role in the invention of the Internet, and his voice/ IP discoveries did the same thing for cellular telephony. But Baran was also, according to some accounts, a difficult man to work with. By comparison, Millard, his partner, was the embodiment of prep-school WASP graciousness and diplomacy—and was often called the most connected man in Silicon Valley. In an earlier life, he had been the VP of a Fortune 500 company responsible for a billion-dollar division.

In the five companies the two men created together, Baran was always the consummate engineer-inventor. But the same could not be said of his interpersonal skills. So, besides locating investors, it was often Millard's job to unruffle employee feathers. Indeed, so much of his time was spent on culture building and personnel challenges that it was often remarked that "Baran did technology and Millard did people." Neither could have built a successful company on his own—or, arguably, without another person of exactly the same, supplementary skill set as his partner. All five companies they founded went public and each had peak market valuations in excess of $1 billion.

Despite their differences, the two men remained a team to the end. On the day of his death, Paul Baran was working on a new company idea in the telemedicine field with Millard.

A more extreme variant of the Counterweight is:

9.1–INSIDE/OUTSIDE: These are "Janus" teams—that is, a close-knit pair that works well together precisely because the two members face in opposite directions—one outward, toward the greater world, and the other inward, toward the operations of teams. You've no doubt seen this type of pairing in daily life in the forms of friendships and marriages. There, they usually take the form of "introvert/extrovert" or "social animal/homebody." Inside/Outside pairs resemble several of the other pairs discussed in this chapter, with the crucial difference that each of the two members is an expert, in skill and temperament, in one of two distinct domains, and rarely enters the other. Indeed, Inside/Outside pairs may interact only rarely, and then just to swap notes.

In the business world, these teams are typically organized around not the relationship itself but the singular demands of different professions. For example, in sales, some of the most potent teams pair a natural salesperson (extroverted, eloquent, affable) with a partner, often a secretary, sales manager, or marketing administrator, who rarely leaves the regional office but knows better than anyone how to package deals, set pricing, and goad manufacturing into making deliveries and giving their team top priority. Similar pairings can be found in other parts of an enterprise, each of them combining some form of outward-looking "face" with another staying back and making the machinery of the system run at peak performance.

You may have noticed that many of the pairs discussed in the previous sections exhibit a lot of Inside/Outside characteristics, especially in the early years of their careers—Larry Ellison and Ray Lane, Walt and Roy Disney, William Durant and Alfred Sloan, Andrew Carnegie and Henry Clay Frick—as well as any number of other pairs we haven't yet mentioned. That's likely because entrepreneurial start-ups, by their very nature, seem to require one figure to run the machinery of the enterprise, including product design and manufacturing, and another to promote that enterprise among potential investors, customers, and employees.

While there are likely a number of different types of these pairings, we have identified three as the most typical and effective:

9.1.1—FINDER AND GRINDER: The term "finder and grinder" comes from law firms (they add a third, the "minder," who runs the business), and it means a division of labor such that one person, the

Outsider, finds new business and handles marking and promotion, while the other, the Insider, grinds away at servicing those new clients, writing briefs, and so forth. You can spot Finder and Grinder pairs in almost every commercial enterprise called an "agency"—in advertising, publishing, public relations, design, marketing, and so on—or "firm," as in law, consulting, accounting, or engineering.

9.1.2–PITCHER AND FIELDER: The Pitcher and Fielder is an even deeper and narrower version of the Finder and Grinder. Whereas the latter typically work in the long term and on a broad scale (that is, the operation of an entire agency or firm), the Pitcher and Fielder are much more specialized and are more often found in large firms or agencies—mostly because small start-ups usually can't afford the luxury of having such specialists. At the heart of this partnership is the deal: the Pitcher sells the potential client or target on the dream, and the Fielder follows up with the details of that dream—or, to maintain the metaphor, the Pitcher delivers the pitch on the deal, the Fielder fields the outline of that deal and turns it into an actual agreement and contract.

9.1.3–EXPLORER AND NAVIGATOR: When you are moving fast through unknown territory, one person has to cut the path and focus on the obstacles and threats ahead, while the other has to follow closely, checking the compass and map and looking for landmarks. If the explorer doesn't do his or her job, the team will quickly get bogged down; if the navigator fails, then the expedition will get lost, or travel in circles, or be unable to arrive home after it reaches its objective. The archetypes for this kind of team can be found among the great explorers: Cook and Bligh, Peary and Henson, Hillary and Norgay, Carson and Frémont.

RELATIONSHIPS DEFINED BY INEQUALITY

10.0—REMEMBER THE FORCE: "Force" pair-teams are mentor partnerships in which the two members are unequal. In a typical case, these teams consist of an older veteran who serves as an adviser and guide to a younger partner. The title of this type of team comes, of course, from *Star Wars* and the relationship between Obi-Wan Kenobi and Luke Skywalker—that is, between an old master and, potentially if he is successful in his teachings, a younger version of himself.

This older-younger version of a "Force" pair is, undoubtedly, the most enduring version of this type of partnership, with roots in monarchal and aristocratic succession—and even more so in the guild system, with its established program of master and apprentice. This type of partnership is likely even older than the teacher-student relationship that is its most common manifestation.

But "master and apprentice" is only one type of Remember the Force pair. And while it may still dominate the trades, another type of mentorship seems to dominate the professional world. In this version, a mentor relationship is created between a veteran male executive and a younger businesswoman in which the older figure guides the younger through the minefield of corporate life.

Interestingly, because of the potential for misinterpretation, these "May to December" mentorships aren't usually talked about. But they are everywhere. One of the authors of this book hosted a nationally syndicated public television interview series (*Betting It All*) in which one season was dedicated solely to top female executives in industries ranging from automobiles to finance to computers. Oblivious to these mentor relationships (they wouldn't become the subject of magazine stories for another couple of years), we were surprised when one subject after another spoke of the crucial role a male mentor had played in her climb up the corporate ladder. By the end of the series, we had learned to ask what we came to call the "mentor question" early in each interview, confident that we would get a positive response.

Needless to say, older man–younger woman relationships carry with them a unique set of dangers, not least the biased or jealous perception by others regarding what the young protégée is doing to get to the top. But the reality is that few of these relationships end in romance. Rather, most seem to be the product of a very different, but equally organic drive: that between a father and daughter. This might suggest that this type of mentor relationship could become rarer as the number of women in senior executive positions increases. But that presumes that these relationships are strictly based on efficiency, when in fact their sources may be deeper.

Another celebrated version of the Force relationship is that of a veteran athlete, now approaching the end of a career or having moved on into coaching, who takes a young athlete under his or her wing and conveys to the newcomer a body of acquired wisdom and experience. Yogi Berra appears to have played such a role over decades with the New York Yankees; and before him, Tony Lazzeri is known for having protected the young Joe DiMaggio when he first came up. Another famous mentor is Stan Musial, who mentored Ken Boyer and a young Lou Brock in one generation, and Albert Pujols in the next. In basketball, the most famous such mentor is coach Phil Jackson, a twelve-year pro himself who then brought along the most famous talent of the next generation, Michael Jordan.

Versions of this sports mentorship model can be found in a wide range of professions, from the theater to the military, in which older noncommissioned officers—chief petty officers, master sergeants, gunnery sergeants—apprentice junior officers who are, officially, their rank superiors. Special forces programs, from the British SAS to the US Navy SEALs and the Army's Delta Force, are particularly noted for their mentoring programs between veterans and new recruits as a way to supplement training in real-life scenarios that are hard to duplicate in training.

"Remember the Force" relationships have a number of crucial advantages:

- *They don't have to reinvent the wheel.* That is, while one member may have an extended learning curve, the other doesn't, so the team itself can be productive almost from the instant of its founding. By comparison, a team like a Castor and Pollux pair will likely be young, and will have to go through their apprenticeship together . . . meaning that it may take years for them to reach top performance.
- *They typically have enormous longitudinal strength.* The senior member may have decades of experience and now be approaching the end of his or her career. By passing that wisdom and experience on to a younger partner, that expertise can still be used at peak performance for decades more . . . and assuming that the junior, now senior, member takes on a new junior partner, that high productivity can last a half century or more. In some of the great and venerable guilds of Europe, such as the livery companies of London (that is, the "Worshipful Companies" of apothecaries, gunmakers, spectacle makers, ironmongers, and, most famously, taxi drivers), the mentor-apprentice relationships form a continuous line of descent dating back to before the thirteenth century. This overcomes the biggest weakness of the May to December duos: they are doomed to lose one member early.
- *They smooth out the variability of a single career.* It goes without saying that the temperament, energy, and goals of a middle-aged person with grown kids looking toward retirement are very different from those of a young college grad without a mortgage trying to make his or her mark on the world. Put those two

together, and if it works, you have a team in which those two extremes counterbalance each other, producing a single entity that is mature and ambitious, prudent and adventurous, patient and tireless. That's a tough combination to beat.

• *They create context.* The problem with young people is that, whatever their energy and talent, they almost always lack a body of experience to tell them when a new idea is viable and worth pursuing, or is simply a repetition of past failures and should be abandoned. The result is a tremendous waste of time and money. By comparison, mature workers typically operate with a huge inner encyclopedia of what works and what doesn't—but they lack any real understanding of new and emerging markets and the newest generation of consumers. Put them together, though, and you may be able to build the perfect beast: a team that is at once hip to the marketplace and with a lifetime of experience in what works and what does not.

In the corporate world, the accounting and auditing giant KPMG is especially noted for its mentorship program, which is based at the company's headquarters in Amstelveen, Holland, and engages all the hundreds of interns whom the company hires each year. Some of those interns will stay on for the summer, other will sign up for the company's national training program, and still others will be sent into KPMG's international program. But whatever direction they take, in a commitment made by KPMG that may be unique, almost every one of the company's interns is teamed with a mentor at the very beginning of the internship—and the company enforces a comparable commitment from those mentors to "offer guidance and help answer day-to-day questions."

Why? In KPMG's own words to those interns, "Mentors can inspire you to meet challenges and achieve success. They enable you to see a wider realm of opportunities, and they provide valuable advice to help you excel in your career."

Will all of those mentors and interns form a Remember the Force relationship? Hardly. No doubt there are many cases of interns who rarely contact their mentors, even when they are interning, much less after they leave or even take a job at KPMG. And equally likely, there are many busy KPMG partners and managers who make a pro forma contact with their young charges, stay in touch just enough to meet the company's requirements, and never speak to the intern again. That said, there are more than enough successful such pairings to justify KPMG's commitment to the program—with many more payoffs as those relationships mature through the years.

There is also a secondary benefit to KPMG's mentoring program. As we've seen over and over, teams are almost always more productive than individuals. But teams also take time to create. A young college graduate dropped into a strange office in a different part of the country (or the world) is going to take time to find someone else with whom to pair up, much less with whom to build a larger team . . . time that individual doesn't have in a comparatively short internship. By teaming the youngster with a veteran, KPMG radically shortens the learning curve, placing the intern into a competent (if not yet productive) pair-term on almost the day of his or her arrival. This newbie-veteran duo may not be optimal, but it is certainly better than legions of lost souls wasting much of their internship just trying to fit in.

11.0–THE DISTANT IDOL: These are the ultimate "distance relationships." One of the biggest bestsellers of the 1920s—indeed of the twentieth century—was *The Man Nobody Knows*. Written in 1925 by an advertising executive named Bruce Fairchild Barton, *The Man Nobody Knows* started a whole new genre of what might be called the "business-spiritual" book. Barton essentially retells the New Testament as a book of business strategy and management theory. Needless to say, the hero of the book is Jesus Christ, whom Barton describes as "the Father of modern business" and "the greatest business executive of all time." It was a clever conceit. Jesus emerges in the pages as a tough outdoorsman, a decisive manager, and an inspiring leader who took his start-up team (the twelve apostles) and built the biggest and greatest organization in history.

While some reviewers lampooned its seriousness and over-the-top theme, millions of businesspeople found in the book a new, very silent partner who had left this world nearly 2,000 years before. This wasn't the first example of a mass movement of people, filling a void of meaning and purpose in their lives, who found inspiration—a partnership of sorts—with a great, if long-dead, figure. Almost a century before Barton's, another book—this one a novel, and written by a truly great writer—explored the same theme. In Stendhal's *The Red and the Black* a young village boy rises to the top of French society largely through his obsession with the exiled Napoleon and his desire to emulate the emperor's ambition and ruthlessness.

Distant Idols are true *ghost partnerships*. In that respect, they take the mentor relationship to its ultimate extreme: one partner is long dead (or at least inaccessible) and has never met the living partner in person. Thus, the relationship in this pair-team is entirely one-directional, with the living partner asking, "What would my idol/ mentor do?"—and that idol can only reply from a fixed repertoire of quotes and aphorisms.

Thus, the central dynamic of Distant Idol partnerships is that the living partner embarks on what can be a lifetime of research into that famous figure of the past to assemble the largest possible body of historical records (especially his or her spoken and written words) on that person, learns from that corpus, and then comes to understand the idol to the point that the living partner can imagine—even to the point of extrapolating new words—the advice the idol would give in this imaginary partnership.

To include this type of pair-team in this book may seem bizarre.

After all, how do you manage such a team? How does it grow? How is the advice of someone gone for centuries, or even millennia, directly applicable to business decision-making in the Internet-based world of the twenty-first century?

In fact, these relationships are more common than we know—and are willing to admit. We've already noted that *The Man Nobody Knows* was one of the great bestsellers of the last century; but so too was *Think and Grow Rich*, which invited readers to imagine asking questions at dinner with a famous historical board of directors, called the "mastermind." If that type of book is an anachronism today (though many older readers will remember a television series on the similar theme of a dinner with great historical figures, produced by Steve Allen, that was broadcast in the early 1980s), it doesn't mean that we've outgrown these relationships.

On the contrary, they've just taken different forms. Thus, witness the hugely popular run of business books distilling career and competitive advice from the most historic figures, such as the Chinese politician and philosopher Sun Tzu, the Prussian military strategist Carl von Clausewitz, and most unlikely, the world-conquering tyrant Attila the Hun. That some of these books are partly tongue-in-cheek doesn't diminish the seriousness with which they have been received—untold numbers of business professionals have taken their messages to heart and applied them to their careers.

Another modern manifestation of Distant Idol relationships derives from business-oriented print biographies and movie idealizations. Both derive from the hagiographies—idealized biographical portraits—of great men that first appeared in the Renaissance and continued into the twentieth century until the publication of Lytton Strachey's *Eminent Victorians*, which introduced a trend of skepticism and warts-and-all biography that continues to this day.

Every year, scores of new business histories and biographies of famous figures appear, whose essential task is to place those idols into the context of modern life and to derive lessons from them that can be applied today. We have hardly been immune to this trend: Rich's *Forbes* column regularly lists the lessons of famous figures in industry, politics, and sports. Mike's history of Hewlett-Packard even offered an appendix of "lessons from Bill & Dave." Meanwhile, some of the most popular books of recent years, from Walter Isaacson's *Steve Jobs* to Doris Kearns Goodwin's *Team of Rivals* have been celebrated not just for their content but also for how their lessons can be applied by readers to their own lives. Some subjects—Lincoln, both Roosevelts, Churchill, Washington—have appealed as idols for generations: the number of books about Abraham Lincoln is in the thousands.

One reason these partnerships have proved so popular and enduring is that they escape a lot of the messiness of two living partners' having to work together on a daily basis. The ghost partners never have annoying habits, they don't have bad days, they never betray you, and the chance of a disagreement or a breakup on their part is zero. Moreover, these idols also never surprise, and they never fail—or at least they don't in an unexpected way. You know they've succeeded, that the story has a happy ending (at least in their place in history)—that's why you picked them. Meanwhile, you will never find another partner of this quality. There's a lot to be said about having a partner with the courage of George Washington, the integrity of Abraham Lincoln, and the decisiveness of Elizabeth I, George Patton, or Alfred the Great.

On the other hand, Distant Idols never really grow or adapt to changing conditions. The ghost in the relationship is essentially a two-dimensional figure who cannot correct misinterpretations of his or her views or beliefs by the living partner, who is the sole (biased) interpreter. With a few exceptions, the pool of wisdom available from the idol is both small and limited in scope, meaning that a lot of that wisdom must be shoehorned—often inappropriately— into most situations.

That said, Distant Idol pairs can operate in the confidence that at least one of the members is world-class—unfortunately, it is the long-dead one.

12.0—THE SWORD AND THE SHIELD: This is a "protection" pair. This duo differs from the Got Your Six pair because one member is strong and responsible while the other is weak and vulnerable. It is also different from the Remember the Force relationship because it is usually briefer and there is a lot more at stake—that is, one member of the pair-team has taken on the duty of protecting the other, renegade, member in the face of fundamental, usually bureaucratic, threats.

If you work in the corporate world, or in government, you have likely seen such a pair—or at least heard of one. They are the stuff of institutional myths. In a typical scenario, a particularly talented employee—often in a single-minded pursuit of a new idea—crashes into the corporate culture. The idea is too new, or too radical, or doesn't properly align with the enterprise's current business strategy, or the creative individual just doesn't have enough political strength to carve out a protected position within the bureaucracy. If left to fend for himself, the maverick will quickly attract swarms of organizational antibodies—bookkeepers, middle managers, cost accountants, operations executives—who will summarily expel that perceived threat to the status quo.

Luckily, our renegade has a protector, a corporate knight-errant who chooses to defend that figure from those institutional threats. Sometimes this hero takes on the task for the right reasons and sometimes for the wrong ones, but ultimately the maverick is saved . . . and, with luck, the company is sent on a bright new path.

One of the least known, but most successful, examples in our time of such a Sword and Shield pairing led to the creation of what has been called the greatest invention of the twentieth century: the microprocessor.

The overall story of Intel's invention of the microprocessor is well known. Busicom, a Japanese electronics firm that was rapidly becoming an also-ran in the desktop calculator wars of the late 1960s, decided to take one last pass at market victory by betting everything on a radical redesign of the integrated circuits used in its products. In particular, Busicom wanted to reduce the current standard chip set of several dozen chips to just eight to twelve—and thus enjoy an unequaled advantage in price, complexity, and size. It shopped the project to Intel Corp., one of many US semiconductor companies that had spun out of Fairchild Semiconductor to create the modern Silicon Valley, not just because Intel was known to be a technological leader but because it was run by Robert Noyce, a coinventor of the integrated circuit and a hero to the Japanese electronics industry.

Intel, a young, struggling company at the time, took the contract. Busicom sent over some of its engineers, and a bright young Intel scientist, Ted Hoff, was assigned as team leader. The plan was for the Busicom team to do most of the work while Hoff acted as an adviser and presided over their efforts. Meanwhile, he was expected to devote most of his time to helping Intel overcome a company-threatening collapse in the manufacturing yields of its memory chips.

Hoff did both jobs, but he soon realized that he had a much better idea for how to build the calculator chip set—this time with just a half dozen or fewer chips—based on the architecture of the revolutionary new VAX minicomputer made by Digital Equipment Corporation. So he went to Noyce and asked permission to pursue the idea. Noyce had every reason to refuse his request. Intel's vice president, Andy Grove, was (rightly) demanding that Hoff, now that the Busicom scientists were nearly done, devote his time to saving Intel's memory business. Meanwhile, the calculator business was now in full collapse and Busicom was headed for bankruptcy—meaning it might not even be able to pay for the work done to date.

But Noyce, one of the greatest visionaries and most fearless decision-makers of the digital age, followed his gut. He hid Hoff and the microprocessor in a corner of Intel's labs and told him to pursue the microprocessor idea wherever it took him. Meanwhile, Noyce not only protected Hoff from Grove—and even, for a time, from cofounder Gordon Moore—but also from the rest of the company, the board of directors, and investors. He even allowed Hoff to form a first-rate team that included the Intel employees Stan Mazor and (hired from Busicom) Masatoshi Shima—and even, when Intel was squeezing its budget, to go outside and hire (from Fairchild) the superstar Federico Faggin, the inventor of the silicon gate. When Hoff was pulled away from the project, it was this team, working over the 1969 Christmas holidays, when the rest of the lab was empty, that built the four-chip set Intel 4004, the world's first microprocessor.

Within the next decade, Intel would abandon the memory chip business and devote itself fully to the design and manufacture of the microprocessor—and make itself one of the most valuable and important companies in history, and the linchpin of the electronics age. Hoff, Faggin, Mazor, and Shima have been showered with honors—and will likely one day win the Nobel Prize. But it is Noyce, the charismatic, reckless, and endlessly lucky Silicon Valley legend, who is the secret hero of this story, betting his reputation and even the survival of his company to help another, much less powerful, man realize his dream.

Sword and Shield pairs are some of the most interesting of all teams, not least because the protectors often have little to gain and much to lose by even entering into such a partnership. They must spend considerable hard-earned political or cultural power to come to the aid of a person they likely barely know, on an initiative for which they will gain little credit. Sometimes the knights' motives are noble—they believe in the idea, they want to shake up the organization from its complacency, they have a natural impulse to help the underdog, or they see their younger selves in the maverick. And sometimes they are base—they want to ride the idea to the CEO's office, they want to get the jump on a despised counterpart by stealing his or her best talent, or they are simply bored and want a new challenge. But whatever the motive—and sometimes they are just plain opaque to the outside observer—they are almost always heroic. The knight chooses to intervene and act, rather than stand back and not take the risk.

As for the renegades, the "Sword" in this pair, they are often portrayed as brave but foolhardy (or at least naive)—the Frodo to the protecting "shield" of Aragorn in *The Lord of the Rings*; David Balfour to Alan Breck Stewart in *Kidnapped*; Tom Canty to Miles Hendon in *The Prince and the Pauper* . . . as well as in scores of lesser novels (that most of these are "children's" books only underscores the parallel of these relationships to that of father-son and father-daughter in family life).

In the worlds of business and politics, this characterization is usually not quite accurate. There, the renegade figure is usually either too young to have much power inside an organization or holds a position of some importance—such as a scientist in the company lab, or a senior figure in a government—but has neither access to nor experience with the halls of power. When this type of individual is actually portrayed—for instance, Jimmy Stewart's character in *Mr. Smith Goes to Washington*—the knight figure (Claude Rains) is often portrayed as one who is initially jaded or corrupt, even an exploiter of the newcomer, but who then comes around and takes on enormous, career- or life-threatening risks to save that vulnerable figure.

Ultimately, Sword and Shield pairs are so valuable and effective because they combine antipodal traits almost impossible to find in one person: experience and energy, technical talent and managerial skills, youthful optimism and mature pragmatism. That's why these teams, when they succeed, don't just change the organizations in which they operate but transform them.

That said, their odds of success, almost by definition, are quite low. The crucial question any "knight" in such a pairing should be asking is: *Is this the right hill to die on?* Just because a corporate insurgency is exciting, it doesn't mean it is right. And just because it is compelling, it doesn't mean it will succeed. Even if you succeed, your reputation may be so tattered that you will have to find work elsewhere. And if you fail, the consequences are likely to be much worse—even competitors don't like mutineers. So, before you become too enamored with your little revolt against the status quo, you had better decide if this is the fight you want to make, if this is what you want to drag your younger, more innocent, partner into, and if the organizational dislocations and recriminations to come at your company are worth it.

We've listed twelve different types of pairs, as well as several variants—and truth be told, if we wanted to be even more specific, we could probably double that number. After all, how many functioning, even successful, pairs—especially in marriages—have you encountered that simply left you scratching your head and thinking "What do *they* see in each other?" Needless to say, there are similarly inexplicable pairs in the business and professional worlds as well. When we speak of love, people often say, with a kind of mystical belief, that *there's somebody for everybody in the world*. We are convinced that's true in the public side of life as well.

MAKING PAIRS WORK

Having such a panoply of pair types can seem a bit daunting, especially when you ponder the challenge of picking the correct one for a particular problem. But the reality is that most pairs will continue to come together into the indefinite future. At minimum, the crucial things to remember are:

- All pairs are not alike.
- Don't recruit pairs based solely on compatibility, or by intuition.
- Some of the most successful pairs do not fit our expectations; rather, the members can be very different in terms of age, talent, character, and temperament. Indeed, one team member may not even physically be there.

The great thing about there being so many pair-types is that, like different shapes of building blocks or Legos, they enable the creation of an almost endless number of larger groups.

Obviously, it is not enough to identify and categorize the different types of two-person teams. In reality, the far more important challenge is to apply that new understanding in productive ways. That is, you need to:

1. **Identify the Need:** First of all, and keeping in mind that usually the smaller the team, the better, ask yourself: Is a duo the best team for the job? And what is that job? Is it embedded in the larger enterprise, with specific duties, or will it work on the fringes of the organization and break new ground? If the role of this duo is to be tightly circumscribed, you will undoubtedly want the type of team you can actually create (Remember the Force, Inside/Outside, Artist-Angel, even Sword and Shield), and not those that are almost always the result of spontaneous formation (such as Castor and Pollux). For the former, recruiting can be just a matter of a résumé search. The latter is much more hit-and-miss, and will likely require testing various pairs for their productivity.

2. **Prepare the Candidates:** An often-ignored threat to successful pairings, especially those composed of individuals with different, even opposing, personalities, attitudes, and skills (like Yin and Yang), is that the members may not recognize or respect each other's achievements. They may not even take each other

seriously. It is incumbent then on a manager to orchestrate these introductions in order to nurture mutual respect. This will prove particularly important with larger groups.

3. **Determine the Goal:** In some cases, you know exactly what you want a duo to do: come up with a new feature for an existing product, prospect and close a particular sales target, open a new office, improve service response times, and so forth. In other cases (Lifeboat, etc.) the goal may be to improve the performance of the team members themselves. And in still others, the goals may be more nebulous—for example, "discover a new market into which the company can expand its offerings"—but no less vital. At the heart of managing pairs—and all teams—is to match the character of the team to the task assigned to it; that is, don't bet the company on an unproven pair of opposites, or give an open-ended assignment to a by-the-book pair.

4. **Establish Metrics:** In most enterprises, this is the easiest step. And, indeed, if you have a pair of scientists who work well together and they are pursuing a particular design goal, then establishing performance benchmarks is pretty straightforward. It is a lot more challenging when you are talking about giving a troubled pair an assignment to save their careers, or asking a pair of corporate superstars to work together to get the company into a new market.

5. **Manage with the Right Intensity:** Finding the right manager is often as important as the right team. An Inside/Outside or Yin and Yang team may work best under a tough taskmaster who doesn't worry much about the emotional health of the team. By comparison, the manager of a Got Your Six team may just establish targets and get out of the way. A Castor and Pollux team manager mostly just needs to make sure the duo stays on track. And for a Sword and Shield team, the manager's primary task is to make sure the team is a positive force and not a destructive or anarchistic one.

6. **Stay Observant:** As you've probably noticed, a lot of especially powerful pair-teams are almost impossible to create by decree; instead, they almost always create themselves, often spontaneously. Sometimes, they are the product of circumstance—such as in response to a deteriorating or dangerous situation. Other times, they are the product of ineffable factors (personality types, backgrounds, interests, maybe even pheromones). This is, in fact, the greatest challenge facing team managers, both external (with pairs) and internal (with larger teams). It all but demands that you work backward; that is, you need to be perpetually vigilant, spotting successful teams when they occur—and then placing them into situations that best fit their skills.

7. **Create Opportunities:** Even when dealing with spontaneous teams, there are ways to improve your odds of finding success. One is to bring people together in physical proximity and see what sparks. Interestingly, this is most likely to happen at two extreme moments: when the enterprise is doing very well and has the luxury of experimentation . . . and when it is in deep trouble and is willing to take unprecedented risks to stay alive.

8. **Keep Records:** Too often, teams, including duos, are formed, then succeed or fail at their task, and then split up, leaving little record of their existence. The message of this book is that every team is distinct, a combination of personality types, structural characteristics, and a record of performance. It is time to start keeping track of *all* these variables—and then use them over time to create new teams with ever-greater chances of success.

9. **Manage Transitions:** Finally, as we shall soon discuss, teams (including pairs), have life cycles—they can behave very differently at their start, at the peak of their activity, and as they approach retirement. By the same token, they cannot be managed in the same manner during these different eras of their existence. A manager not sensitive to this may well begin bril-

liantly, only to unexpectedly fail later on. A smart manager will identify these evolutionary steps as they occur and adjust his or her communications, motivations, rewards, and punishments accordingly.

MATCHMAKER, MATCHMAKER

When it comes to the care and feeding of perfect pairs, you should start as a leader by identifying your most talented people, especially those who are described as difficult, unpopular, eccentric, or odd. Look especially for people who are generally considered the smartest or most creative people in the organization—in particular, those who are unable to accomplish what everyone expects of them, or those who are at risk of quitting or of being driven out of the organization.

Now, don't look at the obvious strengths of these individuals, but instead focus on their weaknesses. Compare these weaknesses to see if they can fit together in a way that neutralizes them. If you can't find a suitable match among this select group of individuals, look elsewhere in the organization. Is there someone in that population who makes an emotional match? Remember, don't go into this process with any preconceptions: the best pairs may be quite alike, complete opposites, or somewhere in between. The key is that, on the job if nowhere else, these individuals fill each other's voids.

Next, put these potential pairs in close proximity, as isolated as possible from outside influences—especially peer groups—which may amplify their differences and undermine their synergies. Do *not* demand that the members of this pair fraternize—office parties, off-sites, business trips, and so forth—outside their actual project activities. Rather, assign the pair a task for which they have the requisite skills but are unlikely to accomplish as solo operators.

You are done with the first phase. You should now step back but continuously monitor what happens. If the team proves to be either dysfunctional or, conversely, enjoying itself too much to get any work done, dissolve it. If it proves to be highly productive—and this will be obvious quickly—keep it intact, find more challenging projects for it, and clear a path for it through the company's bureaucracy. A productive Counterweight team can create miracles.

You've now done the hard part: created a successful team where there was none before, and taken two underperforming employees and made them valuable to the organization. Your task now, over the long term, is to find a way to keep these successful pairs in the company, as they are likely to make a major contribution. But don't be surprised if you lose them. For example, Counterweight teams have a high likelihood of spinning off (after all, why do they need you?) to create their own enterprises.

There are other dangers as well. Magic Moment teams, when successful, can be not only the greatest opportunity but also the greatest threat to any enterprise in which they appear. Even expelling them can be a disaster: they may start a new enterprise and crush your company. You will have created a monster—but one that might just make you successful beyond your wildest dreams.

By comparison, Remember the Force teams are comparatively easy to establish if, like KPMG, you formalize the process into your corporate culture.

Treat Lifeboat teams like the British Army did its "forlorn hope"—men who could avoid a court-martial, imprisonment, or execution by leading an assault on a seemingly impregnable enemy position. The idea was that the odds of survival were so low, and the bravery required so great, that a successful assault would outweigh any black marks against a soldier. Give your Lifeboat pair the most impossible task and short time (say, three months) to achieve it. If they succeed, reward them but don't promote them; if they fail, get them out of the organization.

Artist-Angel and Sword and Shield pairs should be managed lightly but ruthlessly. There is too much talent there to waste on failed efforts—so break them up quickly if they fall behind. Inside/Outside pairs often require the most preparation, because of the antithetical nature of their talents. Loyalty to the enterprise can be an effective motivator. Finally, be ruthless with Here and There pairs. Because there is no emotional involvement between the two members, you can break them up and re-form them at the slightest provocation.

With pair-teams, we are looking at enduring and durable human structures, some of which can last a lifetime. We'll now look at *trios*, the most volatile, and least enduring, of such structures, and then beyond to ever-larger team structures.

Trios

THE PLUTONIUM OF TEAMS

Trios, troikas, triplets—we are endlessly enamored and intrigued with teams composed of three members. Dumas's Three Musketeers—Porthos, Athos, and Aramis—and their cry *Tous pour un, un pour tous!* ("All for one and one for all!") remain endlessly entertaining, as shown by the fact that a cinematic version of the story is filmed every few years.

And yet, though few notice, even this archetypical three-person team really comes to life only with the addition of a fourth player, D'Artagnan. Even then, the three swordsmen remain largely a part of the backdrop, their characters pretty much indistinguishable. Only D'Artagnan, the nonmember—or perhaps more accurately, as the end of the novel underscores, the *fourth* member of the trio— seems fully three-dimensional. Perhaps that's why it is he who devises that famous cry of trio brotherhood for the other three.

As the subtitle of this chapter suggests, if pairs are like inert gases—pairing up and becoming profoundly stable—trios are more like radioactive elements: they seem to exist for only a brief time before they break down to their natural state, pairs. It is important to appreciate that fact up front. Make the most of your trios for as long as they exist, but don't depend on them to survive, and don't be caught surprised when they fail.

A HALL OF FAME TRIO

One of the most successful trios of all time is one you may have watched every Sunday for a decade without ever noticing. It also swapped out its key member once without missing a beat. And of those four members of this trio, three are now in a hall of fame—and, if enough people understood his role, the fourth might be there too. Interestingly, the key to this trio's success lay not in the members themselves but in the person who managed them, who designed a way to deploy the trio in a revolutionary, and devastating, way that changed their industry forever.

We're talking about the trio that was the heart of the offense of the San Francisco 49ers during the seasons between 1985 and 1995. The four members were quarterback Joe Montana, who was effectively replaced by Steve Young in 1991, halfback Roger Craig, and wide receiver Jerry Rice. The coach who recruited this trio and designed the revolutionary "West Coast" offense to make the best use of their talents was Bill Walsh, often listed as the best NFL coach of all time.

To understand why this trio was so effective—it won four Super Bowls, put Montana, Young, Rice, and Walsh in the hall, and made the Niners of the era one of the most celebrated sports teams ever—we need to look more closely at Walsh's much-imitated West Coast offense and the roles that each of these players filled. Interestingly, beyond the obvious talents of these players—Montana's legendary cool under fire, Young's athleticism, and Rice's famous hands—the secret to their success lies with the least celebrated of the group and his singular gift for deception.

Consider the classic play by this trio. It unfolds like this: Montana or Young takes the snap, steps back, and turns. Craig runs forward and either takes the handoff and runs for a gap in the offensive line, or fakes the handoff and does the same maneuver or swings around toward either end. If Montana or Young still has the ball in this "quarterback option" (as the two men are, respectively, right- and left-handed, their moves are mirror images), they can either run with the ball (Young's strength) or follow Craig and throw him a lateral pass, or throw downfield to Rice, who by now has escaped coverage and has the best hands in NFL history.

It is a devastating offense that took a generation for other NFL defensive teams to combat. Even though many of the offenses of those teams tried to copy the West Coast offense, none ever did it as effectively as the 49ers.

So why did it work so well? There are two explanations, one simple and the other complex. The complex one is Bill Walsh. As it happens, both of the authors of this book knew Coach Walsh pretty well. Rich regularly interviewed Walsh for a column in *Forbes ASAP* magazine. Mike helped Walsh organize his thoughts for a potential book on coaching. What we both remember most about the late legend was his extraordinary, almost superhuman mental organization. Even as he sat on the floor, wincing from chronic back pain as he pressed his spine against an office wall, he would say things like, "Coaching has four components: logistics, strategy, tactics and contingencies. Logistics has eight components: recruiting . . ." and so forth. He could go for an hour that way, talking his way through a vast, unbelievably detailed outline in his head.

At the heart of Walsh's coaching model was what might be called *controlled randomness*. It may sound like a non sequitur, but what "controlled randomness" means is that Coach Walsh understood that a sport as fast-moving, unpredictable, and violent as pro football cannot be completely controlled. But it can be given a certain structure at multiple levels that can channel events, if not completely control them. Thus, Walsh's tiered coaching model:

1. Logistics: Recruit the best possible team to match your coaching style and the talents of your key players.
2. Strategy: Plan for the entire season based on the qualities of your opponents; organize to peak at the season's end.
3. Tactics: With that strategy, plan for individual games. Build a strong game plan and stick to it.
4. Contingencies: Like a general, you must understand that all plans begin to fall apart the moment the shooting begins. Don't panic, just act decisively when reacting to the new reality.

Note that at each level, Walsh accepts a level of randomness—of the unexpected—that can show up at any moment. Thus, his famous clipboard, on which he pre-scripted the first ten plays in the game. Many people assumed that Walsh did this so that he wouldn't get so excited by the action on the field and—as many coaches do—start calling plays for the moment and thus deviate from the game plan. This was indeed the case, but less noticed was that the actual plays on that script were specifically selected in order to *inject* randomness into his play-calling—to make the Niners unpredictable and keep the opposing team's defense guessing. This randomness can also be seen in the legendary story that, before the 1990 Super Bowl in New Orleans, Walsh met the team as it arrived at the hotel dressed as a bellhop—a little bit of unexpected humor to keep the team loose.

Now, let's go back to that basic West Coast offense play. Here is the apotheosis of Walsh's controlled randomness. If you look closely, the key figure in this complex dance is Roger Craig. Craig was one of the most balanced halfbacks ever: in 1986, he became the first NFL player to both rush and receive for 1,000 yards in a season. This balance, which was at the heart of Walsh's play-calling, was also critical to his offense.

The idea was that, as Craig approached Montana or Young, the odds of his taking or faking the handoff were, thanks to his history, essentially equal. That meant that the defense—the defensive line and the linebackers behind them—couldn't bet on Craig's dominant skills, as they could with other halfbacks and fullbacks in the league (like, say, John Riggins of the Washington Redskins). As a result, they had to hesitate for a split second for Roger Craig to commit (if they didn't, and went ahead and executed, say, a run defense, Coach Walsh would notice and play-call a fake handoff and pass to take advantage of this early commitment).

This is where Roger Craig's real talent came in. Back in 1983, when he was drafted by the Niners (forty-ninth overall that year), Craig was mostly noted for a high-stepping running style that made him hard to tackle and had led him to several records while playing college football for the Nebraska Cornhuskers. What few noticed—besides Walsh—was that Craig had another talent: duplicity. Roger Craig had one of the best handoff fakes in the business.

So, Montana / Young pivots and moves to hand off the ball. Craig deftly tucks with both arms and charges the line. Does he have the ball or not? Another half second passes as the defensive players hesitate to make sure. . . .

It's a fake! The defense shifts to pass protection mode. Montana steps forward into the pocket, or Young swings to his left. Meanwhile, thanks to that fraction of a second of defensive hesitation that Craig has given Jerry Rice, the most famous hands in NFL history have just gained a step on their defender—which is all Rice has ever needed. The throw, soft and spinning clockwise from Montana, sharp and spinning counterclockwise from Young, is snatched from the air by Jerry Rice's huge hands . . . and he is on his way.

Would Rice still be the greatest receiver in NFL history without that half-second advantage Roger Craig gave him? Probably, but he might not hold as many receiving records. Would Rice, Young, and Montana be the football legends they are without Bill Walsh's strategic genius? That's another matter. What we do know is that under the right leadership (Walsh) and the right organization (the West Coast offense) a trio of extraordinary skill was able to work so well together that it reached the pinnacle of achievement in its industry—and, just as remarkably, was able to repeat that achievement even after replacing one of the three members.

Even now, as his ideas have been assimilated in all of football, from the NFL to Pop Warner, Bill Walsh ("the professor") is regularly acclaimed as the most innovative coach in professional football history, and one of the greatest coaches in all sports. But to fully appreciate what he accomplished, you need to look past the Lombardi trophies and the legends, and, with fresh eyes, look at the game films and his offense in action. Beyond the obvious structural novelty of the West Coast offense, something magical is also going on in those plays when the three players were at their peak.

But the fact that we remember great trios—"Tinker to Evers to Chance"—and that most of them seem to show up in sports, should also be a warning. Dreaming of trios and actually making them work in all but the most synthetic situations are two very different things.[1]

SUCCESSFUL TRIOS IN FOUR TYPES

In our experience, trio teams inevitably take one of four forms:

1.0-2+1: This, the most primitive trio, is really, at its core, a pair—to which has been added a third player in a vital but not an intimate partnerlike role.

The greatest strength of this type of trio is, again, that it's not really a trio, but a pair, with a third peripheral person acting as a consultant or a specialist. In some ways this is the best of both worlds. Pairs are structurally much stronger. They are also usually more efficient. But pairs also, by definition, lack the intellectual heft, and the bandwidth, of trios. Adding that third member as a utility player, who can add expertise, time, and energy when necessary, can be a valuable addition. This is particularly true when the two members of the pair bring their common expertise to a task within that expertise, while the third member, the +1, can add a discrete but vital skill when needed.

A particularly useful scenario in a 2+1 team is one in which the two core members share complementary skills and the third brings his or her own specific expertise—for example, software to two hardware experts, marketing or publicity to a designer and manufacturer—to the project. Ideally, the three should work together, but yet another advantage to the 2+1 architecture is that the +1 participant need only be part-time, dipping in when needed. This opens the door to making that third member a world-class expert who may have only limited time to give.

In the history of science, perhaps the single most famous example of this is the invention of the transistor. Walter Brattain and John Bardeen were physicists at Bell Labs who, in the late 1930s, saw a demonstration of how an insulator (silicon, germanium, and so forth) could be "doped"—that is, impregnated—with certain impurities (such as fluorine) to make it a "semiconductor." An electronic current could then be run through this semiconductor and turned on and off by a second, much smaller, electric current passing through it at right angles (a silicon switch or "gate").

Brattain and Bardeen were eager to start experimenting with these new semiconductors—but World War II got in the way. Returning after the war, the two men began looking at ways in which this new technology could be used to create solid-state electronic switches that would be smaller and cooler, and use less electricity—and most of all, be much more durable—than the fragile glass vacuum tubes currently used for the job.

The timing was perfect. Their boss, William Shockley, then head of Bell Labs' Solid State Physics Group, had been assigned the task of developing a solid-state amplifier. Shockley suggested to the two scientists that one possible approach might be to look into semiconductors. And though he continued to be their official overseer, Shockley mostly left Bardeen and Brattain alone—a good thing, as he is often considered, after driving the "Traitorous Eight" to mutiny at his future company and essentially creating the modern Silicon Valley by default, to have been one of the worst bosses of all time. During the course of the development, he also offered solutions to technical problems when the pair encountered them. Bardeen and Brattain approached the famous scientist only when those problems proved intractable, because Shockley was not only a genius but also almost impossible to work with: arrogant, paranoid, and dismissive of lesser mortals.

When they did approach him, Shockley lived up to his billing—unfortunately, in every way. He not only solved their problems, but when the two other scientists finally demonstrated their new "transistor," an angry Shockley accused them of working behind his back. "There's more than enough glory in this for everybody!" Brattain reportedly shouted at him—but that didn't deter Shockley from going to Bell Labs' corporate headquarters and demanding that it file for a patent on the new device, which he described as a "field-effect transistor," solely under Shockley's name for having suggested the original idea.

Only when it was discovered that a basic patent for a field-effect transistor already existed did Bell Labs decide to put all three names on a patent application for a "point-contact transistor," officially invented on December 23, 1947. Declaring the situation "intolerable," Bardeen soon left for the University of Illinois (where he would win a second Nobel Prize, for his work in superconductors). Brattain asked to be transferred to another division at AT&T. While Bardeen and Brattain remained close friends, they had almost no contact with Shockley. The famous photograph of the three of them in the lab, Shockley sitting at a microscope, was a tense session . . . and the last time the three men would be in one room for almost a decade.

Nine years later, Bardeen, Brattain, and Shockley were awarded the Nobel Prize. By then, Shockley had already walked out of Bell Labs (where there were celebrations at his departure) and had gone to California to start his own company—Shockley Transistor—and get rich. He celebrated his Nobel Prize with the same new employees who would walk out on him a few months later.

When they arrived in Sweden for the Nobel ceremony, the two old lab partners hung out together, like the pair-team they had once been (they were a classic "Yin and Yang" pair: Bardeen the theorist who pondered in his office, Brattain the builder who made Bardeen's vision—in this case the famous arrowhead of plastic, holding two gold wires and embedded in a slab of germanium—a reality). Shockley was largely shunned. Nevertheless, after the ceremony, the three men were seen toasting each other with champagne well into the night. They had, after all, changed the world. And their names would live forever.

2.0-PARALLEL TRIOS: Often what we perceive as a trio is, in fact, two pairs sharing a common member, while the other two members rarely interact.

Parallel Trios are the most powerful of the trio architectures. There are several reasons for this. The first is that because the members of the trio don't actually all work together, it is possible to fill the two outside roles with individuals who are the best at what they do without worrying about their compatibility with the other, only their compatibility with the sole inside member.

This architecture also features its own inherent hierarchy: Inside, because he or she is the traffic cop between the two outsiders, is the uncontested leader of the trio. This solves a lot of the stress found in most trios as the members struggle for dominance. Inside sets the rules, acts as the synthesizer, establishes goals and milestones, and settles differences.

A famous parallel trio story we told on page 150 is worth repeating here: the three scientists at Intel who invented the microprocessor in 1970. That project began when a Japanese calculator company, Busicom, approached Intel, then a memory chip company, with a custom order to reduce the number of chips in its new desktop calculator. Busicom was desperate—the calculator business was undergoing a shakeout and also-ran Busicom didn't think it would survive without a real breakthrough.

The man who fielded the Busicom contract was a young scientist named Ted Hoff. He saw in the Japanese company's problem a way to rethink chip architecture along the lines of the hot new minicomputers then being built by the likes of Digital Equipment Corporation. When the Japanese sent over a team to work at Intel under his supervision, Hoff realized that there was another, even better, way to design this chip set. He then went to Intel's cofounder Bob Noyce (himself the coinventor of the integrated circuit) and proposed a second, "skunkworks" project. Noyce, even though he knew that Intel was at that moment at real risk of bankruptcy from the low yield rates on its memory chip production, gave Hoff the green light and hid the project the best he could.

Hoff, in turn, assembled a design team composed of Federico Faggin (the inventor of the silicon gate, recruited from Fairchild), Masatoshi Shima from Busicom, and a software expert and Intel employee, Stan Mazor. It was this trio that went on to create the Intel model 4004, the first microprocessor, as well as the 8008, the true precursor of all modern processors. But at almost no time were the three scientists working as a trio—indeed, like their direct predecessors Shockley, Brattain, and Bardeen, the three were rarely even in the same room.

In reality, the microprocessor was Faggin's project. He organized the team, established the specifications of the finished product, and led the design and production of the four-chip set. Because Faggin's expertise was hardware, he tended to work more with Shima, assigning him specific tasks on the different chips. He also took over all the hardware design work when Shima returned to Japan. Mazor, being a software expert, tended to work more independently: his job was to deliver the operating code to load into the 4004 when the chips were ready.

So, in practice, the Intel microprocessor trio operated as two overlapping pairs, one composed of Faggin and Shima, the other of Faggin and Mazor. This was a distinctly different arrangement than the Bell Labs trio, which was a tight pair that kept the third player at arm's length. One reason for this is that the microprocessor trio was formed that way (rather than created out of desperation); another is that the Intel trio viewed each other more as equals, and Faggin's supervisory role was clear. The National Medal of Technology and Innovation committee saw it the same way forty years later, when it gave the award to Faggin and Mazor, the two Americans, and to Hoff as the visionary. (Sadly, as with the integrated circuit, Noyce had already died.)

3.0-SERIAL TRIOS: Serial trios differ from Parallel Trios in a temporal way. Rather than the one common member dividing his or her time between the two other members, the various members of the trio simply, and sequentially, work briefly with each other in pairs.

Serial Trios are particularly powerful because there is no need for compromise among the players. You don't have to have the Insider of the Parallel Trio, who is required to bring to the party not only his or her own skills, but also a talent for being a traffic cop and diplomat. Rather, as long as the three can work out an arrangement among themselves to constrain the contact between the pairs that don't get along, and to connect and disconnect for as long or short as necessary, all three are free to run at full speed. And that in turn means that you recruit for that team the very best people for the job. As long as they can stay together, they will be damn near unstoppable.

As it turns out, that famous Parallel Trio that created the microprocessor was managed by the even more famous Serial Trio that ran Intel Corporation. Mike has written a book about this trio of Robert Noyce, Gordon Moore, and Andrew Grove. Arguably, this was the most successful business trio of all time, as Intel would at one point at the beginning of the twenty-first century be the most valuable manufacturing company on the planet. And, as the original guardians of Dr. Moore's legendary law, this trio can also be credited with creating the modern digital world.

If you read the official histories of Intel, this trio is always presented as a troika of equals, working harmoniously as a team leading the company to glory at the vanguard of the semiconductor industry. The reality was much more difficult; the interrelationships between the three men were both complicated and sometimes contradictory—just like real human beings, not mythology.

The three men were very different from each other. Bob Noyce was one of life's natural winners: graceful, charismatic, a wild risk-taker who almost always swept the table, a man who seemed to toy with his career as if it were a game. In a just world—and a longer life—he would have won as many as three Nobel Prizes, one of them for the integrated circuit. Gordon Moore was a local Valley boy, the son of a sheriff, with one of the most powerful minds in high tech. Kindly and self-effacing, he would also devise his law of semiconductors—which would prove to be the metronome of modern life. And Andy Grove: ferociously brilliant and just plain ferocious; arguably the greatest business leader of the second half of the twentieth century.

It should be obvious from just looking at their résumés that there was no way these three men were going to link arms in a kumbaya and together run the most innovative company in the most competitive of all industries of the era. This was especially true in the relationship between Noyce, who seemed to take nothing seriously, and his employee Grove, who took everything seriously. In fact, Noyce didn't even take Grove entirely seriously—remember, he green-lighted the microprocessor project behind Grove's back—and Grove was contemptuous of Noyce, whom he considered irresponsible with the company and its employees. Grove almost didn't join Intel in the first place after he learned that Noyce would be involved. Moore, meanwhile, floated above it all as Noyce's partner and friend, and as Grove's mentor and boss.

It was even more complicated than that, because as much as Grove admired Moore, they never socialized; meanwhile, Grove and Noyce and their families did socialize—at least in the early years. As Grove grew older and played on the global scene, he became more like Noyce. And Noyce found himself engaged in the creation of the government-industry initiative Sematech that forced him to buckle down and manage in a way he never had before . . . and the relentless stress may have contributed to his early death at age sixty-two.

Tellingly (and a real challenge for Intel's marketing), for all their fame as the Intel "trinity" who led the company for almost twenty years—and the surviving two members for more than a decade after that—there is really only one photograph of the three men together. And, once you get past the wide ties and long sideburns, even that photograph is symbolic: Noyce and Moore stand together behind a table, while Grove has kicked one leg up onto it, both team insider and outsider.

So, how did these three very different men not only manage one of the fastest-growing companies in business history but also lead Intel to the top of the pile in a trillion-dollar, cutthroat industry that destroyed scores of its competitors?

The answer is that they managed to work together almost continuously, without ever really working together. There was no single inside person to act as centerpiece of the trio, as there would be with a Parallel Trio. Noyce was officially the top executive of the company—but as we've seen, he sometimes would go renegade and set up side projects. He also was notorious—especially in Grove's eyes—for being conflict-averse: he was almost constitutionally unable to fire anyone. Moore wasn't much better, and his interests were far removed from the day-to-day operations of the company; rather, he was (rightly) focused on keeping Intel the technological leader. As for Grove, he was the one member of the trio who was concentrated on the day-to-day operations of the company. But as the junior member of the trio, he was constantly overruled by the other two—most frustratingly by Noyce—and thus devoted much of his time to angling for the independence and responsibility he thought he deserved.

And yet, for all the frictions and resentments, the trio worked—brilliantly. Why? There are three reasons:

- Their talents and seniority nicely lined up with the classic alignment at the top of a company: CEO (Noyce), R&D director (Moore), and COO (Grove).
- Intel grew so fast, and faced such unrelenting technical and competitive challenges, that it was enough to keep the three members of the trio engaged on a full-time basis.
- Intel's long-term success was such that upward mobility was available at the top. Thus, Noyce slowly detached himself from Intel as he became a national industry figure—leaving room for

Grove to move up to running the company and finding his true destiny. Meanwhile, Moore, now an industry legend and company chairman, could continue in his role as Noyce's friend and Grove's mentor.

It is our sense that all successful Serial Trios are like this: complicated, explosive, dynamic, and constantly readjusting their power alignments. They find a way to deal with each other—sometimes by minimizing direct contact; sometimes by using the third member as an intermediary or a cover or filter; sometimes by simply staying away; and sometimes just by gritting their teeth and waiting for better times. They almost always do (or endure) this because:

- Despite their differences, they respect the unique talents of each other.
- The project upon which they are embarked is so interesting, challenging, or rewarding that it dwarfs any interpersonal differences they may have.

Certainly this was true with the Intel trinity. Noyce put up with Grove's maneuvering because he knew that Andy was tough enough to run Intel in a way that he himself could not. The same for Moore, who stood by Andy in good times and bad. As for Andy, feeling unappreciated and slighted—and not a little jealous of the ease and fame of the other two—his reward for being patient and getting along with Noyce was to become the CEO of the world's most important company, receive recognition as a great business leader, and even become *Time* magazine's person of the year.

4.0-INSTRUMENTAL TRIOS: If 2+1 trios are the easiest to construct, and Parallel Trios the most powerful, Instrumental Trios—three people with carefully defined roles working together on a single, equally well-defined task—are the most consistently successful.

When we think of instrumental trios, we naturally gravitate to sports—where the roles are carefully circumscribed and the results are immediate—and particularly to baseball and the three players of the classic double play combination: shortstop, second base, and first base. And from there, of course, we find ourselves with Joe Tinker, Johnny Evers, and Frank Chance of the Chicago Cubs from 1902 to 1912. Thanks to Franklin Pierce Adams's poem "Baseball's Sad Lexicon" in the *New York Evening Mail* . . .

> These are the saddest of possible words:
> "Tinker to Evers to Chance."
> Trio of bear cubs, and fleeter than birds,
> Tinkers and Evers and Chance.
> Ruthlessly pricking our gonfalon bubble,
> Making a Giant hit into a double—
> Words that are heavy with nothing but trouble:
> "Tinker to Evers to Chance."

"Tinker to Evers to Chance" remains part of the American lexicon as a phrase for an easy series of actions by a trio that results in success—in the case of those old Cubs infielders, the double play, "the pitcher's best friend" for its ability to clear the bases and put two outs on the board.

Joe Tinker, Johnny Evers, and Frank Chance may not have been the greatest double play combination of all time—though Andy Coakley, who played with them and went on to coach baseball (and Lou Gehrig) at Columbia University, believed they were—but they were the first to perfect the play, and to have a great promoter in the journalist Adams. They have also enjoyed a fame unmatched by any other great double-play trio, such as the Dodgers' Bill Russell, Davey Lopes, and Steve Garvey in the 1970s, and Luis Aparicio, Nellie Fox, and Ted Kluszewski of the "Go-Go White Sox" of 1959–1960.

For our purposes, what makes Messrs. Tinker, Evers, and

Chance interesting is not just that they made a whole lot of double plays—fifty-four of them between 1906 and 1910—and helped lead the Cubs to four pennants in those years, but their almost machine-like consistency. In an era when lousy field conditions led to end-less numbers of errors, this consistency made them a synecdoche for hall of fame–level play (and indeed, all three did make the hall, together, in 1946). Each of them not only played his own position well but also played the interfaces of their positions to each other as well as they can be played—that is, each not only successfully fielded the ball as well as anyone in the game but they also placed and timed their throws to each other with unequaled accuracy for the era. And, as it was still the dead ball era of Major League Baseball, they got a lot of practice fielding grounders—and a lot of chances to make errors.

But this is only half of the story. What makes the Tinker-to-Evers-to-Chance trio illuminating is that they performed their historic feats of timing and coordination despite the fact that short-stop Tinker and second baseman Evers basically *hated* each other. In fact, in September 1905 a fistfight broke out between the two of them on the field—and it is believed that they didn't speak to each other again until a radio show in 1938—thirty-three years later. In other words, for fully half of the time the trio played together as baseball's most celebrated well-oiled defensive machine, two of the players didn't even communicate with each other. Yet they still de-fined the art of turning the play at second and firing the ball off to first ninety feet away to beat the running batter there.

This is the essence of the Instrumental Trio—three individuals who do their job, largely independently and at the top of their craft . . . and then combine those labors into a larger production along predetermined lines. When everything goes well, the re-sults are greater than the sum of the three parts.

One of the reasons why we associate these Instrumental Teams with sports is that such teams are the most visible and have the most celebrated successes in that area. The Montana/Young-Craig-Rice trio with which we began this chapter is yet another famous example. Unlike with comparable trios in other fields of endeavor, we can watch the entire functionality of a sports trio unfold over a matter of seconds—and immediately know whether it has been successful or not.

Sports trios also give us a good understanding of the architecture of Instrumental Trios, as it is basically the same whether found in a research laboratory, a code-writing department, a new product development group, or, most of all, in the trades. We've already looked at the 2+1 trio; by comparison, an Instrumental Trio might be called a 3+1, in which the +1 is not another team member or leader, but the rules of the game, project, or corporate function. It is these rules that act as both the disciplining agent for the interactions and as the setter of the boundary conditions for the operation itself.

In essence, in this tightly circumscribed world (infield defense, line of scrimmage offense, application code writing, scientific experimentation, consumer testing, product assembly and testing, service and repair, construction, roofing, and so on), the overall goal is established, the common rules are in place. Now the actual process itself can be divided into three parts and handed out to the specialists of a trio in each area, who are free to use their skills and craft to achieve the best possible outcome.

As with Serial Trios, the greatest advantage of Instrumental Trios is that you don't have to compromise on the players—because all of them are basically independent operators, it is possible to simply go out and get the best talent at each job. Moreover, because there is little need to help them improve at their own jobs, the members of the trio can devote more time to perfecting their interfaces—a process that is, in turn, helped by the fact that the role of this trio is itself severely circumscribed by the overall rules. Get the ball to second base, conduct the spectral analysis, make the handoff, get the shingles up to the roof, acquire the target . . . and it doesn't really matter if you don't get along with the other two members of the team, as long as each of you gets your part of the job done.

Because of this, Instrumental Trios can reach a higher level of performance than any other trio type—indeed, because their goals are usually so carefully defined, these trios can sometimes reach a level of perfection almost unimaginable for any other trio type. Just watch an Olympic-level relay team.

Another advantage of Instrumental Trios is that they are less dependent on their individual members. With the rules carefully defined and the members independent parties, it is relatively easy to replace one or more of them almost seamlessly. The new trio might not be quite as good as the earlier one, or it might be even better—but it can certainly still go on with a new set of members. That's what happened to baseball's most famous double play combination. After a decade together, Chance was hospitalized with a brain injury he received on the field, and in short order Evers was named player-manager of the Cubs . . . which so infuriated Tinker that he asked to be traded to the Cincinnati Reds.

That was the end, except in the lexicon, of Tinker to Evers to Chance. Nevertheless, the Chicago Cubs still fielded an infield in 1913, including Tinker's replacement, Evers, and, eventually, Chance. And they still turned a lot of double plays—just not as famously. Seventy years later, the Cubs would field another double play combination that was likely as good as their legendary predecessor and featuring a better player than any of the originals, Ryne Sandberg. It was the same game, with the same rules, just new names.

THE FINE ART OF TRIO MANAGEMENT

Creating and managing trios can actually be easier than doing the same thing for pairs. That's because trios can exhibit an internal structure and a level of self-management not typically possible with pairs. They can also usually be created simply by taking a successful pair and adding a third player, compatible or not, who brings the requisite skills.

2+1 trios almost never fail because of internal flaws. If Brattain and Bardeen could do it with Bill Shockley, then your pair can deal with anyone you throw at them. Rather, the surefire way to wreck a good 2+1 team is to make the mistake of assuming they are a true trio, treat them that way, reward them as equals, and, worst of all, force them to stay together. Interestingly, this type of team also has trouble dealing with success, because credit is difficult to distribute.

With the Parallel Trio, whoever takes the inside role has to be highly accomplished. He or she must not only make a major contribution to the project—a trio is too small to have a separate leader-manager—but also alternate between consulting and helping the two outside team members. So, by necessity, Parallel Trios, if they are going to work at all, typically include at least one top-notch player—and you have to focus on finding that person. Add to this the opportunity to add two more top-quality outside members without having to worry about their compatibility . . . and the result is a trio that can be like no other.

Remember in chapter 2 how researchers found that trio formats are exceptionally comforting to their members because the members feel as though they have both a valuable role to play and that their voices are being heard? We believe that these Parallel Trios are the groups researchers are talking about.

As for managing Parallel Trios, set goals and performance milestones—and then get out of the way. Manage loosely, and communicate only to the team leader: you want to reinforce that individual's authority. At the same time, when you communicate with that leader, speak of the team as a single unit, not as the leader's venture. When the team leader does update you, ask for a precise description of the two other members' work to date. That'll be your way of determining how well the leader is keeping tabs on the two outsiders.

When the project is completed, you may reward the team leader more, but recognition and honors should be shared equally. That fact should be established from the first to forestall any infighting.

Serial Trios can be treated like Parallel Trios, just extended in time. The biggest mistake that managers make with Serial Trios is to forget to credit that first, departed pair member and instead honor only the final pair.

Instrumental Trios are more recruited than created. The structure of the work is usually already defined, so the challenge is less about finding the right chemistry and more about filling the slot with the best talent available. There can be some challenges here, especially when the performance of one member is clearly inferior to that of the other two: like a precisely tuned mechanism, such a trio can quickly go out of balance if one part carries a different weight. Look at how the grunge band Nirvana quickly found its sound when the old drummer was kicked out and replaced by Dave Grohl.

This raises an interesting question: Is it better to have one or two top-performing members, and the rest lesser players in an Instrumental Trio? Or are you best served by a trio composed of three equally balanced players—even if they are not as high-performing? In sports, the answer is probably the former, but for different reasons: in baseball, for example, the three players have other ways to contribute—such as hitting—that may compensate for weak fielding. In the commercial world, however, an unbalanced team can quickly tear itself apart—so you might be better served by saving the superior talent, if possible, for a different team (say, a pair, or a Parallel Trio, or as the leader of a larger team) and hiring a new third player whose talents are commensurate with those of the other two.

As for managing an Instrumental Trio, you have three basic challenges:

- Keep the trio working at the highest level of productivity and coordination.
- Make sure the trio is never short of the resources it needs to get the job done.
- At completion, assure that all three participants are given full—and just as important—equal credit for the success.

In sports and in most trades, the single most important thing an Instrumental Trio can do is to practice, practice, practice. The team members must continue to perfect their own unique skills, while at the same time working on those interfaces. In business that means training, case studies, quotas, and even competitions. In sports, it means practicing the full array of likely plays over and over, perhaps a thousand times, in spring training, during practices, and in warm-ups before games. As manager, your task is to not only provide the occasions, venues, and equipment for those practices or training sessions, but to also make the team members attend and participate.

Additionally, Instrumental Trios need to be durable. What changes is the composition of these trios. And because they are often made of highly talented and thus highly desirable individuals, you can never be sure how long you'll be able to keep any of the three you've got. They may stay together, like Tinker, Evers, and Chance, for a decade . . . or a headhunter or scout may hire one away tomorrow. That's the bad news. The good news is that you can usually insert a replacement for that lost player pretty easily, and the learning curve to get that new talent up to speed is equally brief.

Finally, track the performance of each trio member—past, present, and future. When the project is completed (or, in sports especially, when an era ends) be gracious and give credit to each member of the trio. After all, these are basically hired guns, and you may want to hire them again.

And that is trios, the most explosive, unstable, and, in many ways, the most interesting, of team architectures. As volatile as they are, when they do collapse they usually revert to pairs, which are the most stable of team forms. And that safe fallback position makes the risk of trios even more worth the attempt.

Next we will look at larger team types, from those with a half dozen members to those with more than a thousand. But ultimately, all of these larger teams can be reduced to pairs and trios—just as nearly all geometric forms can be reduced to squares and triangles. In fact, in these larger arrays, trios can sometimes be made much more stable by surrounding them with other trios and pairs. Thus, all larger teams are basically built from the building blocks we have just described; only the size of the structure varies.

That said, there is one crucial difference between pairs and trios and the larger teams to come: to those building blocks is added the mortar of internal leadership.

Four and More

THE WILD BUNCH

Thanks to marriage and business partnerships, pairings are extremely common in daily life. Trios, because they are so volatile, are much rarer. But so are teams of four, and perhaps for just the opposite reason: because they are so stable. Most of the successful small teams we encounter, however, range in size from five to nine members—what we call 7±2 teams. These 7±2 teams show up almost everywhere: corporate boards of directors, partners in venture capital firms, small law and medical partnerships, sports (baseball, basketball, volleyball, rowing, team handball, water polo, Ultimate Frisbee), the number of key players in romantic comedies and sitcoms (think *Friends*, *Cheers*, *Designing Women*, *The Mary Tyler Moore Show*, *Newhart*—the list is almost endless), rock bands (the Rolling Stones, the Beach Boys, the Temptations), entrepreneurial start-up teams, the Joint Chiefs of Staff, and the United States Supreme Court. Walt Disney's founding animation team was known as the Nine Old Men. Look closely at any modern institution, and somewhere at its center, usually playing a defining role, you will almost always find a 7±2 team.

Sometimes they are there even when, on first glance, they appear not to be. For example, the most famous small team of modern times is equally famous for having four members. Yet, at almost any phase in its brief history, this team actually had anywhere from five to six members—and thus fit perfectly into the archetype of the midsize team.

The Beatles—the Fab Four—will always be John, Paul, George, and Ringo. This is the band that appears in *A Hard Day's Night* and played on the field at Shea Stadium. And it is the band that entered with the first cohort into the Rock and Roll Hall of Fame. It is this lineup that is likely to be as immortal as any team in our time.

But the closer you look at the Beatles' story, the more complicated the story of this team becomes. For example, during the band's formative years, in Hamburg and Liverpool, the Beatles were mostly a *five*-member band, including the group's original leader, Stu Sutcliffe, and Pete Best instead of Ringo Starr on drums. The same is true in the band's later years, when it turned to Eric Clapton for guitar on one track of *The White Album*, and to Billy Preston (the so-called fifth Beatle) for keyboards for the final albums.

But even during the band's most celebrated period, from *Meet the Beatles!* through *Sgt. Pepper's*, the Fab Four lived up to that title only in performance. Until his early death, the Beatles' manager, Brian Epstein, not only played a crucial role in getting the band its recording contract but he even devised the band's signature look. Even more important, and a fact the band itself verified, was the real "fifth Beatle," the producer George Martin. From the tinkling harpsichord-like notes on "In My Life" to the orchestral cyclone that ends "A Day in the Life," Martin somehow made real any outrageous musical sound the band devised. Without Brian Epstein, the world would likely have never heard of the Beatles; without

George Martin at the controls at Abbey Road Studios, it is hard to imagine how the band, for all its talent, could have progressed much beyond *Beatles for Sale*.

Examples like this suggest that, as with pairs, there is something deeply human, even genetic, about gathering in "small midsize" teams of between five and nine members. As we will see later in this chapter, this "natural" human clustering also describes "large midsize" teams of between twelve and eighteen members.

THE SWEET SPOT OF FUNCTIONALITY

Midsize teams can be characterized in a number of ways. We see them as groups that feature:

- No more than two levels of leadership.
- The members knowing each other on a personal basis.

But there are other characterizations as well. If you remember, Robin Dunbar describes these two groups as follows:

- *Five* members: the number of your most intimate friends and partners ("cliques"). Not coincidentally, five is also the number that corresponds to the limits of human short-term memory.
- *Fifteen* is the number of people with whom we can have deep trust in the face of almost any turn of events. Dunbar calls these "sympathy groups."

The noted team scholar Dr. Meredith Belbin identifies small teams as being four to six members—the "sweet spot" of functionality along a continuum of "cultural messages" delivered by teams numbering from four to ten members.[1] Thus:

- Four: "We're well-balanced in our team and good at achieving agreement."
- Five: "One of us tends to be the odd one out."
- Six: "It takes longer to reach agreement, but we get there in the end."
- Seven: "Rather too many random contributions float about."
- Eight: "People speak freely, but no one listens."
- Nine: "We could do with someone taking control."
- Ten: "We now have a leader, but their ideas are the only ones with a chance of acceptance."

You'll also remember, from chapter 2, that Cyril Parkinson, the inventor of the law about the growth of bureaucracies, believed that a team of eight members can never reach a consensus decision.

On the other hand, we also know from our own lives that there are a lot of highly functional eight-person teams, from Boy Scout patrols to Little League teams (minus the pitcher) to army squads. In almost all instances, teams of this size require a strong leader.

In other words, while pairs and trios may be precise in their composition of members, beyond that—as we shall see—our description of teams gets increasingly imprecise. Thus, at the entry level of the midsize team, at the moment when the "team" also becomes a "group" and adds an internal leader, the most accurate we can be in our description of it is as a team of 7 ± 2 members. At the next level, at what we might call (using military terminology) the *squad* or *crew* level, or Dunbar's trust/sympathy level, we are slightly more precise, at 15 ± 3.

Beyond this, at the level of large groups, this variation grows larger in absolute numbers, but settles down at between 10 to 20 percent. Thus, the 4,500-person *division* may feature a swing in actual population of 500 members or more. However, while we will make this variation explicit for small groups, for which the swing is obvious, we will leave that variation unsaid with big teams.

Now let's take a closer look at those two categories, 7±2 and 15±3, of midsize teams. They are of particular importance, because between them they encompass most of the world's operational teams.

7±2 TEAMS

When you think of the word "team," you probably see in your mind's eye a tightly knit group of five to nine individuals. Though this visualization may have some origins in biology, it probably has more to do with the fact that almost every team you've ever seen on television or in the movies, or read about in a book, or joined in an online game, likely has five to nine members.

Another reason for this visualization is that old matter of human short-term memory. Just as we can typically remember only five to nine digits at a time, so too can we keep at once in our frame of interest only about that same number of characters. Think of Snow White's seven dwarfs—of which, as shown by thousands of bar bets, most of us know only six. Or, quick: name more than seven of the Dirty Dozen—yeah, we thought so. *Lord of the Rings?* Four hobbits, one human, one dwarf, one elf. Akira Kurosawa understood this with *The Seven Samurai*, Lina Wertmüller with *Seven Beauties*, and Steven Vincent Benét in the story that became *Seven Brides for Seven Brothers*. And, of course, there's Harry Potter and his four friends (plus the twins) at Hogwarts. Unconsciously or not, novelists and screenwriters understand this, and so they keep the number of major characters in any story down to about a half dozen. If in the course of the narrative they add one character, they compensate by losing one, or putting one in the background. As a result, whenever we encounter a small team of people in a book or onscreen, that team almost always exhibits the familiar 7±2 composition, which further reinforces that size of team in our consciousness.

But this still doesn't fully explain why teams of this size *work* so well. If they didn't, human beings would have long ago found an alternative and superior team size. And yet we still return to this one, so there must be some functional reason why we do.

There are several possible reasons—and the real answer probably lies in some combination of them all.

- **Magic Numbers:** The numbers six and seven have some interesting attributes. Six, for example, has a singular relationship with all the numbers beneath it. Thus it can encompass two trios, or three pairs—or, with a separate internal leader, a pair/trio team or even a five-member team (which still fits in the 7±2 format). That's a lot of flexibility for a small group, and it seems to make the six-member team uniquely adaptable for its size. Meanwhile, the number seven has endless historical resonances connected with good luck. That connection to success came from somewhere, and it wasn't the stars. If human beings hadn't found some advantage to organizing by seven, they would have abandoned it long ago. Instead, they embraced it. Tellingly, the Egyptian pharaohs reserved the number seven to themselves (the average citizen wasn't even allowed to use the number) and organized everything around it.

- **Functionality:** Groups of five to nine, and especially the larger numbers in that set, are basically the smallest teams in which you can have a dedicated internal leader as well as a distribution of tasks with more than one member assigned to each subgroup. In other words, a 7±2 team is the first team that you can actually divide up into robust groups and assign them to work on multiple tasks, in parallel, while still having someone in charge to coordinate their activities.

- **Communications:** Moving up through team size, the 7±2 team basically represents the last time that a team can fulfill Jeff Bezos's "two pizza" rule: the last time that all the members of the team can sit around a single table for a meeting, and the last time that they can all know each other both personally and on a daily basis.

- **Span of Control:** Remember, at seven team members, the number of points of contact among those members has already jumped to twenty-one. By nine members, it reaches thirty-six—and it starts to go vertical from there. As anyone knows who has run such a team, after about nine people in a room it is hard to personally address each member over the course of a meeting. The same is true sitting in a classroom and crouched on a battlefield—which is why the military and leadership training programs are obsessed with the concept of span of control: How many people/subordinates can you not just motivate but actually command in detail? Brig. Gen. Theodore Roosevelt Jr. likely saved the Normandy invasion when, under fire on Utah Beach, he gathered together his commanders, showed them that they'd been landed a mile from their target beach, and announced, "We'll start the war from here!" That decision, expressed directly to probably no more than six battalion commanders, resulted in a coordinated assault that got the US Fourth Infantry Division off the beach with a minimum of casualties.

- **Diversity:** It has become something of a cliché in movies, especially war movies, that whenever you have a team of individuals, it's going to be populated by a carefully selected mixed bag of members—the country boy, the wisecracking kid from Brooklyn, the Southerner, the Hispanic kid from the Southwest, the college intellectual, and so forth. But this predictable feature is also a ham-fisted tribute to reality—which is that 7±2 teams are the smallest teams that can actually show real diversity among their members, and thus can exhibit the advantages that come with the presence of different personalities and talents.

- **Entrepreneurship:** The 7±2 team is synonymous with that most important phenomenon of the modern economy: the entrepreneurial start-up. We often think of the founding teams of great tech companies as being composed of two or three people. And while that may be true for the first few weeks, when the *idea* of the company is first being formulated and the very first "angel" money is being raised, in real life (and we speak from the experience of having been involved in a number of start-ups, including eBay) start-ups do not become actual businesses until they have created an actual start-up team, of five to nine people, and, optimally, six or seven. Only then can one subteam pursue fund-raising, while the others undertake product design and development. This was true not only for Apple, Microsoft, Google, Facebook, and Twitter, but also for some famous intrapreneurial teams, such as the one that created the Macintosh. This is the group that also typically gets the start-up to series A venture investment, and thus to the beginnings of a "real" company. As such, this group (along with the major investors) is considered the "founders."

For these reasons, 7±2 teams are the most flexible, the quickest, and the most cohesive of all internally managed teams. They also have a sufficient number of members to exhibit real diversity, a productive division of labor, and effective mass. As such, this organizational scheme is almost infinitely flexible and can serve as a stand-alone operation (as in start-up teams), as a key component of a larger team (such as a platoon, department, or office), or, by the dozens, as the basic building block of very large organizations. These 7±2 teams can also be assembled and retired quickly and, because they feature only a single layer of management, they are simple to combine into larger organizations.

This doesn't mean that 7±2 teams are entirely ideal. Being small, fast, and flexible is a great advantage, but in the wrong situation it can also be a serious handicap. That is, when the crunch comes, a team with only a half dozen members doesn't have much throw weight—and if you decide to beef up the membership at the eleventh hour, who will have time to train these new members? You? You'll be the busiest person of all.

And how many will you add? Any more than three or four will push your team into the no-man's-land of ten or eleven members, a size that is almost impossible for one person to manage. So that means you add either one or two people (which probably won't be enough) or five or six, including another manager subordinate to you.

But that is a quibble. Because entrepreneurial start-ups are now the driving force of the modern global economy—and not least because these founders are so hugely rewarded in the most successful of these start-ups (they provide much of the ranks of new billionaires)—the survival of the 7±2 team is anything but at risk in the modern world. Indeed, we can expect their numbers only to grow.

Organizing and Managing 7±2 Teams

Managing a 7±2 team usually means that you are a member of that team. And while in theory that shouldn't make a difference, in real life it always does. And so, while you are still trying to assemble the best possible team, in the back of your mind is the lingering thought that whomever you pick you will have to work with closely on a daily basis for the duration of the project.

So if you aren't careful, subjectivity can sneak into what should be a hard-nosed, objective decision. For instance, you may not pick someone who is right for the team but whom you don't particularly like—something that wouldn't happen if you were an external manager. There goes diversity—and you'll end up with a team that has a great time, agrees on just about everything, and enjoys the experience right up until the moment the project craters. It wouldn't hurt to bring in an experienced manager to do a reality check of your work to protect yourself from that error.

You are also the keeper of the team's milestones. You may get some assistance from others (do everything you can to get an assistant or a secretary, as it will make your job, which can be particularly onerous as the sole manager, much easier), but ultimately every milestone and celebration, from meeting an interim development target to team members' birthdays, is your responsibility. Keep careful records and never screw up—in teams this small, *everything* is personal.

15±3 TEAMS

You have probably heard one of two 15±3 teams every day of your life. And the fact that, unless you are a hard-core fan of popular music, you know almost nothing about them is telling: both teams were created purely for effectiveness and not for fame, and they both reached the same magic number in size—the "large midsize team"—only because that grouping worked best for the task at hand.

One of these teams, based at Motown studios in Detroit, was ultimately nicknamed the Funk Brothers. Other than those of the bassist, James Jamerson, and the bandleader, Joe Hunter, it's unlikely that you know any of their names—even if you saw *Standing in the Shadows of Motown*, the 2002 documentary on them. And yet, as Motown's studio musicians from 1959 to 1972, the Funk Brothers, in the words of the documentary, likely "played on more number one hits than the Beatles, Elvis Presley, the Rolling Stones, and the Beach Boys combined." Indeed, every Motown hit during that era, from Smokey Robinson and the Miracles, to the Supremes, the Temptations, and Marvin Gaye, featured the Funk Brothers—who at any given time in the studio numbered about thirteen members.

Meanwhile, at the other end of the country, in Los Angeles, another collection of studio musicians—of almost exactly the same size—was being labeled with the moniker the Wrecking Crew. The crew may not have had quite as many number one hits as the Funk Brothers did, but many of its members went on to much greater fame: Glen Campbell, Dr. John, Leon Russell, bassist Carol Kaye, Sonny Bono, and Frank Sinatra's drummer, Hal Blaine. If the Funk Brothers get credit for "I Heard It through the Grapevine" and *What's Going On*, the Wrecking Crew owns "Good Vibrations" and *Pet Sounds*.

Why don't pop music fans know more about the Funk Brothers and the Wrecking Crew? One reason is that part of their job description was to stay behind the scenes—it was the Four Tops or the original Byrds who went on tour and onstage, not these folks (though sometimes they were in the music pit). But another reason was their sheer numbers; the roll of names is beyond the memories of casual fans.

The same is true of modern progressive rock assemblages like the Polyphonic Spree or Arcade Fire—can you name more than one or two of their members? How about Parliament/Funkadelic: you can probably name George Clinton and bassist Bootsy Collins, and maybe guitarist Eddie Hazel ("Maggot Brain"). And yet all of these groups, allowed to seek their natural size without outside influence, either began with or quickly reached twelve to eighteen members.

Needless to say, music isn't the only place where the 15±3 team is regularly seen. One place where its appearance may have had an even greater long-term impact than on popular music is in the invention of new technologies: Microsoft's founding team and the Apple Macintosh team consisted of twelve and thirteen members, respectively.

Thus even in the furthest corners of popular music and digital technology, natural group sizes still assert themselves.

15±3 Teams—The Organization

15±3 teams are the smallest teams that can actually divide their labor and still have dedicated management for each resulting sub-team. This formulation offers some real advantages; in particular, it means that those subteams can truly operate independently and not have to wait on a single manager racing back and forth among those teams making command decisions. And, of course, the presence of a dedicated manager/leader makes a considerable difference—now you don't just have a fellow team member occasionally stepping back from his or her own work to make, usually under time pressure and with limited knowledge, critical command decisions.

The first teams with real *heft* are 15±3 teams. A full-size 15±3 team, with eighteen members, is more than three times the size of the smallest 7±2 team. That's a lot of firepower to throw at any task—especially when the team has a dedicated management structure that can keep the team continuously on task, and is trained to both bring out the best in each team member and maintain high morale. There's a reason that the platoon is the essential fighting unit.

The 15±3 team features both a true division of labor and a hierarchy of management. As such, it is the first true *organization team.* In particular, it exhibits several characteristics not found in the smaller teams, including:

- **Hierarchal Management:** With the 15±3 team we see for the first time a second layer of management, a kind of proto–executive office that is distinct from the rest of the team. This also means that, for the first time, there is a distinct chain of command, in which a leader is obliged to work through subordinates rather than dealing with the entire team's membership. In fact, because of the limitation of the human span of control, it would be extremely difficult for the team leader to deal with the entire team at one time, beyond a speech or other form of mass messaging.

- **Professional Leadership:** Up to this point, team leaders are also typically active team members. That's why in the military, 7±2 leadership is given to noncommissioned officers—that is, sergeants—who are expected to join in the work, including combat, if necessary. Command of military 15±3 team–type units—*platoons*—is typically given to an officer, usually a second lieutenant or a warrant officer, who has been trained specifically for the task of leadership. (Military platoons are typically larger than commercial 15±3 teams because they add a third 7±2 squad and have a larger command team, including senior sergeants and a weapons team—none of which is, needless to say, usually necessary in the business world.) By the same token, business 15±3 teams are typically led by a professional manager (at this level the equivalent of a second lieutenant: a young MBA) whose job description all but keeps him or her from participating in the actual work of the team. Rather, that person's task, perhaps with the aid of an assistant, is to manage the team—or more precisely, the subteam leaders—full-time, continuously monitor the health and performance of the team, and act as the communications node to the rest of the organization.

In the corporate world, 15±3 teams typically take the form of a sales office, business department, manufacturing line section, or, way up the org chart, the CEO's executive team (C-level executives and group leaders). In R&D, the 15±3 team is usually found in applications, where an original invention is spun out to a full working prototype that can be passed on to manufacturing.

In the world of entrepreneurs, a 15±3 team is usually the size of a start-up as it completes its series A round of venture capital, that is, its first injection of professional capital at the point that it has a demonstrable product.

In an elementary school, a 15±3 team is the teaching staff of fourteen teachers (K–6, two classes each) plus the principal and the vice principal. In a department store, it is an individual department's sales staff plus the department head. And the list goes on and on. Next time you get your car repaired or washed, look around. Same with your dry cleaner, or your local coffee shop (all shifts). Anywhere you have a small-business operation, usually dedicated to a single, vertical task, and led by an owner or a full-time manager, you are likely to have a variant of a 15±3 team.

It can truly be said that small-business America (and most of the rest of the world) runs on 15±3 teams. Once again, these teams come in several forms:

- **Monolithic Teams:** Monolithic teams are the rarest 15±3 teams, and for good reason. Essentially, these are teams in which everyone reports directly to the boss. Since this number of people is well out of the effective span of control of most leaders, these teams typically have a hidden structure that divides up the leadership—such as the owner's spouse who manages personnel and bookkeeping, the veteran employee who serves as the de facto platoon sergeant, the boss's secretary who is the real manager, and so on. Traditional small companies (for instance, those in service or small-scale manufacturing) sometimes exhibit this structure—which usually limits their growth.

- **Professional Teams:** Think of a real estate office. It's filled with a dozen or so Realtors—all of them trained professionals managing their own private rosters of clients—managed by one or two more experienced agents. There is also an agency owner (usually with a secretary) who handles the building's lease, MLS subscriptions, advertising and signage, and commissions. Similar structures can be found in law offices (in which the firm's owner spends more time on administration and client relations than practicing law), doctor's offices, accounting offices, insurance offices, title companies, and so forth. In each case, the organizational structure is minimal because the team members are quasi-independent but still need an umbrella organization to achieve their maximum productivity.

- **Manufacturing Teams:** Small businesses specializing in sequential production activities (custom building, repair, machining, prototyping) typically organize their 15±3 team as a number of small subteams of two, three, and even 7±2, with one or two supervisors and a boss-salesperson (along with a contract bookkeeper and other outside vendors). Watch reality TV on any given night and you'll see these teams building motorcycles, repairing guns, or restoring cars. In real life, just visit any machine shop and you'll see this organizational model played out before your eyes.

- **Development Teams:** Now we enter the world of technology and new product creation and management. The 15±3 member development team is something of a compromise in this world. They are bigger than the typical 7±2 code-writer team we think of in software development, the kind of frat house team we see on television (*Silicon Valley*) and in movies, and in official corporate histories of companies like Google and Facebook. They are also bigger than the standard virtual team that is handing off work in eight-hour shifts to individuals or pairs around the world. And, because of their size, 15±3 development teams can never match the cohesiveness or the flexibility of the smaller design team.

That said, the 15±3 team offers its own advantages in product development. For one thing, it can be faster in certain situations. Code is code, and the more people you have working in parallel, the faster it can be written—a crucial time-to-market advantage when competition is intense—and with a 15±3 team, you don't need to add the risk of contracting out the work to teams of code writers in other countries. In addition, you can divide up the work among twice as many subteams, or conversely, you can double the manpower in each of the same number of teams. Finally, and most important, the presence of a professional manager who is inside the team but not buried in its work makes for much better coordination between the subteams, better continuous monitoring of the team's progress toward its goals, and (because smaller teams have a much greater risk of becoming isolated and insular) better contact with the outside world.

As we've already noted, the rule of the thumb for teams is to go with the smallest team for the task. But here we make a—sort of—exception. If you find yourself with a project that will demand a nine- (or even worse, a ten- or eleven-) member team, seriously consider bumping up the team size to 15±3—and use those additional members to implement an internal management superstructure to the project. The added cost is almost always worth it.

And jumping to the larger size does come with costs. Recall Dunbar's numbers: the 7±2 team is at the upper bound of people with whom you are truly close, who are like family. By comparison, the 15±3 team is at the upper bounds of people you can truly *trust*. There is a very big gap between the two (though perhaps not as big as the one to come), and it can be decisive. In the smaller team, everyone works constantly with everyone else, each knows each other's strengths and weaknesses, and ultimately, honor or blame accrues to everyone just about equally (remember how we apportioned credit for the microprocessor?).

We are also now beyond Jeff Bezos's "two-pizza" rule, and so it is difficult to actually get the entire team together in one place and address every one of them personally. Moreover, for all the advantages of having an internal management, that new apparatus brings with it the problems of transfer and translation—messages and commands can sometimes change subtly (but materially) as they pass down the chain of command.

15±3 Team Creation and Management

Far more than any smaller team type can do, 15±3 teams can recruit for maximum diversity. There are several reasons for this:

- **Mass:** A dysfunctional member of a duo, a trio, or even a 7±2 team can be deadly, especially if he or she isn't excised quickly. But a 15±3 team is big enough to absorb a certain amount of intrateam friction. This in turn means that you can recruit for a much greater range of diversity than ever—which in turn increases the team's likelihood of success.
- **Size:** A 15±3 team is also big enough to allow a certain amount of migration within the team . . . which means that a talented member who doesn't fit in one part of the operation may still find a welcome spot somewhere else.
- **Leadership:** In smaller teams, the leader—already doing his or her own work, plus committing time to supervising—doesn't have time to "sit on" another team member who has huge potential but doesn't quite fit in. But in a 15±3 team, with its two or even three layers of management, it is possible to assign a manager to focus extra time on making sure that a "challenging" member is successful.

As for running the 15±3 team after it is under way, the basic rules of management theory apply: Work through your subordinates but maintain a connection with all the team members; continuously monitor the team's health; recognize hard work and achievement; defend the team against outside challenges; manage the budget carefully; and shepherd the team through major challenges and transitions. If you've built the team properly, it will take care of the rest.

Scaling Up without Blowing Up

Beyond the 15±3 team, each team of increasing size is approximately three times that of the one before. There is no obvious genetic reason for this. More likely it is that the increasing span of control at one level eventually requires a new layer of management—which leads to the jump to a new team size.

Note also that the gaps between the team types also grow greater with each jump—eight from seven to fifteen; thirty-five from fifteen to fifty, one hundred to the next level. These no-man's-lands of team populations quickly become huge, and are only slightly mitigated by the growing margins of error—which means that if you choose to create a larger team over a smaller one, you will inevitably be making a much greater investment. That's yet another reason to keep your teams as small as possible.

At the 50 team level, we leave the world of midsize teams and enter the world of *large teams*, of which there also are two types:

- **Company 1:** These are 50±10 member teams ("50"). In real life, these teams correspond to midsize companies that are either small manufacturers or, with actual products being delivered to customers, start-ups at the series B level of venture financing. These are typically companies based at a single location, with dedicated salespeople, and a growing product catalog. Within larger organizations, this size of team corresponds with the size of a department.

- **Company 2:** These are established companies with 150±30 employees ("150"). They correspond to larger midsize companies than Company 1, but are still privately owned and mostly headquartered at a single location. Whereas Company 1 teams typically feature functional departments and three layers of management, Company 2 teams may have four layers of management and may feature the first appearance of business units or divisions. These larger teams, if a stand-alone enterprise, are typically at series C investment, with an impending acquisition or initial public offering. In a larger organization, this is the size of a product group or small division.

Company 1 and 2 team types represent the last appearance of what we might call *knowing teams*. The 50 team represents the largest team type in which mutual trust remains a defining element, even if it's limited. In a 50 team, you can be pretty sure that no one is actively working against the interests of the group, mostly because you still know everyone, even if you work regularly only with a few of them, and some not at all.

50/150 company teams are the real deal, as underscored by the way they are treated by their employees, customers, investors, and various governments. For employees of 50 teams, they represent the opportunity for long-term employment and bonuses; and for the 150 teams there is even the chance at considerable wealth from an acquisition or an IPO. And, at these sizes—and unlike with many bigger teams—everyone can grab the brass ring. Take the social networking company Whatsapp: three years in business, fifty-five employees . . . and sold to Facebook for $19 billion. That's $120 million for even the least vested employee. Stock option plans are usually distributed more equitably at this level, and the chance for upward mobility through the ranks is greater.

50/150 companies are also more independent and stable than their smaller counterparts, mostly because they can perform all of their necessary duties within their own operations rather than being at the mercy of outside contractors or suppliers—and when they do work with outsiders, it is both from a greater position of strength and with the ability to assign staff to monitor those providers. Having operations inside the team means that 50/150s enjoy a smaller overhead per employee than smaller firms for the same services. On the other end of the scale, 50/150 companies are also more resistant to market shock. They can endure a market downturn better than their smaller counterparts can—and if they can't change direction as quickly as smaller teams, they are also more likely to have the cash, the inventory, and the physical plant needed to survive.

Then there is the matter of innovation: smaller teams are usually better at coming up with that one, big, category-creating product idea. But it takes a 50/150 company (or bigger) to consistently come up with a series of successful new products, all while upgrading their earlier products to push them along the curve to maximum profitability.

Finally, 50/150 teams have a unique ability to *scale*. Unlike with smaller teams, all the pieces are now in place, from line and staff operations to corporate offices to multiple layers of management. The company team, especially the 150 team, can simply grow by expansion, not invention, the former being a much simpler process.

Interestingly, one of the most compelling arguments for the 150 team appeared only in recent years: It can serve as the heart of a virtualized corporation. Mike's 2009 book, *The Future Arrived Yesterday*, argues that the hollowness of the Internet-and-computer-driven "virtual" organization can be filled with the small, solid core of a permanent, tightly knit team that will provide a stabilizing center upon which a vast, infinitely adaptable "protean" corporation can be built from thousands of part-time freelance employees. 50/150 teams, with their last vestiges of teamwide trust, may prove to be the permanent cores of these companies of the future.

Note that 50 is one of the more obscure Dunbar numbers, corresponding (as you may not remember) to "the typical overnight camp size among traditional hunter-gatherers like the Australian Aboriginals or the San Bushmen of southern Africa." That seems a bit of a stretch, a facile attempt to fill a blank space. He might have looked elsewhere. For example, a typical military company—three platoons and a headquarters—fits neatly within the parameters of this team type and, even better, it also bears the name "company." So too do the legendary acting troupes of the Elizabethan era—thus, for example, Shakespeare's King's Men company—which would have performed at the Globe Theatre with twenty-six actors and an equal number of stagehands, seamstresses, and other workers.

By comparison, the 150 team is the most famous Dunbar number—and as such, it may be the most stable human grouping of all. It is the largest team in which all the team members still know each other. That fact, combined with the sheer throw weight of a team of this size—one that can recruit top-notch managerial talent to run it and (thanks to stock options) the best talent to man it—makes the 50/150 team a formidable force indeed. That's why these teams, as companies, clubs, social groups, special forces teams, orchestras, and a thousand other human aggregations, dominate the modern world.

We'll deal with these two company team types as one, because they have more commonalities than differences. From here on out we will be looking at matters of elaboration and scale, unlike the paradigmatic changes we saw when moving from one small team to the next.

In 50 and 150 teams we see the rise of true *departmentalization.* That is, we see teams with internal operations that have sufficiently large memberships and infrastructure to operate all but independently. These departments are organized by professional specialty: manufacturing, research and development, HR, sales and marketing. The difference here between 50 and 150 teams is largely a matter of size and the number of divisions—thus, sales and marketing split, and then the latter divides again into PR, advertising, and marketing. In the larger company type, an IT department appears, as does a full-size finance department. The board becomes more active and formal. And most visibly, the team gains an *administration*—which in Company 2 includes a CEO, a COO, and perhaps a few other C-level executives and division heads.

Interestingly, while they share many of the same strengths, 50 and 150 teams have different weaknesses. The problem with 50 teams is both more complex and more dispiriting. As we've said, beyond 15±3 members, teams begin to lose their internal trust—and this can be a devastating transition.

We can remember one particular meeting with one of Silicon Valley's most celebrated entrepreneurs, Tom Siebel, who founded the industry-dominant sales-force automation software company Siebel Systems and eventually sold it to Oracle for $6 billion. We encountered Tom in his office at about the point when the company was a 50 team. He was deeply depressed.

"What's wrong?" we asked.

Tom replied, "I just got out of negotiations with a potential new vice presidential hire."

"Bad candidate?" we asked.

"No, just the opposite."

"So what's the problem?"

Siebel shook his head. "He started negotiating for which office he wanted and all sorts of other perks."

"So what does that mean?"

"It means that we're not a team anymore. We're not a start-up. We're not all in it together anymore. Now people join the company for what they can get out of it." He frowned. "I knew it was coming, but I didn't think it would be so soon."

Management challenges become amplified when a team grows as large as 150 members; this is typically also the moment when the team becomes visible to the outside world and becomes, for the first time, the target of recruiters. It is the moment when it first begins to bleed the talent it needs to make the next big leap.

ORGANIZING AND MANAGING 50/150 TEAMS

50/150 teams are rarely created from scratch. That is just too complicated and expensive a proposition with little prospect of immediate return on investment. Instead, these teams are usually *grown*—either directly from a smaller team, or through the amalgamation of several teams. The interesting question is: How do you jump the gap between the optimal size of the smaller team to that of the larger one? The good news for 50 teams is that the jump from the 15±3 member team is objectively rather small; the bad news is that this gap, from eighteen members to forty-five, is actually larger than the smaller team.

Management itself must also experience growth, usually just the insertion of a layer of management between the ones already in place. For the 50 team, this means adding a third management layer between the senior management and individual subteam leaders. This is usually accomplished by clustering the subteams (generally two or three) by common technology or market and assigning a *group leader* to manage each of those clusters.

For the 150 team, the growth of management becomes more complicated. At this point, the subteams may have grown to *divisions* (they certainly will at higher levels) with their own internal leadership. It is here that the next layer of management—the restoration of individual team leadership—will usually be added. Needless to say, this will make the 150 a bit bottom-heavy in management, but it beats the alternative—and that situation will be rectified at the next bigger team size.

450 TO 1,500 AND BEYOND—TRIPLING DOWN

Finally, we look at very large teams, which can range from 450 members to 1,500 members and beyond.

These very large teams are considerably different from the smaller teams we've already studied, and there are entire libraries of texts on management and organizational theory addressing these particular organizations, so we feel little need to add to the pile. Instead, we propose to tackle key issues of these large teams that are not usually addressed in those texts.

The first of these is that it is critical to recognize that these large organizations—battalions, regiments, and brigades; faculty, staff, and administrations; publicly traded corporations, governmental agencies, nonprofit foundations, television networks, and so forth—are still, in their essence, *teams*. In fact, they are often dazzling hierarchies of teams, from scores of pairs and trios up through multiple midsize and large teams. This combination is the hidden dynamic of companies—though it is rarely recognized. And it is interesting to speculate just how much greater performance companies could achieve if they did, in fact, recognize that they were actually aggregations of teams and not just masses of individuals, and focus on the care and feeding of those teams.

But the enterprise itself, no matter how large, is also a giant team. It shares the common dynamic of all teams—from the 100,000-member global corporation down to two people sitting in an empty office. Even if it is greatly attenuated, it will also live out the life cycle of teams. In other words, it needs to:

- Stay as small as possible, and as close to the optimal team sizes as it can.
- Focus on and constantly improve communications.
- Maximize the diversity of skills and attitudes.
- Recognize and celebrate achievements and milestones.
- Carefully manage transitions.

We've listed these requirements before, but it can't hurt to serve up a reminder when it comes to the very un-team-looking big organizations. Speaking as journalists who have visited hundreds of companies, we find that too many large organizations assume they have grown too big for the practices that sustained them when they were young and scrappy. Nothing could be further from the truth—in fact, they need to assert those practices even more for the sake of morale, loyalty, and coordination. The need is more acute than ever today: as the market changes more quickly, employees are scattered around the planet with little in-person interaction, and fundamental threats can come from any direction.

In addition, maximizing the performance of big and small internal teams strikes us as one of only two ways to counter the diminishing return on investment per added employee that becomes extreme at this level (the other being productivity tools).

Finally, effective small teams, given freedom of action and strong lines of communications to senior management, may be the only way that a large enterprise can salvage some of the innovation and creativity that first made it a success. That is, this may be the one true answer to Clayton Christensen's "innovator's dilemma" by allowing for the internal creation of disruptive new technologies. In fact, this is exactly what Apple did under Steve Jobs through the first decade of the twenty-first century, with Jobs himself acting as small-team protector for the iPod, iPhone, and iPad.

BEWARE OF A NO-MAN'S-LAND

We finish our team taxonomy with the conversation we've put off until now. By this point you may have already asked yourself this question several times: What do you do in the gaps?

Let's say you have a small business of about fifty-five employees, and you are preparing to grow. But you also know that the next stage, even at the smallest optimal size, is *eighty-five* employees away. That's more than 150 percent larger than you are now.

You certainly can't hire that many people in one or two bursts, for fear of overwhelming every company function. Yet you don't want to be stuck in team no-man's-land for months or even years and increase your vulnerability to your team's shaking itself to pieces or going off the rails. So what do you do?

First, remind yourself that these optimal team sizes are just that: *optimal*. They sit at sweet spots, at the nexus of operational efficiency and human nature. But that doesn't mean that *not* being at one of these optimal sizes is a team death sentence. It just means that you will likely have trouble maintaining your maximum efficiency—though you can still probably cover that gap with greater monitoring and even your recognition (and anticipation) that there may be a potential problem.

By the way, just because you are at one of those sweet spots, it doesn't mean that you are guaranteed success. There is, as yet, no real analysis of the comparative advantages of having the right team size versus other factors from diversity to management competence. And you can still be a textbook team and nevertheless fail—there are no guarantees; you can only improve your odds.

Even though researchers have reached a consensus about ideal team sizes, don't let that always discourage you from composing teams that fall between those benchmarks. This no-man's-land doesn't have to be lethal, but it might diminish a team's chances of reaching its optimal performance. We can't say for sure how much of a risk this poses, but our sense is that if the variant in which the odds don't change is about 20 percent (thus, 15±3, 150±30), the penumbra of acceptable suboptimal team size is possibly 50 percent. This means that the gap between sizes is completely covered for the smaller teams. And only with large and very large teams—450±225 and 1,500±750—do we begin to see any real gaps, and given the size of those operations, those gaps can be vaulted quickly.

So, the real question becomes: How much of a shortfall from your potential optimal team performance are you willing to accept in exchange for the cost and trouble it will take to get there? There is no universal answer to that—each team leader must make his or her own choice based on a calculus of many variables, including funding, time to market, and the available talent pool. With luck, tools will also soon emerge to help with that decision.

Now let's look at teams in action.

The Birth and Life of Teams

The most important team in American history officially retired at noon on December 4, 1783. The location was the Long Room of Fraunces Tavern in one of the oldest parts of New York City. The location was picked not only because it was a popular saloon and gathering place, but also because much of the city, including many of its public buildings, had been burned down during the war.

Nine days before, the defeated British Army—along with a large number of Tories who, rightly, believed they were no longer welcome—had packed up, boarded Royal Navy ships, and sailed away. The parades and celebrations following the embarkation of the enemy were largely over, the city was secure, and the members of the team—many of whom had rarely been home over the previous six years—were eager to get back to their families for the holidays.

None was more so eager than the leader of the team, General

George Washington, who had visited his Virginia home, Mount Vernon, just once during all those years. Now he was going home. His possessions were packed, his horse, Nelson—who had crossed the Delaware with him at Trenton, stood like a rock on the bridge under fire at Monmouth, and carried the general to Cornwallis's surrender at Yorktown—was brushed and fed, and the honor guard was pacing impatiently.

Everyone knew that this would be the team's last time together. So they put on their best uniforms and left their homes and barracks early enough to be sure they were on time, knowing that this moment would be remembered for as long as the new nation they had helped create endured.

One man who rushed to the tavern knew the city well. Colonel Benjamin Tallmadge was the son of a New York City police commissioner, and during the war, as Washington's chief of intelligence, he had run the Culper Espionage Ring—which had played a crucial role in the war—in Manhattan. Almost fifty years later, in his memoirs, Tallmadge recorded his memories of the day:

> At 12 o'clock the officers repaired to Fraunces Tavern in Pearl Street where General Washington had appointed to meet them and to take his final leave of them. We had been assembled but a few moments when his excellency entered the room. His emotions were too strong to be concealed which seemed to be reciprocated by every officer present. After partaking of a slight refreshment in almost breathless silence the General filled his glass with wine and turning to the officers said, "With a heart full of love and gratitude I now take leave of you. I most devoutly wish that your latter days may be as prosperous and happy as your former ones have been glorious and honorable."

After the officers had taken a glass of wine General Washington said "I cannot come to each of you but shall feel obliged if each of you will come and take me by the hand." General Knox being nearest to him turned to the Commander-in-chief who, suffused in tears, was incapable of utterance but grasped his hand when they embraced each other in silence. In the same affectionate manner every officer in the room marched up and parted with his general in chief. Such a scene of sorrow and weeping I had never before witnessed and fondly hope I may never be called to witness again.[1]

Not many teams have members the likes of Knox, Greene, and Hamilton. And fewer yet are led by someone who is, in the immortal words of one team member, Henry "Light-Horse Harry" Lee: "First in war, first in peace, and first in the hearts of his countrymen."

But if you step back from the extraordinary achievement of this team in defeating the most powerful army in the world and winning independence for the United States of America, you are reminded that it was still just a team—one that feuded, exhibited near-fatal inexperience and incompetence, and lost more battles than it won. Indeed, just nine months before, in the so-called Newburgh Conspiracy, many of this team of officers (including several at Fraunces Tavern that day) had come very close to mutinying over lack of pay. It took a famous bit of theatrics by General Washington (showing his age by putting on a pair of glasses to read a letter) to end the mutiny and probably save the young nation.

THE MARCH OF LEADERSHIP

General Washington's sense of theater and drama, combined with his astonishing bravery, integrity, and self-control, made him one of history's greatest leaders. He didn't, however, start out that way. The young man who first made his reputation in the French and

Indian War was less decisive and more hotheaded, if no less brave. It is interesting to speculate how much of the general's behavior that day at Fraunces Tavern was real and how much was calculated. Some historians have even suggested that some of his tears were in frustration for having (thanks to the Continental Congress) failed to fulfill the promises he made at Newburgh.

It was probably all three and more. Washington, who willed himself to almost never show emotion, was obviously deeply moved by the moment. Understandably so; he and his team had just won a great victory. But Washington, as much as any leader, and certainly since the Enlightenment stripped away the role of religion in such events, understood the importance of the sacred in secular events. He knew that his tears would shock the room, so he let them flow. That Henry Knox, the big, emotional bookseller turned artillery commander, stood beside Washington for the toast probably wasn't a coincidence either. Washington must have realized that his own tears would turn General Knox into an emotional wreck.

Then, in the crowning moment, the one captured in paintings over the next two centuries (and likely for many centuries to come): the stricken commander-in-chief asks that his fellow team members come to him, where he says not a word, but takes each man's hand and, through tears, dips his head in gratitude for their service.

You could not script a better scene. It all could have turned into a chaos of rushed words and improvised speeches. Instead, the general controls the event: the weeping attendees come forth and shake the Great Man's hand with an almost unbearable (and certainly unforgettable) intensity of emotion. Washington is spared having to improvise a comment for each officer and thus betray how he ranks each man in his memory and esteem; and the moment passes quickly without dragging on and losing its emotional punch.

Cynical? No, genius. As always with his eye on history and perception, Washington crafted an almost mythical moment that gave every man in the room exactly what he needed and wanted—and yet rings through history. And he does so speaking just two sentences, neither particularly memorable. And the tears on both sides of those handshakes are real. Like all memorable and great leaders, Washington has both played his part and lived the character.

The event ends quickly. The officers, many of them now barely able to maintain their composure, follow the general to the nearby Whitehall wharf. There he takes his leave of them—there is no record of his words, if indeed there were any—and boards a barge to today's Jersey City. Then he travels on to Annapolis, where, in yet another theatrical moment—maybe the most important in the history of democracy—he stands before the Continental Congress, resigns his commission, and goes home. He arrives at Mount Vernon just in time for Christmas Eve.

THE HEART OF THE TEAM

In order to gain the deepest understanding of teams and how they operate, one must appreciate the dynamic of teams. The everyday term is "team spirit." We prefer the term "dynamic," because until this point we have largely been speaking of teams in a static manner. But, as we mentioned earlier, teams do have a beginning, a middle, and an end; they are born, take form, accelerate from a standing start, reach peak speed and productivity, and then, for some interval, preferably short but sometimes drawn out, they decline—with luck, *after* they've achieved their goals.

And then they die. Sometimes this ending is happy because a team has achieved the goal set for it, its members are lauded and rewarded, and they move on to new challenges. Sometimes a team ends because it reaches a temporal deadline set for it; its results are then measured or audited, and with luck the team has achieved an acceptable result and the members are proud of their contributions.

And sometimes a team fails to reach its goals and disassembles itself. Or worse, through some internal dysfunction—the wrong skill combination, incompatible personalities, poor management, misguided or impossible goals—the team dissolves in acrimony and accusations of bad faith.

But whatever the reason—and we hope that after you've read this book, your teams will have the happier conclusions—the fact is, for good or bad, teams do not experience these things all at once. In this chapter, we intend to look at how the stories of teams play out over time, and how at each step of the way—even after the team's death—you can, with the right management, improve the outcome.

ALL TEAMS HAVE LIFE CYCLES

Every team is a narrative, a story that typically begins with a *formation phase* in which strangers (or near strangers) are thrust together under unusual circumstances and then are forced to quickly establish their relationships with each other even as they rush to understand their assignment, divide it up, and then parcel out the pieces to the right members. Soon thereafter, the team enters into an *establishment phase*, in which it needs to establish rules, metrics, milestones, and its communication apparatus. And all of this must be done even as those same members begin to work on their task itself. That shift of focus from organization to actual work on the assignment marks the transition to the *operational phase*.

As time passes, and as the initial results of its work are known, the team inevitably has to adjust—resetting milestones and deadlines, and coping with the personalities, idiosyncrasies, and the strengths and weaknesses of its members. This is the *functional phase*. External forces are in play as well: new competitors with threatening new products or services may appear unexpectedly;

deadlines may change; budgets may shift; product descriptions may be rewritten to meet the evolving needs of the parent company. All of this puts further stress and confusion on the team, whose still-immature interpersonal relationships may not yet be strong enough to handle them.

But assuming the team survives, these events ultimately have another effect: they become elements in the team's growing story, the legends and experiences that help define its internal culture. It is from this evolving story that the team derives an even greater internal cohesion, as well as a body of best practices to draw upon while facing future challenges. This is the *cultural phase*.

There are new challenges as well. For example, the longer a team endures, the more likely it is to lose original members. Some leave voluntarily, their work done. Others go, often regretfully, because their talents are needed elsewhere and the company transfers them. A third group leaves not only the team but also the company itself—often to work for a competitor.

This third type of departure can be particularly unsettling—because of its betrayal, because it enhances the competition, and most of all, because it may transfer the team's proprietary knowledge to its biggest threat. These departures can lead to a lot of mistrust, bad blood, and time wasted on depositions and litigation.

A fourth type of departure can have the opposite effect: when a difficult or dysfunctional member of the team is forced out. In the short term, this can raise the overall paranoia of the team ("Will I get fired next?"), but in the long term it is almost always a salutary event.

No matter the reason for a team member's departure, the immediate concern afterward is the recruiting and training of his or her replacement. Even if the rookie is a good fit, this process is always a test of the team's personality, solidarity, and culture. It's also a good reason for the development of the team's narrative, its story; it is the assimilation of that story by the newcomer that quickly acculturates him or her to the team. The healthier a team's culture, the less productivity it will lose to newcomers making their way up the learning curve. This is the *sustainable phase*.

Assuming the team survives these challenges, overcomes any technical obstacles, and approaches its goals, it now moves into a *maturation and consolidation phase*. The challenge now is to resist the desire to rush ahead, and instead to maintain the pace and finish the project properly. It is a task more difficult than it appears, because pressures will build from every direction—the company wants to introduce or implement the project's results; recruiters want to steal away the team's top talent; the team members themselves want to move on to new challenges; and, you, as the internal or external manager of the team, are exhausted and want to wrap things up. Those pressures only grow as the project approaches the finish line, and they serve as distractions and impediments to finishing the job right.

Bad teams disintegrate or implode. Good teams survive to enter the *completion phase*. Now that the invention, prototyping, and testing are completed, the task becomes one of packaging the results (which can include a demonstration or a finished product, an operations manual, preparing presentations of test results, patent filings, facility dismantlement, and team member reassignment) for senior management or, in the case of an entrepreneurial start-up, for investors. Usually, there is a handoff of the completed project to another team that specializes in commercialization or reverse engineering in preparation for large-scale manufacturing. In recent years, as products and services are increasingly released to the public while still prototypes—Google's search engine officially remained a work in progress for more than a decade—a team's life cycle may not end until its offering has a hundred million users and is sold to another company.

Once everything is packaged, bundled up, and either handed or sold off, the team reaches its *end phase*. Successful teams "end" in two different ways. They are either shut down or they transform, often with many of the same members, into a new team with a new task. Either way, the best teams (as with General Washington and his staff) mark that transition with some kind of ceremony that both celebrates their success and officially demarks the team's conclusion along with the beginning of the next phase in the members' lives.

The open-ended era that follows the retirement of a team might be called the *aftermath phase*. These are the months and years that follow the end of a team's existence, during which each member, the company, and sometimes even the world put their experience with that team into perspective. Needless to say, many teams exist for such a short duration or take on such minor tasks that the members' memories of them are insignificant or even nonexistent. Rather, in this discussion we are talking about teams working together for an extended period on a common task.

In the next few sections we'll look at each of those phases in turn.

THE FORMATION PHASE

One reason that so many teams fail is that they are doomed from the start.

As we've shown, an enormous amount of research has been conducted over the last fifteen years into the dynamics of teams—how they should be composed, how they should operate, what types of individuals they should employ, and how those members should interact over the course of the team's life. Unfortunately, few of these findings have been put to use in any systematic way—much less in combination with each other—but here are four key lessons we hope leaders will use for team recruitment:

- Diversity: Look past surface differences such as race and gender, and focus instead on real differences in culture, life experiences, skills, and thought processes. The larger the mix you have of these qualities—as long as the members can build a team culture that will keep them together—the greater the chance the team will be successful.
- Proximity: Teams work better the closer the members are to each other. That's true even in the age of virtual work teams. So if you can't put the members in the same room, then find communication tools to close the gap.
- Size: Bigger isn't better for teams; in fact, it usually makes them worse. Determine the smallest-size team for the task at hand and recruit for that size, or a size not much larger.
- Hierarchy: Layers of management increase efficiency but not necessarily productivity. Keep the leadership of the team to the smallest number of managers and the fewest layers of control. The best teams have few leaders and a flat organization with little hierarchy. Eschew titles.

Finally, resist the desire of team members to recruit their friends to the team. Even if those friends are talented, their presence will almost inevitably reduce the diversity of the team.

In recruiting a team leader, look for someone who has been part of a successful and healthy team in the recent past. Or choose a proven leader coming off a "successful failure." As much as it sounds like the right thing to do, resist the strategy of letting the team leader select his or her own team, as those choices will almost always lack the necessary diversity needed for true team genius.

The number two person in the team should also be, if possible, someone coming from a successful team. Also recruit that one person, even if he or she is not an expert in the subject at hand, for his or her transactional skills—that is, for the ability to maintain records, become the team's memory, act as the interface among all the other members, and be the unofficial contact to the outside world.

Now build out your team and prepare to fire them up.

THE ESTABLISHMENT PHASE

At the heart of the establishment phase is a process as old as humankind. It is the creation of a sacred space.

There is a reason we open school days, troop meetings, church services, graduations, city council meetings, sporting events, trials, and the United States Congress with a series of rituals—a flag ceremony, the pledge of allegiance, the stating of oaths, a prayer. All serve to emotionally and psychologically separate the participants from what came before (everyday life) and launch them into a different reality, a different plane of heightened experience.

Over time we tend to become jaded about these rituals. We go through the motions. But remember what it was like when you were young and you encountered these rituals for the first time—or even now when you find yourself in a different institution or culture and in the midst of a ceremony that is alien to you. You cannot help feeling different—intimidated, exalted, confused. Whatever the response, you can't help but feel yourself in a different place, one in which your concentration is more focused and your senses heightened. If you are a member of the institution in question, you feel unleashed and part of something larger than yourself; and if you are not a member, no matter how much you know about these rituals and no matter how much you have been welcomed into the group, you can't help but feel like an outsider.

These are not shallow emotions, but rather emotions that go right to the heart of being a social creature. Many species of social animals, if forced out of the pack or herd, will die from loneliness

and isolation. By comparison, being part of a team gives us an identity, a bigger purpose, and a way of interacting trustfully with other
team members without the wariness and fear we experience with
strangers.

Thus, the rituals that are established at the formation of a team,
and regularly repeated in an abbreviated form thereafter, establish
a threshold through which we depart the vast and dangerous real
world and enter into a smaller, sacred space where we are safe and
surrounded by others who accept us and whom we can trust.

Put simply, teams need an official beginning as much as they
need an official ending—an event to mark the official start of the
team's endeavor, to establish the team's culture, and to initiate
mechanisms for ongoing communication.

It doesn't have to be an elaborate ceremony—though sometimes
that's not a bad idea. For two people who have been paired up on a
project of comparatively short duration, the official beginning may
be a casual lunch or drinks after work to get to know each other, to
talk about their lives and aspirations, to scope out the task ahead,
to swap email addresses and phone numbers, and to establish times
and locations for regular meetings.

At the other end of the scale are the elaborate ceremonies, gatherings, and investitures that mark our entry into established and
exclusive groups—freshman orientation, fraternity and sorority
initiations, Eagle Scout Courts of Honor and Order of the Arrow
ordeals, Little League opening-day ceremonies, the first day of
boot camp, professional society ceremonies, secret investitures into
fraternal organizations. All of these have a highly ritualized atmo-
sphere, often as the result of years, even centuries, of accumulated
experience, and are usually intentionally strange, even frightening,
so as to create an indelible shared memory among all the members, new and old. In the case of the military, those nightmarish
first days of "boot" are also designed to be an equalizer—to strip
the new recruit of whatever prejudices and attitudes he or she may

have from civilian life in order to create a tabula rasa upon which the service can write its own rules of conduct.

For most teams, such rituals will fall somewhere between these two extremes. But whatever form the kickoff event takes, they all share common goals:

1. **Set an Official Start.** Without an official starting time ("We begin tomorrow morning at eight a.m., so get a good night's sleep"), human nature will lead some team members to jump the gun for advantage, start late to show their independence, and so forth. An official start, even if it is pretty much arbitrary, synchronizes the team from the outset—and reminds them that they will begin together, work together, and end together.

2. **Establish Relations.** Team success depends on reducing the barriers to communication among team members. And that starts on day one. Time spent on name tags, introductions, sharing details about oneself, distributing phone numbers and email addresses, and even small-group exercises and brainstorming sessions—all of these activities serve the important purpose of establishing rapport and connection among all members of the team. Sometimes we may cut these efforts short (or even roll our eyes when we see them noted on the agenda), but don't underestimate the positive effect they can have in the long run.

3. **Set Rules.** When it comes to rules of behavior, establishing them early and clearly is paramount. Setting the rules at the start and sticking to them for everyone, including yourself, is both democratizing and (unless you are a controlling martinet) liberating, because everyone knows what the rules are and appreciates that they are shared by everyone on the team—no one gets special favors. By the way: Announce those rules, keep them simple, and write them down to be distributed to everyone. That will minimize disputes.

4. **Seed the Culture.** Like it or not, the cultural life of the team begins at that kickoff event. Every member of the team leaves that meeting with a gut feeling about the quality of the team and its likelihood of success. They will have already formed opinions about other individuals on the team. As team leader—and even more so if you are the more senior team creator—it is incumbent on you to plumb the feelings of the team members about their new team as quickly as possible. That's why well-run teams typically feature a round of interviews with each member immediately after that kickoff event. Ostensibly, these interviews are about the member's skills and potential contribution to the team, but they are also about gaining insight into the initial impressions and expectations of the group. Everything you do will affect the overall culture of the team, so design the kickoff meeting so that it showcases the kind of culture you want the team to have.

5. **Set Attitudes.** Natural leaders instinctively understand that they have the power to shape the tone and attitude of the team through the force of their own personalities. That's why they continuously project a persona that will color the team in the way they want it to behave: loose or intense, playful or serious, big thinking or detail-oriented. Great leaders, like George Washington (as his youthful notes to himself about public behavior underscore), live this persona so completely that eventually they *become* it.

Unfortunately, many leaders make the mistake of allowing a team to find its own attitude and "style," which in reality means that the most strong-willed members dominate and even emotionally hijack the team. Even worse, some leaders allow their own negative emotions and moods to infect the team. We recommend when recruiting a team leader that you do not leave this process of attitude creation entirely up to that individual, but rather that you demand an *explicit plan* as to how that leader will manage that task, including the rituals, beginning from the first gathering and carrying through the entire life span of the team. Giving that person a little training in dress and presentation wouldn't hurt either.

6. **Establish Communications.** As research shows, and as great leaders know, healthy and frequent communications ensure that team members and the team's work are synchronized, which, in turn, allows the team to adapt quickly to difficulties and to calm rough waters. It starts at that all-important first meeting and should continue at every regular team gathering, whether these meetings are in person or are virtual, asynchronous exchanges. Having clear expectations and "rules of engagement" is even more important when teams work across geographies and time zones. We recommend establishing clear but flexible routines that will reinforce intrateam communications. Keep these meetings short, purposeful, and tightly managed.

The lesson is: Set the personality and the attitude of the team early, and you will spare yourself a lot of frustration and misery later. And you'll improve the team's odds of being successful in the process.

THE OPERATIONAL PHASE

Among the most tragic types of teams might be those called "process teams." We've encountered only a few in our careers, and we've always come away both stunned that people would actually participate in such a surreal situation, and appalled at the waste of time, talent, and treasure these teams represent.

These process teams tend to take one of two forms, one obvious and the other dangerously subtle. The former is a team so dysfunctional that it devotes all of its time and energy just to keeping the group together and trying to get the members on task. These teams are obviously destined to fail, and the best solution is to follow the advice from earlier in this book and break them up immediately. They will never right themselves—and if by some miracle they do, it'll probably be long after it is too late to get the job done.

The second type of process team is much more difficult to identify. It is important to look closely at supposedly healthy teams that have nevertheless failed in their task to make sure they really represent "good failures." Sometimes the reason for the failure is that the team spent too much of its time in a group kumbaya and not enough on the task at hand, or, worse, that it created only a simulacrum, a Kabuki play of a real team, and merely went through the motions. Management—that is, *you*—never noticed, because the team seemed to be doing so well; it had "great chemistry."

The best way to prevent this kind of fiasco—and it will be one, embarrassing everyone involved, especially you, and leaving the company desperately behind the competition—is to force yourself to look beyond the morale of the team and to set some early and precise milestones for the team to reach. Demand that the leader convey those milestones to the entire team (a good leader will want to do so anyway). You can loosen up later if the team is both humming along *and* productive. If the team doesn't hit those early milestones—no matter what its explanation—consider breaking it up. At the very least, set even tighter and more explicit milestones. If the team fails to reach those, remove its leader, no matter how beloved by the team. Don't be unreasonable in your targets—almost every new team has growing pains—but don't accept excuses either. Do *not* buy into their self-delusion; do *not* become their advocate— your job is to be the sane, even ruthless, adult. If the team can't do the job at the beginning, it is unlikely to do so at the end.

THE CULTURAL PHASE

One of the most famous stories in high-tech history is that of Bill Hewlett and the bolt cutter.

A half century ago, William Hewlett, the cofounder of the largest electronics company of them all, Hewlett-Packard, dropped by the then-small company on a Saturday just to check up on things. When he got there, he was appalled to find that scores of company engineers were standing around doing nothing. When he asked why, Hewlett was told that all the equipment needed by the staff to do their work was locked in a storage room, and only one person owned the key: the lab supervisor, who hadn't arrived yet.

History often turns on one leader—Alexander, Sherman, Ted Roosevelt Jr. on Utah Beach—who encounters an obstacle and, instead of fighting it, just cuts through the problem and resets the rules. That's what Hewlett did that morning. He searched around until he found a pair of bolt cutters and promptly cut the padlock right off the storage room door. He then announced to the surprised engineers that the new rule at HP was that there would never be a lock on any storage room door in the company ever again—and if anyone tried to install one, they would be fired on the spot.

When one of the engineers demurred, saying that the reason for the lock was to keep employees from taking equipment home for their own use, Hewlett replied that he didn't give a damn about that, either; they might invent something great on their free time, and, besides, he trusted them to bring the equipment back.

Cutting a padlock off a door may seem like a minor matter, but the resonance of that single act transformed modern business and still affects corporate life today. That's because the story of Hewlett's actions quickly spread across HP and underscored what came to be known to insiders and outsiders as the HP Way. It was a corporate philosophy built on trust in HP employees to find their own best path to achieving the company's objectives.

The HP Way, of course, is the most famous and esteemed corporate culture ever devised—and its innovations (flextime, stock options, profit sharing, and so forth) have been imitated by companies throughout the world. And it all began with that little bit of theater of Bill Hewlett brandishing the bolt cutters.

The stories we tell ourselves and each other about our work have proved to be incredibly powerful. Great teams invariably have great stories—and not just drunken anecdotes and tales of screwups, but also stories that help define the personality of the team, that underscore its pride and morale, and most of all, stories that help the team explain its own specialness to itself.

Unhealthy teams have stories too, but they are usually about failure and the foibles of others, and most are laced with resentment and contempt. In fact, that's one of the best ways to gauge the health of a team: listen to the stories the team tells about itself. Healthy teams and healthy companies tend to recount major turning points and dramatic episodes with a sense of pride, good humor, and confidence (even with stories of mistakes). In unhealthy teams and unhealthy companies, even their stories of victories carry an unmistakable reek of pessimism, as if their successes are undeserved or ill gotten.

Stories can also be an insight into the relative health of a company. Here are three types of team "stories" that suggest a poor leader who should be watched and possibly replaced:

- If all the stories are about the boss—it could mean that the CEO is mean or domineering. Or that the team's communications are almost entirely vertical (that is, the boss does all the talking and decision-making) and insufficiently horizontal across the team.

- If they are all about meeting important people—you may have a process team on your hands. Worst of all,
- If a team has no stories—it may not really be a team at all, but merely an aggregation of individuals suffering from insufficient diversity, personal contact, and a broken communication apparatus.

At first the use of storytelling to engender a culture may seem like an evanescent hope, something you can't force into creation, but just the opposite is true. Having been in the professional storytelling business all of our professional lives (and in Mike's case, having even been a novelist), we are, of course, biased. Nevertheless, our experience is that other than a few (tragic) people, *everyone* enjoys a story, and most people also like to tell them. So the manager of a team has three duties in this area:

- Create a setting in which team members not only feel free to tell stories but are encouraged to do so.
- Help the process of selecting and repeating those stories that aid in the health and productivity of the team, and that are reflective of the team's desired culture.
- Establish occasions and settings in which these stories can be regularly shared, especially with new team members.

Good sales managers—probably because sales departments have long been the domain of storytellers—have known this for a long time. That's why sales meetings, typically held in exotic locales, are usually less about training and seminars than about creating an environment that cultivates both story creation and story swapping. That explains why a lot more of the positive work usually takes place in the resort bar each night than in the meeting rooms during the day. All team leaders can learn something from those priorities.

THE SUSTAINABLE PHASE

Any team that stays together for any length of time is likely to see some turnover. This is not only inevitable but particularly painful, because the members who leave are often the team's most valuable contributors; it is precisely their talent that gets them transferred to new and important projects. Other factors can cause members to leave the team midcourse for reasons ranging from dissatisfaction (often a good thing, as it removes a growing threat to team harmony) to life changes (personal health, retirement, even death).

When these departures occur, one thing should happen, and another thing must happen:

- Should happen. Conduct some kind of departure ceremony, even if the member is happy to go and the team is even happier to see that member gone. This ceremony can be as simple as a quick office meeting to make the announcement and wish the member good luck. Or it could be a dinner, and even a going-away gift, for a longtime or beloved member.

The purpose of the departure ceremony is to recognize the member's contribution to the team—and thus hold out the promise of recognition to other team members who will receive the same recognition someday. It also creates a distinct and sharply defined closure to that member's tenure with the team; it ends an era. By comparison, allowing a member to simply pack up and silently leave creates a void, an unanswered question about the reasons for the departure, and a sense that things aren't quite over, that the departing figure (for good or bad) might come back.

- Must happen. Create some kind of event to welcome the new team member replacing the departing one. As we've shown, it is crucial to assimilate new members into the team, acculturate them into the team's culture, and equip them with all the necessary communications tools as quickly as possible.

Most of us have had the miserable experience of joining a new group or team, being left on our own, and feeling like we've walked into someone else's family, or arrived at a cocktail party two hours late. The more pronounced this alienation, the more difficult it becomes to ever feel part of the team. Conversely, the team misses out on increased productivity, diversity, and a new source of intellectual capital as long as a newcomer remains an outsider.

The goal should always be to assimilate a new member into the team as quickly as possible. There are a lot of proven ways to do this: a group announcement of the newcomer's arrival; a team gathering to make the introduction in person, including telling personal anecdotes that humanize the newcomer; making one-on-one introductions with every team member; assigning a team member to act as temporary host, mentor, and teller of the team's stories; and providing personalized training for the new member in using the team's communications apparatus.

In other words: welcome the new team member, embed him or her into the culture and operations of the team as quickly as possible, and then get back to work.

THE CONSOLIDATION AND MATURATION PHASE

"Maturing" is a dreaded fate for most companies because it's associated with losing the innovative edge and entrepreneurial fervor and, worst of all, becoming a corporate dinosaur waiting to be made extinct by some fast-moving furry little start-up.

But maturity is a good thing for teams, because this is the era in their history when they bring together and consolidate their disparate operations and work in harmony toward a final goal. Whether a team can navigate through this phase usually determines whether it will be ultimately successful or not.

There are very few teams whose members all work together doing the same thing at the same time throughout the life span of that team. Rather, most teams, at the very beginning, divide the assigned task into subtasks based on differences in the work, in the skills required, completion dates, and sometimes just size. Think of the army patrol moving through the jungle: it isn't just a dozen undifferentiated soldiers, but an officer in charge setting course and strategy, a sergeant managing the soldiers, a radio operator, a point man out front, and a two-man heavy weapons team. Each member of that platoon has a different job to do.

Most teams are like that. An even better analogy might be the newsroom of a newspaper or television station. Say that there are 150 people working in that newsroom putting out a daily newspaper or an evening newscast. Of that cohort, about one-third is actually reporting—each taking on a different story, gathering data, interviewing subjects, writing the article under deadline. A second third is working in support of those reporters—everything from the newsroom phone operators to the art department to clerks to layout experts, secretaries, interns, and assistants. Largely unrecognized, they are the glue that holds the whole operation together, helping the reporters or running the newsroom's infrastructure. The remaining third are editors: at newspapers these include copy editors, department editors (sports, business, living, and so forth), news editors, assignment editors, city or metro editors, national editors, international editors, managing editor, executive editor, and editor in chief. At television stations, the editors carry many of the same titles, though their actual duties may differ.

The reporters typically operate alone, or in pairs, but they are also part of teams that make up the different departments and report to their respective editor and assistant editor. The support group is composed almost entirely of teams. And the editors (which also includes the department heads) form essentially one large team filled with multiple overlapping teams, the largest being the group of copy editors (in newspapers they sit together at the circular table called "the slot" and piece together the paper to fit the editorial "hole" defined at the last minute by whatever advertising has been sold.

From a distance, this newsroom may look like a single large team, a hive of individuals, busy at work. But in truth this one big team is made up of dozens of subteams, each with assignments and each racing in a different direction over the course of a shift, most of them slightly out of phase with each other.

Thus, the reporters arrive early and start chasing stories. So do the senior editors, who will determine the contents of that day's edition. The department heads arrive early too, to decide which stories their reporters will follow, and to look at the first version of the day's layout. But others—the art people, most of the support staffers, and the copy editors—arrive later; they aren't needed until the stories are under way and the first completed ones are delivered.

By afternoon, the newsroom is crowded and humming. Almost every desk is filled—and those that are empty belong to reporters who are still out chasing their stories. Streams of editorial copy are now being created, converging first in the departments; and from those departments larger streams emerge, to converge again at the slot, where the copy editors are now cutting and mixing stories produced in the newsroom with those coming from outside bureaus and wire services.

By late afternoon, a decision has been made on the final layout of the paper—what stories will make it and where. Now the copy editors use their unique skill and rush to write compelling and succinct headlines (or prepare the copy and titles at the TV station). Meanwhile, many of the reporters, especially those covering breaking news, are cleaning off their desks and preparing to go home. The newsroom now looks half-empty, but in the slot, in the art department, and in some of the special sections, the staff is busier than ever.

At the newspaper, this second phase of activity will continue into the evening, with a skeleton crew still working at midnight in case of a sudden news break. Should that happen, they will stay until the morning edition can be recomposed. At the TV station, the on-air talent, which has arrived in the afternoon, prepares for the evening broadcast, as does the studio crew. Some will stay on for the late-night news broadcast, or hand their duties off to their late-shift counterparts. By the time of the late-night broadcast, the studio and control room will be busy, but the newsroom will be mostly darkened and empty.

Keep in mind that this complex choreography of multiple sub-teams working largely independently, with their results then consolidated in a sophisticated finished product, takes place in these newsrooms *every day*. The finished product, in the case of the newspaper, is the equivalent of a small book, filled with all-new material, published every twenty-four hours; in the case of the evening news, it is the equivalent of a multisubject half-hour documentary created in the same brief cycle.

This is the consolidation phase in one of its most exciting and compressed forms. It cannot be accomplished without a robust infrastructure, clearly established lines of communication, rules of behavior (editorial ethics and standards, deadlines, grammar and editorial style), consideration of precedent and practice ("maturity"), and a lot of experienced team members. That's one reason young newspaper and television reporters have to pass through a long training process that begins with local media and can take years, even decades, to reach a major-market paper or news station.

Newspapers and TV news may represent extreme cases of consolidation and maturation, but they are far from unique. Established teams in many fields—those found in emergency rooms, special forces operations, government, police and fire departments, and even fast-food restaurants—find themselves dividing into sub-teams, working at a furious pace that allows for few mistakes, and then coming together quickly and precisely to deliver the final product or service.

But it can also be said that *every* team, small or large, short-lived or long-lasting, in one way or another must pass through this consolidation and maturation phase along the path toward its resolution. Even pairs divide up their work, and at some point the two must come together, merge their work into the synthesis that will ultimately represent the team, and then perfect and polish that result in preparation for the final presentation.

This consolidation is not always easy. Egos are often involved—and if the assignment's boundaries haven't been made precise and explicit from the start, there can be a lot of frustrating overlap. Tempers can get short as subteam leaders realize that hundreds of hours of their group's work may never see the light of day.

Among the most dangerous and destructive types of teams is one in which one or two members, recognized as the "idea" people, are given too much control—usually by an awed leader. These teams *never* consolidate—rather, as one idea approaches fruition, the "genius" suddenly comes up with an "even better idea" and the entire team shifts direction to pursue it; just when that idea is almost realized, the genius comes up with another one, ad infinitum, until the team runs out of money, energy, or senior management's patience. In the meantime, the team has wasted immense amounts of time, talent, and capital toward no good end. Teams must be kept on track—even if it means kicking out the top talent in the shift into consolidation. Such a move will be hugely disturbing but necessary. And if the genius really does have a great new idea, you can always start a new team for him or her.

More than at any time since the founding days of the team, the consolidation moment is when the team leader is tested. Final decisions have to be made. The creative work has to be stopped—even when some members beg for just a little more time for an impending breakthrough. Ruffled feathers must be smoothed. And the team must be brought together for the final assault on the goal. If the leader has done his or her job along the way—establishing precise duties, setting subteam milestones and interim goals, and, most of all, keeping all the members feeling that they are part of the larger group and its work—then this reintegration of the team should occur with the minimum of friction.

But friction or not, consolidation and maturation must take place. The team and its members must quickly transform from a band of semi-independent creators to a coordinated and structured group of organizers for the final rush to completion.

The Retirement and Death of Teams

From the time we are young we are taught, through both demonstration and aphorisms, the importance of finishing well ("It ain't over 'til it's over"; "80 percent of the value comes from the last 20 percent of the work"). And yet, like the value of compound interest, it is a lesson we typically fail to observe. It is human nature to be eager to get something done and to run on to the next new thing when we approach the end of something. It is usually only later in life that we finally learn this lesson, and we are left to regret all of those things in our lives that we didn't finish well.

Unfortunately, the need for a good finish grows more important by the year. In the mechanical age, a team could usually complete a prototype, show that it operated properly, and walk away, leaving the tasks of disassembling, reverse engineering, adapting for large-scale manufacturing, and writing manuals to others. But today, when product cycle times grow shorter by the day, tackling these secondary and ancillary duties typically falls to the team it-self. Moreover, when a basic microprocessor design can have more feature details than the map of every building, street, and utility line in a full-size city, the need for mountains of documentation becomes particularly acute. This places three historically unprece-dented duties on most team leaders:

- To *assume*, while still in the consolidation and maturation phase, many of the tasks heretofore put off until after a project is com-pleted and until now usually done by others. This will almost certainly include heavy documentation and the measurement of performance specs, but may also include creating manuals, training materials, emulators, and even marketing and sales tools.
- To *design* these expanded completion-phase duties into the proj-ect from the very beginning. Traditionally, teams didn't have to worry that much about how they finished until they had reached their goals and were down to the final wrap-up. Now the completion phase—because it is likely to be drawn out and costly, and to require considerable labor—needs to be incorpo-rated into a team's schedule and milestones. As it is unlikely, given the press of competition, that the team will be allowed extra time to finish the task, the best alternative may be to add more team members either at the beginning, or (here's yet one more place where quick assimilation comes in) at the start of the consolidation phase.
- To *prepare* the team for the added work that will be required at the end of the project. Completing the actual subject of a project greatly reduces the motivation of a team: employees (and lead-ers) naturally see it as the end of the hard work and the begin-ning of the hard celebrations of what they've achieved. There is a no more depressed group of people than a successful team that returns on Monday morning to discover that instead of merely

tying up some loose ends, they are now expected to take on a whole new phase of supplemental work. The answer—and admittedly it is a limited one—is to prepare the team for this bad news from the beginning. That is, from the start, in all calendars, targets, and milestones, incorporate these "after" duties—and regularly remind the team of their existence—such that they subconsciously reset their notion of "end" to the completion of this work. Finally, sad to say, you may also want to consider postponing any celebrations until all the work is done (and look the other way when team members still choose to celebrate early—just don't let it be official).

As a leader, beware of mission creep, especially considering these additional responsibilities. It's pretty easy to know when the core mission of a team—a fully tested new product or service—has been completed. It is not so easy when the work expands to intrude into other company departments. The creation of documentation, publications, development tools, and so forth has a tendency to be an open-ended process, and other corporate departments are sometimes quite happy to let you do their work for them. So it is incumbent on you as leader to establish boundaries on this work at a project's beginning.

When you do reach that end, formally announce that fact—and then *celebrate*. This is not a time for reserve, or weary acceptance, or polite acknowledgment of a job well done. Even if you've failed to achieve all of your goals, your team deserves a full-blown recognition of its loyalty and hard work if it is healthy and strong. And if the team has succeeded, that's even more reason for a party. Make it an event that every team member will always remember: if they stay all night because they don't want to leave, if they get drunk, weep, make fools out of themselves, let them. Just remember to cover the following in the course of the celebration:

- Recount their achievements.
- Remind them of the team's beginnings, how they didn't know each other and how close they've become since.
- Reminisce about the high points (and the low points overcome) in the team's history.
- Most of all, recognize the work of every team member individually, both before the rest of the team and one-on-one.
- Retreat at the right moment. Every leader plans the beginning of these events; smart ones plan the ending—especially the part about exiting quickly and on a high note.

THE AFTERMATH PHASE

The future of a team's members, and how you deal with the legacy of the team, depends on which of the following four categories the team falls into:

Unhealthy, Unsuccessful Teams

Unhealthy, unsuccessful teams are either intentionally forgotten or indelibly scar their members. Not only have they failed—damaging both their parent company and the résumés of their members—but the miserable experience will likely make those members less effective in the future, and almost impossible to put together as another viable grouping. In most cases, the members aren't even around anymore but have moved on to happier work environments. These teams can be considered failures in every way: the wrong members, the wrong leader, the wrong task or direction, poor oversight by the organization, and a failure to shut the team down early.

It is usually the best strategy to admit that failure, let the members leave the organization, and conduct a postmortem to determine what went wrong and make sure it doesn't happen again.

That said, some of these teams may have a member or two who may appear to be worth keeping. Whether they really are revolves around the word "worth." Because of his or her recent history with a dysfunctional, failed team, the worth of this team member must be measured differently from someone with a clean slate. With such a person you need to look past the standard résumé highlights and dig down into her behavior with the team. That means interviews, at least with that employee, in order to determine how she dealt with the team during its existence, how bitter she is from the experience, and how much she holds (perhaps rightly) senior management responsible for what happened.

Unhealthy, Successful Teams

Unhealthy, successful teams are in many ways the most dangerous of all teams. You can easily, and with justification, get rid of an entire unhealthy, unsuccessful team and minimize your risk. But success camouflages a lot of bad things. Moreover, remove a successful team and all the other teams in the organization will suffer a serious drop in morale ("If they got punished, are we next?").

The challenge, then, is to look past the success and see the truth of the team in stark relief. And since you can't know if a successful team is also unhealthy, you will have to scrutinize all successful teams in this way, even the ones that, on the surface, look happy and functional.

During his career as a newspaperman, Mike was once warned by an editor, "Don't ever hire a Pulitzer Prize winner." Only with time did he understand what the veteran journalist had meant: too many people who won top prizes did so because they happened to be in the right place at the right time, or because they were put in a team with others of superior talent, or because they were rewarded for the wrong reasons—a fan on the selection committee, their organization's "turn" for an award, larger national or global events that make their story timely, and so on. Whatever the real reason, the fact that they had received the award cast a penumbra of achievement around them that demanded a higher salary, bigger stories, and greater independence whether they deserved it or not.

Dysfunction in a successful team takes several forms:

a. A team that, despite its internal strife, just gets lucky.
b. A team that features so much talent that, despite itself, still manages to get across the finish line—though much less successfully than it might have otherwise.
c. A team that is composed of some top-quality members, and others who just played easy riders but took a share of the credit.
d. A team that fakes results to look like it succeeded.

The reason successful, unhealthy teams are so dangerous is not (with the exception of [d]) because of what they've accomplished, but what happens to them in the aftermath phase. Unless exposed, every member of these teams will carry the afterglow of the success—and it will reward them with raises, promotions, fame, and recruitment into even more important teams. There, they threaten to poison their new team's health, or through their lack of ability prevent that team from achieving its potential. Meanwhile, you may have deluded yourself that these players are winners, but—trust us—everybody else in the company, especially their peers, will soon know the truth and grow increasingly resentful. Everybody despises fellow employees who have so obviously fallen upward—as they despise the bosses who allowed it to happen.

By being successful, however, these unhealthy teams do— especially if their damaging influence can be detected and stopped—contribute to the success of the enterprise. On the other hand, (d)-type teams are destructive, unethical, and perhaps even criminal. That kind of pathology needs to be spotted early and punished quickly.

Healthy, Unsuccessful Teams

Healthy, unsuccessful teams are the trickiest to judge. Silicon Valley likes to pride itself as the place where failure is both understood and rewarded. The cliché is that the Valley's venture capitalists are clever enough to recognize "good failures," while downplaying "bad successes." It sounds good in theory—and indeed, our own experiences with this in the Valley were one of the sources of this section—but answers are a lot more elusive in real life. The heart of the matter is that phrase "good failure." What exactly does that mean? Can failure actually be good?

The standard answer to that question is "Of course." You can run a healthy, productive team, hit all of your milestones, do everything right, and deliver on time, and still fail because of forces outside your control: a new technology, a market shift, a quicker or more powerful competitor, an economic downturn, bad senior management, and so on.

But that answer is too facile; and it raises even more questions. After all, if you had done a good job, wouldn't you have adapted to those challenges? Wouldn't you have anticipated them and prepared a response? And if your failure was the result of bad decisions by your superiors (budget cuts, wrongheaded interventions, last minute changes), why didn't you quit? Thus, the meaning of a "good failure" is that you failed, but the mistakes you made would likely have been made by any prudent person in your position at that moment—including the person currently calling your enterprise a "good failure."

So the most important questions you should be asking in your postmortem of a failed but seemingly healthy team include the following:

- In retrospect, did the team have a viable strategy that would have worked without the interference or incompetence of senior management?
- Did the team function harmoniously throughout its life, including even during the interval when its impending failure was apparent?
- When it encountered the event that would prove fatal to the team's efforts, did the team recognize it as such, or were the members oblivious?
- How did the team react to this news? Did it try to react? Develop a new strategy? Or just surrender?
- Did the team leader keep the team on point in the aftermath of this shock?
- Did the team search for new and relevant talent in its response? Was that talent quickly incorporated into the team's work?
- Did the team leader quickly present the changed situation, with alternative responses, to senior management—or did he or she and the rest of the team try to hide it from outsiders?
- Was blame cast and recriminations made among team members for the failed outcome?
- Did the team leader help the team members with recommendations and job placement in the aftermath of the failure, or were the team members jettisoned and forgotten?
- Finally, and this is the question you must ask of yourself: *Not knowing what was to come, would you have done anything differently?*

In answering those questions, you will find the truth about whether this team was as healthy as you thought, and whether indeed it suffered a "good failure." If the answer is that it did, then your response should be to hold the members to as little blame as possible and move them on to the next project. If possible—and this would be best for company morale—keep that team together . . . and give them a "win" for their next project if you can.

On the other hand, if you determine that this team was not as healthy as you first thought, break it up and treat the members as if they were members of the unhealthy, unsuccessful teams described earlier in this chapter.

Healthy, Successful Teams

Healthy, successful teams will prove the most difficult to manage. The members of the team know what they've accomplished, and they've had a satisfying time doing so. Unlike the members of unhealthy, successful teams, all the members know that they are good at what they do, that they made substantial individual contributions, and that they deserve to be properly rewarded.

For that reason, you will have a tough time keeping this team together. First of all, thanks to salary increases, the cost of operating this team in the future will be much higher. Second, the Peter Principle will soon be at work, as the team members start getting promotions to better jobs (for which they may or may not be suited). This will be especially the case for the team leader: successful team leadership—in business, in science, in the military—is almost always the prerequisite for advancement to senior management. (The good news is that you'll likely be promoted too.) Finally, news of the success will hardly be confined to your own organization, and it won't be long before some of those team members will be recruited by other divisions in your company and by competitors. In some cases, team members will decide to become entrepreneurs and start their own companies.

This can be disappointing; but it can also be good news. Healthy, successful teams can be lucky too. And because a team managed to remain healthy and achieve success on one project, the odds that it will do the same the next time around are only increased—they aren't guaranteed. Indeed, the best strategy at the end of one of these teams may be to accept the inevitable and allow it to break up—but to do so in a managed and strategic way.

That is, let the team leader get promoted; it's probably best for the company's future anyway. But identify the other team members with the most managerial talent, and make them the leaders of new teams pursuing new goals. With luck, you will multiply the success and functionality of the original team, as the new team leaders pass on what they've learned about winning. Then take the other members of the original team and place them in other teams that have a high chance of success in the hope that they will push those teams over the line to victory. This may seem counterintuitive: If a team is already likely to be successful, why waste on it the talents of another winner, when that person could instead be used to turn around, or at least improve the odds, of a failing team? Two reasons:

- You go for the win. Life doesn't offer that many wins, so you take them when you can. You are better off achieving a guaranteed victory, especially one that accomplishes more than expected, than trying to push a failing team over the finish line.
- Failure breeds failure as much as success breeds success. Adding a winner to a failing team rarely turns things around, as the team is failing either because it can't win in a changed environment, or because it is unhealthy, in which case the newcomer has almost no chance of turning it around. Either way, those teams, as we've already noted, should be *shut down*, not be transformed into a black hole for time and resources trying to resuscitate them.

Handled properly, a healthy and successful team can become the farm team for a whole host of new teams that carry with them the parent team's DNA and that, with luck, are just as healthy and successful.

L'ENVOI

Why, after nearly a quarter millennium, does the story of Washington's farewell at Fraunces Tavern still resonate so deeply?

One obvious reason is that, combined with General Washington's official retirement before the Continental Congress a few days later, the farewells mark a major historical turning point in Western civilization. Much more so than now, the officers and delegates at those two gatherings knew their history—and that the last victorious general who had laid down his sword and submitted to the dictates of an elected legislature had been the Roman consul Cincinnatus. On learning the news, even King George III, the ruler defeated by Washington, was heard to mutter, "If he does that, he will be the greatest man in the world." And he was.

But we think it is more than that. After more than two centuries of living in a democracy, we Americans (and the citizens of those nations with leaders, like Nelson Mandela, who followed Washington's lead) have grown comparatively inured to the bounties of democracy. What was a thunderbolt to the officers in Fraunces Tavern—many of whom still wanted the general to declare himself king—is just everyday life today.

No, what appeals to us about that moment is that *we wish we could have been part of that team.* That feeling is best captured in the famous illustration of that day, in which Washington embraces a weeping officer who is so distraught that he has buried his face in the general's shoulder, while circled around them a dozen other officers bow their heads or wipe their eyes.

Life is short and our chances to do something great are few, and, as we hope this book has convinced you, the best chance for doing so is as part of a team of smart, hardworking people—a team of genius—working together in harmony to create something greater than themselves.

Those officers at Fraunces Tavern—George Washington's team

of senior officers and his headquarters staff—had done just that, and in the process they had accomplished as much as any team in history. They had taken on the world's most powerful army and greatest empire, and beaten it. In seven years, they had literally changed the trajectory of human history, and for the better. And they had done so not only against impossible odds but against a third of the local population and, in Washington's case, against both a stingy Continental Congress and even some of his own generals. They had held together through the worst times imaginable—the Battle of Long Island, Valley Forge, the winter of 1779–80. And despite that, they had emerged victorious, with military successes culminating in "the world turned upside down" at Yorktown.

Many of the original team members were now gone—dead, sick, captured—and one reason the general may have composed the moment as he did was that there were some new and perhaps unfamiliar faces in the crowd. As homogenous as the team now looked, especially in their buff-and-blue uniforms, anyone who had seen them at the beginning of the war would have known how diverse they really were: Southern aristocrats, New England merchants, college students, new immigrants like Alexander Hamilton and "Baron" von Steuben. Even Washington's generals comprised an amazing range of personalities: profane backwoods warrior Dan Morgan, studious bookseller Henry Knox, Quaker Nathaniel Greene, the French aristocrat Marquis de Lafayette.

Somehow—it seemed miraculous even to his contemporaries—Washington had not only held them all together, but also turned them into a formidable army that, at Cowpens and Monmouth, had gone toe to toe with the world's best soldiers and beaten them. Across the colonies, Washington had sent these generals, entrusting them to do their tasks independently—and then, in the end, he had brought everything together on a peninsula in Virginia and sealed the victory. Through all of this, the general had also protected his troops from slaughter, represented their interests against a mercurial Congress, dealt with the demands of a strategic partner (the French navy), established an intelligence apparatus that supplied key information about the opposition, and regularly taken greater risks than the people he led. Where everyone else at some point wavered, the general alone stood firm, unleashed his titanic temper only when premeditated and useful, and put on one of the greatest "performances" of a leader ever seen.

And now it was all ending on a perfect note. The team had done everything it said it would. And now its leader was fulfilling his most important promise to the team and to the people for whom the team worked (the citizens of the new United States of America). Already one team member, General Knox, had organized an alumni group (the Society of Cincinnatus) with the boss's blessing, a group that would still be led by the team members' descendants more than two centuries later.

Most of the team members stayed in touch for the rest of their lives, not least because their singular achievement was the subject of endless celebrations. They would also visit their old boss at the office and at his home for the rest of his life. And when it was time, six years later, to build his next team—his presidential administration—General Washington would draw on many members of that original team, notably Knox (secretary of war) and Hamilton (secretary of the treasury).

Once again, Washington would lead this new-old team to great things, and they in turn would remain intensely loyal to him. As the end of this second team approached, and with it the end of Washington's public life, the team members began positioning themselves against each other for their future careers. But even in the intense competition that followed, they maintained their allegiance to their late leader's legacy, keeping it alive for another generation—long enough to set the former colonies on the path to being the most successful and enduring republic in history.

In an era in which we obsessively collect and share "best practices," the group gathered at Fraunces Tavern on that December afternoon still stands as the very model of a great and successful team. But just as important—and this too is a lesson—this team was far from perfect. As noted, it lost far more battles than it won. Their leader was so inexperienced that he almost wrecked the team on multiple occasions. And, incredibly, the team had at least one traitor (Benedict Arnold), and maybe two (Charles Lee), in its midst. Even their employer faced bankruptcy (and capture, imprisonment, and execution) on multiple occasions.

And yet, against all odds, this team succeeded—it, and its leader, *learned* how to win—and its victory was so complete and so extraordinary that it still rings down through history.

Whatever our dreams and ambitions, it is highly unlikely that any of us will be part of a team as important and successful as the leadership of the Continental Army. And as team leaders, we would be wildly presumptuous to compare ourselves to George Washington, one of the greatest figures of the last millennium. But that doesn't mean that we cannot aspire to be the best possible leaders of the healthiest and most successful teams.

Revolutionary America needed a great natural leader and a whole lot of luck. Against all odds, it got both. But in twenty-first-century America, and in other developed nations throughout the world, teams, big and small, fleeting and enduring, don't need luck (well, perhaps a little). We now have decades of precedent and example to learn from. More than ever before, we can determine not just the optimal team size but also the best team *type*.

Equally important, we now have more than a decade of deep empirical research into the psychological, sociological, and anthropological heart of successful (and unsuccessful) teams. And in the next few years, as digital technology comes to bear, we may even have assistance in team member recruitment.

Finally, we now also have, more than ever before, an understanding of the life cycle of teams. We also, for the first time, have a template for the different phases in this life cycle, and crucial clues about how to lead a team through each of them in turn, as well as through the difficult transitions to the next phase.

The teams in which we work, and the teams we lead, may not change the world. But they can make the world a better place, make our company (and everyone who depends on it) more successful and secure, and give ourselves and our teammates a more rewarding and fulfilling career. And most of all, we can increase the odds of our team's success. Given all of that, why wouldn't we want to apply the latest discoveries and experiences about teams to our own lives and careers? Why wouldn't we want to create and be part of teams of genius?

Not every team can do something great. But every team can *be* great. Even if we can't be at Fraunces Tavern in 1783, we can be at our own team's final party someday in the future, celebrating our victory, making teary promises to stay in touch with each other, and, best of all, knowing that the last few months, or years, of our lives have been well spent.

And who doesn't want that?

Acknowledgments

Rich

This book would not have the depth of research, in chapters two through five especially, if not for the work of Faiiza Rashid, a doctoral candidate at Harvard Business School. Thanks to Jeff Leeson of Benson-Collister for the introduction to Faiiza, and for his invaluable advice on the book's organization. Thanks also to Professor Amy Edmundson of Harvard Business School.

To my coauthor Mike Malone, Silicon Valley's most gifted writer and knowledgeable historian. *Team Genius* marks the latest of many collaborations with Mike, beginning with *Upside* magazine in the 1980s and continuing through *Forbes* ASAP in 1990s, when we tricked the great Tom Wolfe into writing a 9,000-word grand essay ("Sorry, But Your Soul Just Died") for a tiny fee. To future capers and collaborations, Mike!

There is no better book agent than Jim Levine, who, once he believes in you, can sell a project faster than anyone. Thanks for believing in us, Jim, and for saving us the drudge of a long and tedious proposal. Thanks to superstar editor Hollis Heimbouch and to Eric Meyers and Joanna Pinsker of Harper Business.

I'd like to thank Steve Forbes and his brothers Kip, Bob, and Tim for welcoming me aboard a new world back when *Forbes* Magazine was seventy-five years old, and to Mike Perlis for navigating this ship toward our hundredth anniversary in 2017. To T. C. Yam, Wayne

Hsieh, and Sammy Wong for their wise stewardship and guidance. To George Gilder, who taught me to think exponentially, and to Danny Stern, who said I had the chops to be a professional speaker.

My patient wife, Marji, and kids, Katie and Peter, must wonder whether I'm writing my *Forbes* Innovation Rules column, the next book . . . or else sneaking a peek at Real Clear Sports or aviation websites . . . when I'm in my home office, half-supine on my Relax The Back recliner, with my laptop on a thick pillow and drugstore reading glasses on my nose. My wonderful family puts up with me, and I'm grateful.

Mike

To Rich's recognition of Faiiza and Jeff I add my own. Their talents and hard work took this book to a level the two of us could not have reached without them.

As Rich noted, this book marks thirty years of collaboration—creating controversies, putting out some of the best magazine issues of the era, and now, after all of these years, writing our first book together. I hope it's just a prelude to even more fun in the years to come.

Speaking of teams, being part of a trio now for the last seven years with Hollis Heimbauch as my editor and Jim Levine as my agent (in Jim's case, for another decade before that) has been one of the most rewarding experiences of my career. I consider myself very lucky to be able to work with the two best people in their professions—and grateful they were willing to break that rule to work with me. Eric Meyer has now kept me on track for four books (no easy task), and Joanna Pinsker is the best publishing house publicist I have ever worked with, bar none.

At the Malone household, professional writing has now moved on to the next, fifth generation. I hope that the family's newest writer finds the same wonderful teammates on his books as I have found with this one.

Notes

1: CHANGE KILLS

1. Plesu, A. October 10, 2005. "How Big Is the Internet?" Sofpedia.com, http://news.softpedia.com/news/How-Big-Is-the-Internet-10177.shtml
2. Internet World Stats. 2014. "Internet Usage Statistics," www.internet worldstats.com/stats.htm.
3. Value of the Web, www.valueoftheweb.com/.
4. Karlgaard, R. "Are You Maneuverable?" *Forbes*, November 3, 2014, http://www.forbes.com/sites/richkarlgaard/2014/10/15/are-you-maneuverable/.

2: THE MAGIC NUMBERS BEHIND TEAMS

1. Heathfield, S. M. "What Team Size Is Optimum for Performance?" About.com, http://humanresources.about.com/od/teambuildingfaqs/f/optimum-team-size.htm.
2. Hasrati, V. 2007. "Is Five the Optimal Team Size?" InfoQ.com, www.infoq.com/news/2007/11/team-growth-and-productivity.
3. Parkinson, C. N. 1955. "Parkinson's Law." *Economist*, www.economist.com/node/14116121.
4. Ibid.
5. Ibid.
6. Hayes, T., and Malone, M. S. 2009. *No Size Fits All*. New York: Portfolio, pp. 30–31.
7. Bennett, D. January 10, 2013. "The Dunbar Number, from the Guru of Social Networks." *Bloomberg BusinessWeek*, www.businessweek.com/articles/2013-01-10/the-dunbar-number-from-the-guru-of-social-networks#p1.
8. Dunbar, R. 2010. *How Many Friends Does One Person Need?* Cambridge, MA: Harvard University Press, p. 33.

9. Snowden, D. December 10, 2006. "log(N) = 0.093 + 3.389 log(CR) (1) (r2=0.764, t34=10.35, p<0.001)." Cognitive-edge.com, http://cognitive-edge.com/blog/entry/4403/logn-0.093-3.389-logcr-1-r20.764-t3410.35-p0.001/.

10. Social Science Bites. November 4, 2013. "Robin Dunbar on Dunbar Numbers." Socialsciencespace.com, www.socialsciencespace.com/2013/11/robin-dunbar-on-dunbar-numbers/.

11. Coutu, D. "Why Teams Don't Work." May 2009. *Harvard Business Review*, http://hbr.org/2009/05/why-teams-dont-work.

12. Ibid.

3: THE NEW SCIENCE OF TEAMS

1. Wolpert, D., and Frith, C. 2004. *The Neuroscience of Social Interactions: Decoding, Influencing, and Imitating the Actions of Others*. Oxford: Oxford University Press.

2. Clarke, D. D., and Sokoloff, L. 1999. "Circulation and energy metabolism." In G. J. Siegel, B. W. Agranoff, R. W. Albers, S. K. Fisher, and M. D. Uhler (eds.), *Basic Neurochemistry: Molecular, Cellular and Medical Aspects*. Philadelphia: Lippincott-Raven, pp. 637–70.

3. Dunbar, R. 1998. "The social brain hypothesis." *Evolutionary Anthropology* 6(5), pp. 178–89.

4. Humphrey, N.K. 1976. "The social function of intellect." In Bateson, P. P. G., and Hinde, R. A. (eds.). *Growing points in ethology*. Cambridge: Cambridge University Press, pp. 303–17.

   Emery, N. J., Clayton, N. S., and Frith, C. D. 2007. "Introduction. Social intelligence: from brain to culture." *Philosophical Transactions of the Royal Society B* 362 (1480), pp. 362, 485–88.

5. McNally, L., Brown, S. P. and Jackson, A. L. 2012. "Cooperation and the evolution of intelligence." *Proceedings of the Royal Society B* 279(1740), pp. 3027–34.

6. Nowak, M. A. 2006. "Five rules for the evolution of cooperation." *Science* 314, pp. 1560–63.

7. Keltner, D., Kogan, A., Piff, P. K., and Saturn, S. R. 2014. "The Sociocultural Appraisals, Values, and Emotions (SAVE) Framework of Prosociality: Core Processes from Gene to Meme." *Annual Review of Psychology* 65, pp. 425–60.

8. Hill, K. R., Walker, R. S., Božičević, M., Eder, J., Headland, T., Hewlett, B., Hurtado, A. M., Marlowe, F., Wiessner, P., and Wood, B. 2011. "Coresidence patterns in hunter–gatherer societies show unique human social structure." *Science* 331, pp. 1286–89.

9. Dean, L. G., Kendal, R. L., Schapiro, S. J., Thierry, B., and Laland, K. N.

2012. "Identification of the social and cognitive processes underlying human cumulative culture." *Science* 335(6072), pp. 1114–18.

10. Rand, D. G., Greene, J. D., and Nowak, M. A. 2012. "Spontaneous giving and calculated greed." *Nature* 489, pp. 427–30.

11. Rilling, J. K., Gutman, D. A., Zeh, T. R., Pagnoni, G., Berns, G.S., and Kilts, C.D. 2002. "A neural basis for social cooperation." *Neuron* 35(2), pp. 395–405.

Decety, J., Jackson, P. L., Sommerville, J. A., Chaminade, T., Meltzoff, A. N. 2004. "The neural bases of cooperation and competition: an fMRI investigation." *NeuroImage* 23(2), pp. 744–51.

Tabibnia, G., and Lieberman, M. D. 2007. "Fairness and cooperation are rewarding: evidence from social cognitive neuroscience." *Annals of the New York Academy of Sciences* 1118, pp. 90–100.

12. Camerer, C. F. 2003. *Behavioral Game Theory: Experiments in Strategic Interaction.* Princeton, NJ: Princeton University Press.

13. Warneken, F., and Tomasello, M. 2007. "Helping and cooperation at 14 months of age." *Infancy* 11(3), pp. 271–94.

14. Fehr, E., and Fischbacher, U. 2004. "Social norms and human cooperation." *Trends in Cognitive Sciences* 8(4), pp. 185–90.

15. Cialdini, R. B., and Trost. M. R. 1998. "Social influence: social norms, conformity, and compliance." In D. T. Gilbert, S. T. Fiske, G. Lindzey (eds.), *The Handbook of Social Psychology.* New York: McGraw-Hill. 4th ed, pp. 151–92.

16. Gurven, M. 2004. "Reciprocal altruism and food sharing decisions among Hiwi and Ache hunter/gatherers." *Behavioral Ecology and Sociobiology* 56(4), pp. 366–80.

Henrich, J. 2004. "Cultural group selection, coevolutionary processes and large-scale cooperation." *Journal of Economic Behavior and Organization* 53(1), pp. 3–35.

Sober, E., and Wilson, D. S. 1998. *Unto Others: The Evolution and Psychology of Unselfish Behavior.* Cambridge, MA: Harvard University Press.

17. Henrich, J. "Cultural group selection, coevolutionary processes and large-scale cooperation."

Henrich, J., Boyd, R., Bowles, S., and Camerer, C. 2001. "In search of homo economicus: behavioral experiments in 15 small-scale societies." *American Economic Review* 91(2), pp. 73–79.

Henrich, J., Boyd, R., Bowles, S., Camerer, C., Fehr, E, et al. 2005. "'Economic man' in cross-cultural perspective: behavioral experiments in 15 small-scale societies." *Behavioral and Brain Sciences* 28(6), pp. 795–815.

Henrich, J., Boyd, R., Bowles, S., Camerer, C. F., Fehr, E., and Gintis, H. 2004. *Foundations of Human Sociality: Economic Experiments and Ethnographic Evidence from Fifteen Small-Scale Societies.* Oxford: Oxford University Press.

Henrich, J., McElreath, R., Barr, A., Ensminger, J., Barrett, C., et al. 2006. "Costly punishment across human societies." *Science* 312, pp. 1767–70.

18. McNeill, W. H. 1995. *Keeping Together in Time.* Cambridge, MA: Harvard University Press.

19. Fuchs, A., Kelso, J. A. S., and Haken, H. 1992. "Phase transitions in the human brain: Spatial mode dynamics." *International Journal of Bifurcation and Chaos* 2, pp. 917–39.

    Kelso, J. A. S. 1995. *Dynamic Patterns: The Self-Organization of Brain and Behavior.* Cambridge, MA: MIT Press.

    Kelso, J. A. S., Bressler, S. L., Buchanan, S., Deguzman, G. C., Ding, M., Fuchs, A., et al. 1992. "A phase transition in human brain and behavior." *Physics Letters A* 169, pp. 134–44.

    Kelso, J. A. S., Fuchs, A., Lancaster, R., Holroyd, T., Cheyne, D., and Weinberg, H. 1998. "Dynamic cortical activity in the human brain reveals motor equivalence." *Nature* 392, pp. 814–18.

20. Néda, Z., Ravasz, E., Brechet, Y., Vicsek, T., and Barabasi, A. L. 2000a. "The sound of many hands clapping—Tumultuous applause can transform itself into waves of synchronized clapping." *Nature* 403, pp. 849–50.

    Néda, Z., Ravasz, E., Vicsek, T., Brechet, Y., and Barabasi, A. L. 2000b. "Physics of the rhythmic applause." *Physical Review E* 61, pp. 6987–92.

21. Oullier, O., de Guzman, G. C., Jantzen, K. J., Lagarde, J., and Kelso, J. A. S. 2008. "Social coordination dynamics: Measuring human bonding." *Social Neuroscience* 3(2), pp. 178–192.

22. Insel, T. R., and Fernald, R. D. 2004. "How the brain processes social information: Searching for the social brain." *Annual Review of Neuroscience* 27, pp. 697–722.

23. Dunbar, R. "The social brain hypothesis."

24. Grist, M. 2009. *Changing the Subject: How New Ways of Thinking about Human Behavior Might Change Politics, Policy and Practice.* London: Royal Society of Arts.

25. Norman, G. J., Hawkley, L. C., Cole, S. W., Berntson, G. G., and Cacioppo, J. T. 2012. "Social neuroscience: The social brain, oxytocin, and health." *Social Neuroscience* 7(1), pp. 18–29.

26. Carter, C. S. 1998. "Neuroendocrine perspectives on social attachment and love." *Psychoneuroendocrinology* 23(8), pp. 779–818.

    Ross, H. E., Freeman, S. M., Spiegel, L. L., Ren, X., Terwilliger, E. F., and Young, L. J. 2009. "Variation in oxytocin receptor density in the nucleus accumbens has differential effects on affiliative behaviors in monogamous and polygamous voles." *Journal of Neuroscience* 29(5), pp. 1312–18.

    Williams, J. R., Insel, T. R., Harbaugh, C. R., and Carter, C. S. 1994. "Oxytocin administered centrally facilitates formation of a partner preference in female prairie voles (Microtus ochrogaster)." *Journal of Neuroendocrinology* 6(3), pp. 247–50.

27. Norman, G. J., et al. "Social neuroscience: The social brain, oxytocin, and health."

28. Heinrichs, M., Baumgartner, T., Kirschbaum, C., and Ehlert, U. 2003. "Social support and oxytocin interact to suppress cortisol and subjective responses to psychosocial stress." *Biological Psychiatry* 54(12), pp. 1389–98.

29. Witt, D. M., Winslow, J. T., and Insel, T. R. 1992. "Enhanced social interactions in rats following chronic, centrally infused oxytocin." *Pharmacology, Biochemistry, and Behavior* 43(3), pp. 855–61.

30. Di Simplicio, M., Massey-Chase, R., Cowen, P. J., and Harmer, C. J. 2009. "Oxytocin enhances processing of positive versus negative emotional information in healthy male volunteers." *Journal of Psychopharmacology* 23, pp. 241–48.

    Guastella, A. J., Mitchell, P. B., and Mathews, F. 2008. "Oxytocin enhances the encoding of positive social memories in humans." *Biological Psychiatry* 64, pp. 256–58.

31. De Dreu, C. K. W., Greer, L. L., Handgraaf, M. J. J., Shalvi. S., Van Kleef, G. A., et al. 2010. "The neuropeptide oxytocin regulates parochial altruism in intergroup conflict among humans." *Science* 328, pp. 1408–11.

    Kosfeld, M., Heinrichs, M., Zak, P. J., Fischbacher, U., Fehr, E. 2005. "Oxytocin increases trust in humans." *Nature* 435, pp. 673–76.

32. De Dreu, C. K. W., Greer, L. L., Van Kleef, G. A., Shalvi, S., and Handgraaf, M. J. J. 2011. "Oxytocin promotes human ethnocentrism." *Proceedings of the National Academy of Sciences of the United States* 108(4), pp. 1262–66.

33. Penner, L. A., Dovidio, J. F., Piliavin, J. A., and Schroeder, D. A. 2005. "Prosocial behavior: multilevel perspectives." *Annual Review of Psychology* 56(1), pp. 365–92.

    De Waal, F. B. M. 2008. "Putting the altruism back into altruism: the evolution of empathy." *Annual Review of Psychology* 59, pp. 279–300.

34. Decety, J., and Svetlova, M. 2012. "Putting together phylogenetic and ontogenetic perspectives on empathy." *Developmental Cognitive Neuroscience* 2(1), pp. 1–24.

    Panksepp, J. 2007. "The neuroevolutionary and neuroaffective psychobiology of the prosocial brain." In R. I. M. Dunbar and L. Barrett (eds.). *The Oxford Handbook of Evolutionary Psychology*. Oxford: Oxford University Press, pp. 145–62.

35. Donaldson, Z. R., and Young, L. J. 2008. "Oxytocin, vasopressin, and the neurogenetics of sociality." *Science* 322, pp. 900–904.

36. Schneiderman, I., Zagoory-Sharon, O., Leckman, J. F., and Feldman, R. 2012. "Oxytocin during the initial stages of romantic attachment: relations to couples' interactive reciprocity." *Psychoneuroendocrinology* 37(8), pp. 1277–85.

37. Kosfeld, M., et al. "Oxytocin increases trust in humans."

38. De Dreu, et al. "The neuropeptide oxytocin regulates parochial altruism in intergroup conflict among humans."

De Dreu, C. K., et al. "Oxytocin promotes human ethnocentrism."

39. Norman G. J., et al. "Social neuroscience: The social brain, oxytocin, and health."

40. Meinlschmidt, G., and Heim, C. 2007. "Sensitivity to intranasal oxytocin in adult men with early parental separation." *Biological Psychiatry* 61(9), pp. 1109–11.

41. O'Gormon, R., Sheldon, K. M., and Wilson, D. S. 2008. "For the good of the group? Exploring group-level evolutionary adaptations using multi-level selection theory." *Group Dynamics: Theory, Research, and Practice* 12 (1), pp. 17–26.

42. Brewer M. B., and Caporael L. R. 1990. "Selfish genes vs. selfish people: sociobiology as origin myth." *Motivation and Emotion* 14, pp. 237–43.

43. Barry, A. M. 2009. "Mirror Neurons: How We Become What We See." *Visual Communication Quarterly* 16(2), pp. 79–89.

44. Rizzolatti, G. 2005. "The Mirror Neuron System and its Function in Humans." *Anatomical Embryology* 210, pp. 419–21.

45. Rizzolatti, G., and Craighero, L. 2004. "The Mirror-Neuron System." *Annual Review of Neuroscience* 27, pp. 169–92.

46. Goleman, D. 2006. *Social Intelligence: The New Science of Human Relationships.* New York: Bantam Books.

47. Goleman, D., and Boyatzis, R. 2008. "Social intelligence and the biology of leadership." *Harvard Business Review* 86(9), pp. 74–81.

48. Ibid.

49. Ibid.

Sala, F. 2003. "Laughing all the way to the bank." *Harvard Business Review,* pp. 16–17.

50. Clouse, R. W., and Spurgeon, K. L. 1995. "Corporate Analysis of Humor." *Psychology: A Journal of Human Behavior* 32, pp. 1–24.

51. Bettinghaus, E., and Cody, M. 1994. *Persuasive Communication.* Fort Worth, TX: Harcourt Brace College Publishers. 5th ed.

Foot, H. 1997. "Humor and laughter." In O. Hargie (ed.). *The Handbook of Communication Skills.* London: Routledge. 2nd ed.

52. Vissera, V.A., van Knippenberga, D., van Kleef, G. A., and Wissec, B. "How leader displays of happiness and sadness influence follower performance: Emotional contagion and creative versus analytical performance." *Leadership Quarterly* 24(1), pp. 172–88.

53. Barsade, S. G., and Gibson, D. E. 2007. "Why does affect matter in organizations?" *Academy of Management Perspectives* 21, pp. 36–59.

54. Dasborough, M. T. 2006. "Cognitive asymmetry in employee emotional reactions to leadership behaviors." *Leadership Quarterly* 79, 163–78.

55. Hatfield, E., Cacioppo, J. T., and Rapson, R. L. 1993. "Emotional conta-gion." *Current Directions in Psychological Science* 2(3), pp. 96–99.

Christakis, N. A., and Fowler, J. H. 2009. *Connected: The Surprising Power of Our Social Networks and How They Shape Our Lives.* New York: Little, Brown.

56. Algoe, S. B. and Haidt, J. 2009. "Witnessing excellence in action: the 'other-praising' emotions of elevation, gratitude, and admiration." *Journal of Positive Psychology* 4(2), pp. 105–27.

Schnall, S., Roper, J., and Fessler, D. M. 2010. "Elevation leads to altru-istic behavior." *Psychological Science* 21(3), pp. 315–20.

Schnall, S., and Roper, J. 2012. "Elevation puts moral values into ac-tion." *Social Psychological Personality Science* 3(3), pp. 373–78.

57. Jonas, E., Martens, A., Kayser, D. N., Fritsche, I., Sullivan, D., and Greenberg, J. 2008. "Focus theory of normative conduct and Terror-Management Theory: the interactive impact of mortality salience and norm salience on social judgment." *Journal of Personality and Social Psy-chology* 95(6), pp. 1239–51.

58. Krupka, E., and Weber, R. A. 2009. "The focusing and informational effects of norms on pro-social behavior." *Journal of Economic Psychology* 30(3), pp. 307–20.

59. Ramnani, N., and Miall, R. C. 2004. "A system in the human brain for predicting the actions of others." *Nature Neuroscience* 7(1), pp. 85–90.

Sebanz, N., Knoblich, G., and Prinz, W. 2003. "Representing others' actions: Just like one's own?" *Cognition* 88(3), pp. 11–21.

60. Gallese, V., Fadiga, L., Fogassi, L., and Rizzolatti, G. 1996. "Action recog-nition in the premotor cortex." *Brain* 119(2), pp. 593–609.

Rizzolatti, G., Fogassi, L., and Gallese, V. 2001. "Neurophysiological mechanisms underlying the understanding and imitation of action." *Na-ture Reviews Neuroscience* 2(9), pp. 661–70.

61. Hommel, B., Colzato, L. S., and van den Wildenberg, W. P. M. 2009. "How social are task representations?" *Psychological Science* 20(7), pp. 794–98.

62. Koban, L., Pourtois, G., Vocat, R., and Vuilleumier, P. 2010. "When your errors make me lose or win: Event-related potentials to observed errors of cooperators and competitors." *Social Neuroscience* 5, pp. 360–74.

63. De Cremer, D., and Stouten, J. 2003. "When do people find cooperation most justified? The effect of trust and self–other merging in social dilem-mas." *Social Justice Research* 16(1), pp. 41–52.

Sommerville, J. A., and Hammond, A. J. 2007. "Treating another's ac-tions as one's own: Children's memory of and learning from joint activ-ity." *Developmental Psychology* 43(4), pp. 1003–18.

64. Koban, L., et al. "When your errors make me lose or win: Event-related potentials to observed errors of cooperators and competitors."

65. In a 2005 interview with Diane L. Coutu, a senior editor at the *Harvard Business Review*, Kasparov explained:

> People who see chess as a scientific pursuit played by some kind of human supercomputer may be surprised, but it takes more than logic to be a world-class chess player. That's because chess is a mathematically infinite game. The total number of possible different moves in a single game of chess is more than the number of seconds that have elapsed since the Big Bang created the universe. Many people don't recognize that. They look at the chessboard and they see 64 squares and 32 pieces and they think that the game is limited. It's not, and even at the highest levels it is impossible to calculate very far out. I can think maybe 15 moves in advance, and that's about as far as any human has gone. Inevitably, you reach a point when you've got to navigate by using your imagination and feelings rather than your intellect or logic. At that moment, you are playing with your gut.

66. Goleman, D., and Boyatzis, R. 2008. "Social intelligence and the biology of leadership." *Harvard Business Review* 86(9), pp. 74–81.

67. Algoe, S. B., Haidt, J., and Gable, S. L. 2008. "Beyond reciprocity: gratitude and relationships in everyday life." *Emotion* 8(3), pp. 425–29.

68. Grant, A. M., and Gino, F. 2010. "A little thanks goes a long way: explaining why gratitude expressions motivate prosocial behavior." *Journal of Personality and Social Psychology* 98(6), pp. 946–55.

69. Rolls, E. T., O' Doherty, J., Kringelbach, M. L., Francis, S., Bowtell, R., and McGlone, F. 2003. "Representations of pleasant and painful touch in the human orbitofrontal and cingulate cortices." *Cerebral Cortex* 13(3), pp. 308–17.

70. Holt-Lunstad, J., Birmingham, W. A., and Light, K. C. 2008. "Influence of a 'warm touch' support enhancement intervention among married couples on ambulatory blood pressure, oxytocin, alpha amylase, and cortisol." *Psychosomatic Medicine* 70(9), pp. 976–85.

71. Hansen, A. L., Johnsen, B. H., and Thayer, J. F. 2003. "Vagal influence on working memory and attention." *International Journal of Psychophysiology* 48(3), pp. 263–74.

72. Kraus, M. W., Huang, C., and Keltner, D. 2010. "Tactile communication, cooperation, and performance: an ethological study of the NBA." *Emotion* 10(5), pp. 745–49.

    Kurzban, R. 2001. "The social psychophysics of cooperation: nonverbal communication in a public goods game." *Journal of Nonverbal Behavior* 25(4), pp. 241–59.

73. Craik, K. H. 2009. *Reputation: A Network Interpretation*. New York: Oxford University Press.

74. Anderson C., John, O. P., Keltner, D., and Kring, A. M. 2001. "Who attains

social status? Effects of personality and physical attractiveness in social groups." *Journal of Personality and Social Psychology* 81(1), pp. 116–32.

Anderson, C., and Shirako, A. 2008. "Are individuals' reputations related to their history of behavior?" *Journal of Personality and Social Psychology* 94(2), pp. 320–33.

75. Milinski, M., Semmann, D., and Krambeck, H-J. 2002. "Reputation helps solve the 'tragedy of the commons.'" *Nature* 415, pp. 424–26.

76. Holt-Lunstad, J., Smith, T. B., and Layton, J. B. 2010. "Social relationships and mortality risk: A meta-analytic review." *PLoS Medicine* 7(7), e1000316.

77. Cacioppo, J. T., Hawkley, L. C., Crawford, L. E., Ernst, J. M., Burleson, M. H., Kowalewski, R. B., et al. 2002. "Loneliness and health: Potential mechanisms." *Psychosomatic Medicine* 64(3), pp. 407–17.

78. Cohen, S., Doyle, W. J., Skoner, D. P., Rabin, B. S., and Gwaltney, J. M., Jr. 1997. "Social ties and susceptibility to the common cold." *Journal of the American Medical Association* 277(24), pp. 1940–44.

Pressman, S. D., Cohen, S., Miller, G. E., Barkin, A., Rabin, B. S., and Treanor, J. J. 2005. "Loneliness, social network size, and immune response to influenza vaccination in college freshmen." *Health Psychology* 24(3), pp. 297–306.

79. Henry, R. A. 1993. "Group judgment accuracy: Reliability and validity of post discussion confidence judgments." *Organizational Behavior and Human Decision Process* 56, pp. 11–27.

Henry, R. A. 1995. "Improving group judgment accuracy: Information sharing and determining the best member." *Organizational Behavior and Human Decision Processes* 62, pp. 190–97.

Sniezek, J. A., and Henry, R. A. 1990. "Revision, weighting and commitment in consensus group judgment." *Organizational Behavior and Human Decision Processes* 45, pp. 66–84.

Laughlin, P. R., Bonner, B. L., Miner, A. G., and Carnevale, P. J. 1999. "Frames of reference in quantity estimations by groups and individuals." *Organizational Behavior and Human Decision Processes* 80, pp. 103–17.

Bonner, B. L., Sillito, S. D., and Baumann, M. R. 2007. "Collective estimation: Accuracy, expertise, and extroversion as sources of intra-group influence." *Organizational Behavior and Human Decision Processes* 103, pp. 121–33.

80. Henry, R. A. 1993. "Group judgment accuracy: Reliability and validity of post discussion confidence judgments." *Organizational Behavior and Human Decision Process* 56, pp. 11–27.

81. Henry, R. A. 1995. "Improving group judgment accuracy: Information sharing and determining the best member." *Organizational Behavior and Human Decision Processes* 62, pp. 190–97.

82. Bonner, B. L., et al. "Collective estimation: Accuracy, expertise, and extroversion as sources of intra-group influence."

83. Schultze T., Mojzisch, A., and Schulz-Hardt, S. 2012. "Why groups perform better than individuals at quantitative judgment tasks: Group-to-individual transfer as an alternative to differential weighting." *Organizational Behavior and Human Decision Processes* 118, pp. 24–36.

84. Howe, C. 2009. "Collaborative group work in middle childhood: Joint construction, unresolved contradiction and the growth of knowledge." *Human Development* 52, pp. 215–19.

   Howe, C. 2010. *Peer Groups and Children's Development.* Oxford: Wiley-Blackwell.

85. Schulz-Hardt, S., Brodbeck, F. C., Mojzisch, A., Kerschreiter, R., and Frey, D. 2006. "Group decision making in hidden profile situations: Dissent as a facilitator for decision quality." *Journal of Personality and Social Psychology* 91, pp. 1080–93.

86. Howe, C. 2009. "Collaborative group work in middle childhood: Joint construction, unresolved contradiction and the growth of knowledge." *Human Development* 52, pp. 215–19.

   Howe, C. 2010. *Peer Groups and Children's Development.* Oxford: Wiley-Blackwell.

87. Pentland, A. 2012. "The new science of building great teams." *Harvard Business Review* 90(4), pp. 60–68, 70.

88. Will, U., and Berg, E. 2007. "Brain wave synchronization and entrainment to periodic acoustic stimuli." *Neuroscience Letters* 424, pp. 55–60.

89. Stevens, R. H., Galloway, T., Berka, C., and Sprang, M. 2009. "Neurophysiologic collaboration patterns during team problem solving." *Proceedings: HFES 53rd Annual Meeting,* October 19–23, 2009, San Antonio, TX.

   Stevens, R. H., Galloway, T., Berka, C., and Behneman, A. 2010. "Identification and application of neurophysiologic synchronies for studying team behavior." In *Proceedings of the 19th Conference on Behavior Representation in Modeling and Simulation,* pp. 21–28.

   Stevens, R. H., Galloway, T., Wang, P., Berka, C., Tan, V., Wohlgemuth, T., Lamb, J., and Buckles, R. 2013a. "Modeling the neurodynamic complexity of submarine navigation teams." *Computational and Mathematical Organization Theory* 19(3), pp. 346–69.

90. Stevens, R. H., Galloway, T., Campbell G., Berka, C., and Balthazard P. 2013b. "How tasks help shape the neurodynamic rhythms and organizations of teams." *Foundations of Augmented Cognition Lecture Notes in Computer Science* 8027, pp. 199–208.

4: THE POWER OF DIFFERENCE

1. Woolley, A. W., Hackman, J. R., Jerde, T. J., Chabris, C. F., Bennett, S. L., and Kosslyn, S. M. 2007. "Using brain-based measures to compose teams: How individual capabilities and team collaboration strategies jointly shape performance." *Social Neuroscience* 2, pp. 96–105.
2. Rypma, B., Berger, J. S., Prabhakaran, V., Bly, B. M., Kimberg, D. Y., Biswal, B. B., et al. 2006. "Neural correlates of cognitive efficiency." *NeuroImage* 33(3), pp. 969–79.
3. Woolley, A. W., Gerbasi, M. E., Chabris, C. F., Kosslyn, S. M., and Hackman, J. R. 2008. "Bringing in the experts: How team composition and work strategy jointly shape analytic effectiveness." *Small Group Research* 39(3), pp. 352–71.
4. Kozhevnikov, M., Kosslyn, S. M., and Shephard, J. 2005. "Spatial versus object visualizers: A new characterization of visual cognitive style." *Memory and Cognition* 33, pp. 710–26.
5. Woolley, A. W., et al. "Bringing in the experts: How team composition and work strategy jointly shape analytic effectiveness."
6. Hackman, J. R., Brousseau, K. R., and Weiss, J. A. 1976. "The interaction of task design and group performance strategies in determining group effectiveness." *Organizational Behavior and Human Decision Processes* 16, pp. 350–65.
   Wittenbaum, G. M., Vaughan, S. I., and Stasser, G. 1998. "Coordination in task-performing groups." In R. S. Tindale, L. Heath, J. Edwards, E. J. Posavac, F. B. Bryant, Y. Suarez-Balcazar, E. Henderson-King, and J. Myers (eds.), *Theory and Research on Small Groups*. New York: Plenum, pp. 177–205.
7. Wegner, D. M. 1986. "Transactive memory: A contemporary analysis of the group mind." In G. Mullen and G. Goethals (eds.), *Theories of Group Behavior*. New York: Springer-Verlag, pp. 185–208.
   Wegner, D. M. 1995. "A computer network model of human transactive memory." *Social Cognition* 13, pp. 319–39.
   Mohammed, S. and Dumville, B. C. 2001. "Team mental models in a team knowledge framework: Expanding theory and measurement across disciplinary boundaries." *Journal of Organizational Behavior* 22, pp. 89–106.
8. Masuda, T., and Nisbett, R. E. 2001. "Attending holistically vs. analytically: Comparing the context sensitivity of Japanese and Americans." *Journal of Personality and Social Psychology* 81, pp. 922–34.
9. Weiss, H. M., and Shaw, J. B. 1979. "Social influences on judgments about tasks." *Organizational Behavior and Human Performance* 24(1), pp. 126–40.
10. Miron-Spektor, E., Erez, M., and Naveh, E. 2012. "To drive creativity, add some conformity." *Harvard Business Review* 90(3), p. 30.

11. When we speak of left- and right-brained people, we may not be speaking literally. A two-year study of the brain scans of more than one thousand people ages seven to twenty-nine was conducted as recently as 2103 by Dr. Jeff Anderson, the director of the fMRI Neurosurgical Mapping Service at the University of Utah, and his colleagues. The result? They found no evidence of left- and right-brained people. So we may be talking only of personality types here, not brain hemisphere dominance. Time will tell. In the meantime, our concern is that people do seem to come in either creative or empirical types.

12. Leonard, D. A., and Straus, S. 1997. "Putting your Company's Whole Brain to Work." *Harvard Business Review* 75(4), pp. 110–22.

13. Ibid.

14. Hackman, J. R. 2002. *Leading Teams: Setting the Stage for Great Performances.* Boston: HBS Press.

    Hackman, J. R., and Wageman, R. 2005. "When and how team leaders matter." *Research in Organizational Behavior* 26, pp. 37–74.

15. Uzzi, B., Mukherjee, S., Stringer, and M., Jones, B. 2013. "Atypical Combinations and Scientific Impact." *Science* 342(6157), pp. 468–72.

16. Shih, M., Pittinsky, T. L., and Ambady, N. 1999. "Stereotype susceptibility: Identity salience and shifts in quantitative performance." *Psychological Science* 10, pp. 80–83.

17. Hong, L., and Page, S. 2001. "Problem solving by heterogeneous agents." *Journal of Economic Theory* 97, pp. 123–63.

18. Williams, K. Y., and O'Reilly, C. A. 1998. "Demography and diversity in organizations." *Research in Organizational Behavior* 20, pp. 77–140.

19. Milliken, F. J., and Martins, L. L. 1996. "Searching for common threads: understanding the multiple effects of diversity in organizational groups." *Academy of Management Review* 21(2), pp. 402–33.

    Williams, K. Y., and O'Reilly, C. A. 1998. "Demography and diversity in organizations." *Research in Organizational Behavior* 20, pp. 77–140.

20. Cox, T.H. 1993. *Cultural Diversity in Organization: Theory Research and Practice.* San Francisco: Berrett-Koehler Publishing.

    Ibarra, Herminia. June 1995. "Race, opportunity, and diversity of social circles in managerial networks." *The Academy of Management Journal* 38(3), pp. 673–703.

    Martin, J., and Pettigrew, T. 1989. "Shaping the organizational context for minority inclusion." *Journal of Social Issues* 43, pp. 41–78.

21. Gladstein, D. L. 1984. "A model of task group effectiveness." *Administrative Science Quarterly* 29(4), pp. 499–517.

    Jehn, K. A. 1995. "A multi-method examination of the benefits and detriments of intragroup conflict." *Administrative Science Quarterly* 40(2), pp. 256–82.

    Jehn, K. A., Northcraft, G. B., and Neale, M. A. 1999. "Why difference make a difference: A field study of diversity, conflict, and performance in workgroups." *Administrative Science Quarterly* 44(4), pp. 741–63.

22. Bell, M. P., and Berry, D. P. 2007. "Viewing diversity through different lenses: Avoiding a few blind spots." *Academy of Management Perspectives* 21(4), pp. 21–25.

  Klein, K. J., and Harrison, D. A. 2007. "On the diversity of diversity: tidy logic, messier realities." *Academy of Management Perspectives* 21(4), pp. 26–33.

23. Bell, M. P. and Berry, D. P. 2007. "Viewing diversity through different lenses: Avoiding a few blind spots." *Academy of Management Perspectives* 21(4), pp. 21–25.

  Klein, K. J., and Harrison, D. A. 2007. "On the diversity of diversity: tidy logic, messier realities." *Academy of Management Perspectives* 21(4), pp. 26–33.

24. Van Vugt, M. and Hart, C. M. 2004. "Social identity as social glue: The origins of group loyalty." *Journal of Personality and Social Psychology* 86, pp. 585–98.

25. Homan, A. C., van Knippenberg, D., van Kleef, G. A., and De Dreu, C. K. W. 2007. "Bridging faultlines by valuing diversity: Diversity beliefs, information elaboration, and performance in diverse work groups." *Journal of Applied Psychology* 92, pp. 1189–99.

26. Chatman, J. A., and Flynn, F. J. 2001. "The influence of demographic composition on the emergence and consequences of cooperative norms in groups." *Academy of Management Journal* 44(5), pp. 956–74.

  Ely, R. J. 2004. "A field study of group diversity, participation in diversity education programs, and performance." *Journal of Organizational Behavior* 25(6), pp. 755–80.

  Harrison, D. A., Price, K. H., Gavin, J. H., and Florey, A. T. 2002. "Time, teams, and task performance: Changing effects of surface- and deep-level diversity on group functioning." *Academy of Management Journal* 45(5), pp. 1029–45.

27. Huckman, R. S., and Staats, B. 2013. "The hidden benefits of keeping teams intact." *Harvard Business Review* 91(12), pp. 27–29.

28. Polzer, J., Milton, L., and Swann, W. 2002. "Capitalizing on diversity: Interpersonal congruence in small work groups." *Administrative Science Quarterly* 47, pp. 296–324.

29. Bunderson, J. S. 2003. "Recognizing and utilizing expertise in work groups: A status characteristics perspective." *Administrative Science Quarterly* 48, pp. 557–91.

  Cronin, M. A., and Weingart, L. R. 2007. "Representational gaps, information processing, and conflict in functionally diverse teams." *Academy of Management Review* 32, pp. 761–73.

30. Mintzberg, H., Raisinghani, D., and Theoret, A. 1976. "The Structure of

'Unstructured' Decision Processes." *Administrative Science Quarterly* 21, pp. 246–75.

Yen, J., Fan, X., Sun, S., Hanratty, T., and Dumer, J. 2006. "Agents with shared mental models for enhanced team decision making." *Decision Support Systems* 41, pp. 634–53.

31. Okhuysen, G. A., and Eisenhardt, K. M. 2002. "Integrating knowledge in groups: How formal interventions enable flexibility." *Organization Science* 13, pp. 370–86.

32. Henry, R. A. 1995. "Improving group judgment accuracy: Information sharing and determining the best member." *Organizational Behavior and Human Decision Processes* 62, pp. 190–97.

Stasser, G., Stewart, D. D., and Wittenbaum, G. M. 1995. "Expert roles and information exchange during discussion: The importance of knowing who knows what." *Journal of Experimental Social Psychology* 31, pp. 244–65.

33. Bunderson, J. S., and Sutcliffe, K. M. 2002. "Comparing alternative conceptualizations of functional diversity in management teams: Process and performance effects." *Academy of Management Journal* 45, pp. 875–93.

34. Lazar, D., and Friedman A. 2007. "The network structure of exploration and exploitation." *Administrative Science Quarterly* 52, pp. 667–94.

35. Nemeth, C. J., Personnaz, B., Personnaz, M., and Goncalo, J. A. 2004. "The liberating role of conflict in group creativity: A study in two countries." *European Journal of Social Psychology* 34, pp. 365–74.

36. Uzzi, B., and Spiro, J. 2005. "Collaboration and creativity: The small world problem." *American Journal of Sociology* 111(2), pp. 447–504.

37. Hornsey, M. J. 2005. "Why being right is not enough: Predicting defensiveness in the face of group criticism." *European Review of Social Psychology* 16, pp. 301–34.

38. Esposo, S. R., Hornsey, M. J., and Spoor, R. 2013. "Outsiders critical of your group are rejected regardless of argument quality." *British Journal of Social Psychology* 52, pp. 386–95.

39. Gilkey, R., and Kilts C. November 2007. "Cognitive fitness." *Harvard Business Review* 85, pp. 53–54, 56, 58 passim.

40. Lee, K., Brownstein, J. S., Mills, R. G., and Kohane, I. S. 2010. "Does collocation inform the impact of collaboration?" *PLoS ONE* 5(12), e14279.

41. Ibid.

42. Moreland, R. L., and Myaskovsky, L. 2000. "Exploring the performance benefits of group training: Transactive memory or improved communication?" *Organizational Behavior and Human Decision Processes* 82(1), pp. 117–33.

Newell, A., and Rosenbloom, P. 1981. "Mechanisms of skill acquisition and the power law of practice." In J. Anderson (ed.), *Cognitive Skills and Their Acquisition*. Hillsdale, NJ: Erlbaum, pp. 1–55.

Wegner, D. M. 1986. "Transactive memory: A contemporary analysis of the group mind." In G. Mullen and G. Goethals (eds.), *Theories of Group Behavior*. New York: Springer-Verlag, pp. 185–208.

43. Haleblian, J., and Finkelstein, S. 1993. "Top management team size, CEO Dominance, and firm performance: The moderating roles of environmental turbulence and discretion." *Academy of Management Journal* 36(4), pp. 844–63.

    Reagans, R., and Zuckerman, E. W. 2001. "Networks, diversity, and productivity: The social capital of corporate R&D teams." *Organization Science* 12(4), pp. 502–17.

44. Moreland, R. L., Levine, J. M., and Wingert, M. L. 1996. "Creating the ideal group: Composition effects at work." In E. H. Witte and J. H. Davis (eds.), *Understanding Group Behavior: Small-Group Processes and Interpersonal Relations*. Volume 2. Mahwah, NJ: Erlbaum, pp. 11–35.

45. Bray, R. M., Kerr, N. L., and Atkin, R. S. 1978. "Effects of group size, problem difficulty, and sex on group performance and member reactions." *Journal of Personality and Social Psychology* 36(11), pp. 1224–40.

46. Hoegl, M. 2005. "Smaller teams—better teamwork: How to keep project teams small." *Business Horizons* 48, pp. 209–14.

47. Zenger, T. R., and Lawrence, B. S. 1989. "Organizational demography: The differential effects of age and tenure distributions on technical communication." *Academy of Management Journal* 32(2), pp. 353–76.

48. Brooks, F. 1975. *The Mythical Man-Month: Essays on Software Engineering*. New York: Addison-Wesley.

    Chen, G. 2005. "Newcomer adaptation in teams: Multilevel antecedents and outcomes." *Academy of Management Journal* 48(1), pp. 101–16.

49. Kravitz, D. A., and Martin, B. 1986. "Ringelmann rediscovered: The original article." *Journal of Personality and Social Psychology* 50(5), pp. 936–41.

50. Harkins, S. G., and Petty, R. E. 1982. "Effects of task difficulty and task uniqueness on social loafing." *Journal of Personality and Social Psychology* 43(6), pp. 1214–29.

51. Mueller, J. 2012. "Why individuals in larger teams perform worse." *Organizational Behavior and Human Decision Processes* 117, pp. 111–24.

52. Liden, R. C., Wayne, S. J., Jaworski, R. A., and Bennett, N. 2004. "Social loafing: A field investigation." *Journal of Management* 30(2), pp. 285–304.

53. Ancona, D. G., and Caldwell, D. F. 1992. "Bridging the boundary: External activity and performance in organizational teams." *Administrative Science Quarterly* 37, pp. 634–65.

54. Hoegl, M., Weinkauf, K., and Gemuenden, H. G. 2004. "Interteam coordination, project commitment, and teamwork in multiteam R&D projects: A longitudinal study." *Organization Science* 15(1), pp. 38–55.

    Hoegl, M. 2005. "Smaller teams—better teamwork: How to keep project teams small." *Business Horizons* 48, pp. 209–14.

5: MANAGING TEAMS TO GENIUS

1. Wageman, R., and Gordon, D. 2005. "As the twig is bent: How group values shape emergent task interdependence in groups." *Organization Science* 16, pp. 687–700.

2. Wageman, R. 1995. "Interdependence and Group Effectiveness." *Administrative Science Quarterly* 40(1), pp. 145–180.

3. Ginnett, R. 1990. "Airline cockpit crew." In J. R. Hackman (ed.), *Groups That Work (And Those That Don't)*. San Francisco: CA: Jossey-Bass.
   Ginnett, R. 1993. "Crews as groups: Their formation and their leadership." In E. Wiener, B. Kanki, and R. Helmreich (eds.), *Cockpit Resource Management*. San Diego, CA: Academic Press, pp. 71–98.

4. Hackman, J. R. 2002. *Leading Teams: Setting the Stage for Great Performances*. Boston: HBS Press.

5. Ibid.

6. Steiner, I. D. 1972. *Group Process and Productivity*. New York: Academic Press.
   Forsyth, D. R. 2006, 2010. *Group Dynamics*. Belmont, CA: Wadsworth, Cenpage Learning.

7. Edmondson, A. C. December 1999. "Psychological safety and learning behavior in work teams." *Administrative Science Quarterly* 44(4), pp. 350–83.

8. Liden, R. C., Wayne, S. J., Jaworski, R. A., and Bennett, N. 2004. "Social loafing: A field investigation." *Journal of Management* 30(2), pp. 285–304.

9. Van Dick, R., Tissington, P. A., and Hertel, G. 2009. "Do many hands make light work? How to overcome social loafing and gain motivation in work teams." *European Business Review* 21 (3), pp. 233–45.

10. Köhler, O. 1926. "Kraftleistungen bei Einzel- und Gruppenarbeit." ["Physical performance in individual and group work."] *Industrielle Psychotechnik* 3, pp. 274–82.

11. Weber, B., and Hertel, G. 2007. "Motivation gains of inferior group members: a meta-analytical review." *Journal of Personality and Social Psychology* 93(6), pp. 973–93.

12. Hertel, G., Deter, C., and Konradt, U. 2003. "Motivation gains in computer-mediated work groups." *Journal of Applied Social Psychology* 33(10), pp. 2080–2105.

7: SUCCESSFUL PAIRING

1. In terms of an effect on modern life, perhaps no one has ever been better at spotting and developing these "perfect pairs" than Frederick Terman Jr., the professor who set up the first electrical engineering program in

the western United States at Stanford University, where his father had been president. Terman is rightly celebrated as the father of Silicon Valley because of his lab, his students who went out to build the electronics industry, and his successful advocacy of the creation of the first great industrial park.

Less noticed is that Terman, perhaps alone among any academic or business executives, helped create and then successfully managed two Castor and Pollux pair-teams, each exemplifying a different type. The most famous of these perfect pairs is, of course, Bill Hewlett and Dave Packard. Both men had crossed paths for years but didn't really meet until they were in Terman's lab. It was Terman who suggested that the two men work together, beginning in the celebrated Packard garage. He also found them employees, contracts, and clients, and even gave them business advice until their skills far outpaced his own.

Bill and Dave in time created what is still generally considered among the greatest companies of all time. Less appreciated is their almost superhuman friendship: over the course of nearly sixty years, the table-pounding Packard and the genial Hewlett appear never to have had an argument, much less a fight. Not only did they work together every day, but their families often vacationed together—despite the stress of presiding over one of the fastest-growing and most innovative technology companies in history.

Also in Terman's lab in the mid-1930s was an even more unlikely Castor and Pollux team, the Varian brothers. The two men may have been siblings, but in person few would have guessed that fact. Russell Varian was a gentle giant, with a great square jaw and huge hands; phlegmatic and slow moving. Sigurd Varian ("Sig") was small and handsome. They were the sons of Irish theosophists and had been raised in the utopian community of Halcyon, California. As boys, the brothers had built and flown their own airplanes, a swashbuckling career that Sigurd pursued (he flew for Pan Am, opening new routes over Latin America) after dropping out of college. Russell took a different path. Developing a deep interest in the emerging field of electronics, he was accepted to Stanford. Because the family was poor, he chose to hike the 220 miles to school—and during his years studying under Terman, he often lived off the fruit growing on campus. Turned down for work on a PhD, Russell took a job in private industry.

It was Sigurd who came up with the idea for a new kind of microwave device, the klystron tube. This might seem surprising, but in fact Sig Varian had a good reason: dealing with old flight maps that sometimes showed swamps when there were mountains instead, he wanted a way to see the flight path ahead at night or through inclement weather. Thanks to one of Russell's old classmates, now a professor at their alma mater, Russell was invited back to Stanford with his brother to work on building a klystron.

What happened next was something that no one who saw it ever forgot. In exchange for giving away half of any royalties, the brothers set up in a physics lab near Terman's and began to work. In the weeks and months that followed, the brothers seemed to work continuously, day and night. Visitors, including Hewlett and Packard, were astounded by what they saw: despite being so different, and having lived such different lives, Russell and Sigurd worked together like a kind of perpetual motion machine—rarely taking a break, seemingly sharing the same thoughts, finishing each other's sentences, like two minds in one. Officially, Russell was responsible for the design, Sig for the building of the prototype, but each was deeply involved in the work of the other.

In August 1937, the Varian brothers completed and successfully fired up the prototype klystron. Within a year, it was licensed by Sperry Gyroscope—and just in time. The British, facing the prospect of German attack, were desperate to build a low-weight version of their new radar technology to put into planes and ships. The Varian klystron was the perfect solution. In radar, it played a crucial role in the Allied victory.

After the war, the Varian brothers founded Varian Associates to build multiple versions of the klystron. Interestingly, one of their most important customers was Stanford University, where Russell's old professor and supporter William Hansen lined up scores of klystrons on a mile-long path and created the linear accelerator. By then, Russell and Sigurd had gone back to their old lives: Sigurd to building machinery and flying (he would die in a plane crash off the coast of Mexico) and Russell to helping design the equally monumental MRI technology for the medical world.

8: TRIOS

1. By the way, some NFL teams learned to counter the West Coast offense by taking a cue from the other Niner hall of famer of those years, the defensive safety Ronnie Lott. Lott's solution was to break up the precision of the offense, and thus Walsh's controlled randomness, by asserting a randomness of his own, improvising his own play responses on the fly, shortening his decision-making time to what almost seemed like intuition, unmatched open field tackling, and sufficiently intimidating receivers so that *they* hesitated and he regained any lost time. This response resulted in a new kind of defensive back, the hybrid "elephant" linebacker—huge, fast, and free to take any role from pass coverage to rushing the quarterback—best exemplified by Charles Haley of the Cow-

boys (though trained by the Niners) and Lawrence Taylor of the New York Giants. This underscores the fact that one of the *biggest* weaknesses of trios is coordination and the time it takes to achieve it.

9: FOUR AND MORE

1. Belbin M. 2011. "Size matters: How many make the ideal team?" Belbin .es, www.belbin.es/rte.asp?id=153&pressid=31&task=View.

11: THE BIRTH AND LIFE OF TEAMS

1. Scheer, George F., and Hugh F. Rankin. 1957. *Rebels and Redcoats: The American Revolution Through the Eyes of Those That Fought and Lived It.* New York: World Publishing Company, p. 504.

Index

ghost partnerships, 146, 148
Gilbert, John, 118
Gilbert, William, 121
Gillespie, Dizzy, 118, 122
Glaser, Joe, 131
Goleman, Daniel, 36
Goodwin, Doris Kearns, 148
Google, 2, 5, 8, 11, 20, 30, 70, 190, 197, 217
Got-Your-Six pairs, 116–17, 130, 149, 155
Grant, Ulysses S., 127, 130
Greene, Nathaniel, 212, 247
Grove, Andrew, 20, 122, 150–51, 171–74
Guggenheim, Peggy, 134

Hackman, J. Richard, 31–32, 95
Hamilton, Alexander, 212, 247–48
Hammerstein, Oscar, 122, 131
Hardy, Oliver, 125
Harrison, George, 184
Hart, Lorenz, 122, 131
Hatch, Orrin, 137
Hazel, Eddie, 193
healthy teams
    successful, 244–45
    unsuccessful, 242–44
Heathfield, Susan, 20, 21
Henrich, Joe, 42
Henson, Matthew, 140
Here-and-There pairs, 124, 159
Hewlett, William, 8, 27–29, 126–27, 226–27

Hewlett-Packard (HP), 27–29, 120, 127, 148, 226–27
hierarchy, 194–95, 198–99, 206, 219
Hillary, Edmund, 140
Hines, Earl, 118
HireVue, 34
hiring, 33–34, 74, 103
Hirshberg, Jerry, 69
Hoff, Ted, 150–51, 169–70, 170
Holiday, Billie, 118
Holliday, Doc, 116
hominids, 16–17, 21
Hope, Bob, 122
Hopkins, Margaret, 50
HP Way, The (Packard), 27
Huawei, 20
Hunter, Joe, 192
hunter-gatherers, 16–17, 21, 26–27, 38, 203
Hutterites, 25

IBM, xii, xiii, 5, 13, 18
independence, 66–68, 93–94
information, 76, 80, 84, 96
innovation, xiii, 67–68, 208
Inside/Outside pairs, 138–39, 154–55, 159
Instrumental Trios, 174–78, 181
integration, 79, 83, 89, 99
Intel, 1, 20, 122, 137, 150–51, 169–74
interdependence, 92, 94–98
Internet, 2–3, 30–31, 138
interpersonal congruence, 82
interpretations, 73, 74

intuition, 53–54, 68
Isaacson, Walter, 148
Iwerks, Ub, 132

Jackson, Michael, 131
Jackson, Phil, 142
Jamerson, James, 192
James, LeBron, 81
Janus teams, 138
Java, 40
Jeter, Derek, 49
Jobs, Steve, xii, 9–15, 119–20, 131, 208
John, Elton, 131
Johnson, Kelly, xii
Jones, Ben, 71
Jones, Quincy, 131
Jordan, Michael, 142

Kandinsky, Wassily, 134
Kasparov, Garry, 53
Kaye, Carol, 193
Keeping Together in Time (McNeill), 42
Kellogg, Harry, 81
Kennedy, Ted, 137
Kenobi, Obi-Wan, 141
Kern, Jerome, 131
key employees, 65
King, Don, 135
kin relations, 38–39
Kirk, Captain, 136
Kleiner, Eugene, 126
Kluszewski, Ted, 175
Knight, Phil, 109
knowing teams, 201
knowledge, 88
Knox, Henry, 212, 247–48
Köhler effect, 98
KPMG, 144–45, 158
Krzyzewski, Mike, 49
Kurosawa, Akira, 187

About the Authors

RICH KARLGAARD is the publisher of *Forbes* magazine, where he writes a featured column, Innovation Rules, covering business and leadership issues. An accomplished entrepreneur as well as a journalist and speaker, he is a cofounder of Upside magazine, Garage Technology Partners, and Silicon Valley's premier public business forum, the 7,500-member Churchill Club. He is also the author of Life 2.0, and *The Soft Edge: Where Great Companies Find Lasting Success*. He lives with his family in Silicon Valley.

MICHAEL S. MALONE is one of the world's best-known technology writers. A veteran newspaper reporter and columnist, magazine editor, and entrepreneur, he is the author or coauthor of nearly twenty award-winning books, notably the bestselling *The Virtual Corporation*, *Bill and Dave*, and *The Intel Trinity*, which was named the Best Book of 2015 by 800CEOread.com.